T0419644

Water Resource Planning, Development and Management Series

INTEGRATED WATER RESOURCE MANAGEMENT IN THE KURDISTAN REGION

WATER RESOURCE PLANNING, DEVELOPMENT AND MANAGEMENT SERIES

Planning and Managing of Water Resources
Peter A. Unwal (Editor)
2006. ISBN 1-59454-757-2

Water Resources Research Progress
Liam N. Robinson (Editor)
2008. ISBN 1-60021-973-X

Trends in Water Resources Research
Alan B. Prescott and Thomas U. Barkely (Editors)
2008. ISBN 978-1-60456-038-1

Integrated Water Resource Management in the Kurdistan Region
Almas Heshmati
2009. ISBN 978-1-60741-295-3

Water Resource Planning, Development and Management Series

INTEGRATED WATER RESOURCE MANAGEMENT IN THE KURDISTAN REGION

ALMAS HESHMATI

Nova Science Publishers, Inc.
New York

Library of Congress Cataloging-in-Publication Data
Heshmati, Almas.
  Integrated water resource management in the Kurdistan region / Almas Heshmati.
     p. cm.
  Includes bibliographical references and index.
  ISBN 978-1-60741-295-3 (hardcover)
  1. Water-supply--Kurdistan--Management. 2. Water--Purification--Kurdistan. 3. Water--Government policy. 4. Integrated water development--Kurdistan. I. Title.
  TD313.I7H47   2009
  363.6'1095667--dc22   2009008025

Published by Nova Science Publishers, Inc. ✛ *New York*

CONTENTS

LIST OF TABLES

LIST OF FIGURES

LIST OF MAPS

PREFACE

This book examines the current economic practices of water management in the Southern Kurdistan Region (SKR) and suggests ways to change environmental conditions to encourage the region's decision makers to pursue sustainable resource development through interstate and within Kurdistan Region KRG-consumers' co-operation. The focus is on:

- making a comparative study of water resources between Iraq, its neighboring countries, MENA and the world averages,
- conducting a sector analysis to identify and quantify available water resources, the needs and sub-optimality in their uses,
- analyzing current allocation of water and quantifying and suggesting necessary reductions in wasteful use of water resources,
- designing water policies and suggesting measures that improve regional water planning and management practices,
- developing techniques and models in the projection of demand, supply and future utilization patterns and quantification of the water gap,
- suggesting alternatives for provision of water to areas facing scarcity on the basis of sustainable long-term and minimum cost solutions,
- suggesting necessary mechanisms for approaching interstate cooperation and for participating in the building of interregional institutions,
- proposing economically and environmentally optimal practices for within region and interstate cooperation and resource management, and
- suggesting opportunities for increased government investment in the development and management of the water market.

FOREWORD BY THE
MINISTER OF WATER RESOURCES

Throughout the history of humankind, water has always been the central element for the existence and survival of societies. Wars have been fought over this valuable resource and risks of future conflicts are prevailing in different parts of the world, where water is in short supply. Presence of and access to fresh water are two of the main factors for sustaining a natural balance in the environment we live in.

About seventy percent of our planet is covered by water. The vast majority of this water is in salty oceans. About two-thirds of the freshwater is frozen in the ice caps and glaciers, which leaves only a small fraction, less than 1%, accessible for human use. Demand on this limited resource is increasing rapidly due to fast population growth. Population concentration in small geographical areas (mainly cities, which grow rapidly) also presents a challenge. In most cases, this leads to an imbalance between water supply and demand, which may result in compromising policies on water quality and its sustainable management.

Between the two main sources of fresh water (i.e. surface water (lakes, rivers and streams) and groundwater (water in underground aquifers)), surface water is more widely used because it is easier to access. In the Kurdistan Region, where rate and amount of precipitation is high compared to the rest of Iraq, surface water is the main source of fresh water. However, there is a large temporal and spatial (lowlands and highlands) variability in annual precipitation. This, together with a forced shift in population densities, has increased stress on water resources in the Kurdistan Region. This shift in population distribution is a hangover of the previous political regime, when several thousand rural communities were forcefully displaced to the cities or other areas far from their natural territories. Prior to this, most villagers were using nearby water sources (streams or springs) for daily use and cultivation. These water sources were naturally recharged during winter and spring, when most of the precipitation occurs in the Kurdistan Region. Today, a sizable number of these villagers are still living either in or close to the cities.

Iraq's dependence on the water resources of the Kurdistan Region is likely to increase in the future. This is because of the heavier upstream use of the main tributaries of the Euphrates and Tigris by the neighboring countries (Turkey, Syria and Iran). The increasing number of dams built on these two rivers in these countries has had an obvious impact on the rate and amount of water that flows into Iraq. International agreements on these trans-boundary water sources are vital to maintain a fair and balanced distribution of water resources in the future. Such agreements enable us to see these rivers as bridges of peace rather than sources of conflict. Due to its geographic position, the Kurdistan Region which is the source region for some of the main tributaries, would be able to play a responsible role in building bridges of peace.

The lack of well-defined projects which enable a sustainable management of surface water in the Kurdistan Region and absence of momentum to shift the dependence of irrigation from less reliable seasonal precipitation to well-established, long-term solutions, have caused severe water-related problems in the Kurdistan Region. In addition to their effect on agriculture, implementation of such projects would have an immediate impact on all other sectors of the society and enable government agencies and municipalities to be more prepared in the drought and flood seasons.

The future of water is the responsibility of us all and depends on investments of individuals, communities, and the government at all levels to ensure that water resources are protected and managed in a sustainable manner. The very first step in achieving sustainable water management is outlining the temporal and spatial distribution of water resources. Without acquisition of such valuable knowledge, governments would neither be able to meet the water needs of their societies nor to draft adequate legislations to sustainably manage water resources.

Defining water-related problems and outlining the main sources of water in the Kurdistan Region is the first step towards establishing well-defined solutions to water shortages and providing a framework for sustainable management of water in the Region. I endorse this report as a sound attempt in this direction, in which, based on the currently available data, both spatial and temporal distribution of the sources of water in the Kurdistan Region and the problems associated with them are defined.

I would like to thank Professor Dr. Almas Heshmati for undertaking the task of preparing this document. Thanks are also due to the specialists and other personals at the Ministry of Water Resources of the Kurdistan Regional Government for their help in preparing this valuable document. Last but not least, I would like to thank Professor Dr. Hemin Koyi for his thorough review and constructive comments on this document.

Tahsin Kader Ali
Minister of Water Resources
Kurdistan Regional Government-Iraq

March 28, 2009

ACKNOWLEDGEMENTS

This study of "Integrated Water Resources Management in Kurdistan Region" was initiated by Tahsin Kader Ali, Minister of Water Resources, Kurdistan Regional Government, Almas Heshmati, at the time Professor of Economics at the University of Kurdistan Hawler and Nabaz Tahir Abdullah, Senior Advisor at the Ministry of Water Resources.

The research was conducted at the University of Kurdistan facilities during July and August 2008 for the purpose of researching the integrated management of water resources in the Kurdistan Region which is a challenge that faces the regional government.

During the process Nabaz Tahir Abdullah, Binar Jawhar, Aumed Muhammed, Zozan Othman, Fatima Osman, and Shehin Salah contributed to parts of the report. Fatima Osman also served as project secretary. The team's research assistance and Rhona Davis review of the text is acknowledged with gratitude.

In conducting this study, the research assistants consulted a wide range of interested ministries, to whom we are grateful for information shared and comments and suggestions received. In particular we wish to thank Mohammed-Reza A. Rasoul, Ministry of Industry, Dr. Jamal M. Ameen, Ministry of Planing, and Narmiekhan and Kameran, Ministry of Water Resources for sharing data with us. Special thanks go to Husain A. Rassoul, Planning Manager, Mohammad Hassan, Aman Farman, and Rasul T. Baba, in the General Directorate of Studies and Design, all other employees of the Ministry of Water Resources, in particular Lashkiry Koye the support service manager, for provision of data, various documents and for their valuable cooperation.

I thank Abdulrahman Khani (Director of Darbandikhan Dam), Dler Koyi (General Director of Studies and Design), Hama Taher (Director of Dukan Dam) and Najmaddin Hawrami, for their support and assistance during site visits to Garmiyan area.

The first draft of the report will be presented at the workshop to be held at the University of Kurdistan Hawler on August 25. Valuable comments and suggestions from Professor Hemin Koyi, Dr. Carel Dohnald, Nabaz T. Abdullah, Ali Rashid and Cheman Bajalan gratefully appreciated.

Finally, the research team on its own behalf and on the behalf of the Ministry of Water Resources wishes to thank Rector Robin Brims for his full support and the Staff of University of Kurdistan Hawler for allowing the team to access the University research and conference facilities.

I also wish that the propositions in this report may contribute to continuous prosperity and the development of the Southern Kurdistan Region, its water resources and the activities of the Ministry of Water Resources. None of the persons above are responsible for any error in this report.

Any remaining errors are those of mine and the views expressed in this report are not necessarily those of the Ministry of Water Resources.

Almas Heshmati
Professor of Economics
Seoul National University, South Korea and
Ministry of Water Resources, Kurdistan Region, Iraq

March 28, 2009

ABBREVIATIONS

ADR	Alternative Dispute Resolution
BOD	Measure of industrial organic pollutants
CBA	Cost-Benefit Analysis
CO2	Carbon Dioxide emission
EC	European Community
EPDC	Dam Design Company
EU	European Union
FAO	Food and Agriculture Organization (of the UN)
FDI	Foreign Direct Investment
GAP	Turkish Southeast Anatolia Development Project
GD	General Directorate
GDP	Gross Domestic Product
ICOLD	International Commission on Large Dams
IT	Information Technology
ICT	Information and Telecommunication Technology
KRG	Kurdistan Regional Government
MCU	Million Cubic Meters
MDG	Millennium Development Goals
MENA	Middle East and North Africa
MOWR	Ministry of Water Resources
MST	Ministry of Science and Technology
MULINO	Project addressing complexity of EU water planning
MWh	Megawatt hours
NGO	Non-Governmental Organization
NPK	Nitrogen, Phosphorous and Potassium fertilizer type
SKR	Southern Kurdistan Region
SQ KM	Square kilometer
UKH	University of Kurdistan Hawler
UN	United Nations
UNDP	United Nations Development Program
UNICEF	United Nations Children's Fund
USA	Unites States of America
WDI	World Development Indicators database
WFD	Water Framework Directive
WSSD	World Summit on Sustainable Development

Chapter 1

INTRODUCTION AND BACKGROUND TO THE PROJECT

1.1. BACKGROUND TO THE PROBLEM

The Middle East is a region characterized by scarce water resources and rapid population growth increasingly concentrated in urban areas. Water scarcity is both increasing and expanding in the region. Accordingly water is a binding constraint on sustainable future economic and social development in the region which in turn increases demands especially for fresh water. Improved efficiency in water use must be combined with provision of new and additional water to the region to satisfy the water needs and to minimize the shortage of water. There is a prediction that the region's future war will be over water rather than on land or as a religion-based conflict. However, due to interconnected water resources and environmental security, water is likely to be a factor for promoting interstate cooperation in the region. Economic, technical and regional water sharing agreements are sufficient instruments for conflict avoidance. Therefore, governance and the sustainable development of a common pool of water resources of the Middle East should be given more attention.[1]

A comprehensive strategy for regional co-operation in development and management of water resources, exchange of agricultural products within the region, development of regional institutional arrangements, joint regional water planning is both necessary and beneficial to all regional parties. The logic of collective action has already in several cases, like Israel-Jordan-Palestine, made it possible to develop co-operation in water issues, although in practice the principle of equality in access to water is not fully respected. Institutional development is a binding constraint on the capacity to respond effectively to the water problem, but the energy-rich countries in the Middle East can afford to finance water development projects, while other non-oil producer countries with low GDP per capita must rely on finances through external loans or contributions from international aid agencies or non-governmental organizations.

---

[1] The current disputes over renewable international water resources in the Middle East and North Africa concern Euphrates/Tigris (shared by both Northern and Southern Kurdistan as well as the rest of Iraq, Syria and Turkey), the Nile (shared by Burundi, Congo, Egypt, Ethiopia, Kenya, Rwanda, Sudan, Tanzania and Uganda), the Jordan (shared by Israel, Jordan, Palestine and Syria), and the Orontes (shared by Israel, Lebanon, Syria and Turkey). For quantitative data on the various water sources and distribution of their uses refer to respective country's related authorities and national statistics.

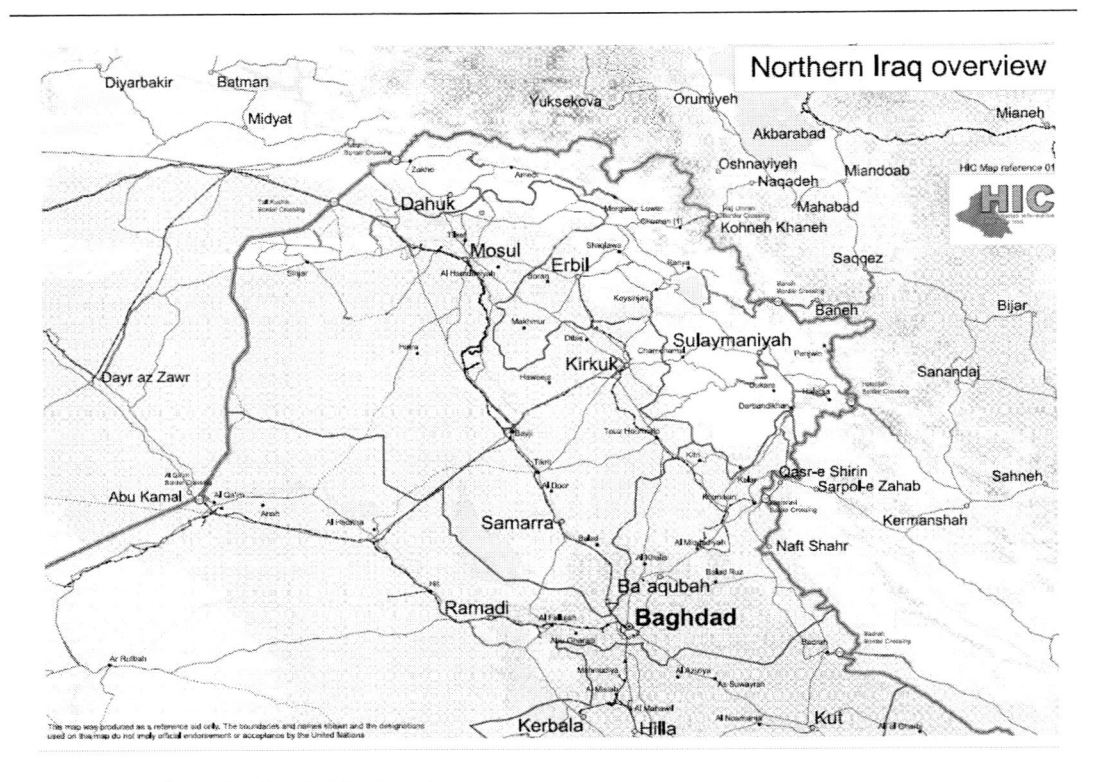

Map 1.1. Kurdistan Region in Northern Iraq.

Kurdistan Region in Northern Iraq is not an exception to the rest of the Middle East. Similar conditions apply to this region as well (see map 1.1). Water scarcity is increasing and has a binding constraint on economic and social development in the region. The scarcity of water is often a result of neighboring countries active policy of divergence of water, changes in population structure and concentration within the region, climate changes, as well as the increasing use of water in hydropower-based electricity production. It is important to investigate the current economic, social and water resource conditions in Kurdistan Region and evaluate alternative sources of water. This will be helpful in proposing measures to enhance the effectiveness in the use of water resources, to reduce the shortages in its supply and to mitigate negative environmental effects.

1.2. THE OBJECTIVES OF THIS PROJECT

This study examines the current economic practices of water management in Souther Kurdistan Region (SKR) and suggests ways to change environmental conditions to encourage the region's decision makers to pursue sustainable resource development through interstate and within Kurdistan Region KRG-consumers' co-operation. The project will focus on:

- making a comparative study of water resources between Iraq, its neighboring countries, MENA and the world averages,

- conducting a sector analysis to identify and quantify available water resources, the needs and sub-optimality in their uses,
- analyzing current allocation of water and quantifying and suggesting necessary reductions in wasteful use of water resources,
- designing water policies and suggesting measures that improve regional water planning and management practices,
- developing techniques and models in the projection of demand, supply and future utilization patterns and quantification of the water gap,
- suggesting alternatives for provision of water to areas facing scarcity on the basis of sustainable long-term and minimum cost solutions,
- suggesting necessary mechanisms for approaching interstate cooperation and for participating in the building of interregional institutions,
- proposing economically and environmentally optimal practices for within region and interstate cooperation and resource management, and
- suggesting opportunities for increased government investment in the development and management of the water market.

1.3. IMPLEMENTATION OF THIS PROJECT

This project was financed by Kurdistan Region's Ministry of Water Resources and implemented under the supervision of Professor Almas Heshmati. A team of research assistants from the University of Kurdistan and researcher/research assistants currently employed at the Ministry was set up which had the necessary skills. A preliminary report was completed during July and August 2008 and presented at a full day workshop organized by the Ministry of water Resources held at the University of Kurdistan Hawler on August 25, 2008. The report was revised, following the workshop to get views, comments and suggestions by experts in water resources. The final report is intended to be used by the Ministry of Water Resources as a handbook for the efficient use of water resources, for policy analysis and in the region's co-operation with NGO's and in relationship with other users of common pool water resources in the region.

Since the water challenge in Southern Kurdistan Region is not much different from that experienced elsewhere, the results could provide valuable information to common pool water issues in the rest of Iraq, the Middle East and North Africa and be useful to other regions' decision-makers. In addition, it can be instrumental for international organizations with an interest in the field and in the global management of water resources.

1.4. ORGANIZATION OF THE PROJECT

This project was financially supported by the Ministry of Water Resources but conducted at the University of Kurdistan-Hawler. The University of Kurdistan-Hawler supported the project by providing access to the university's research facilities and a number of research assistants mainly consisting of Masters but also Bachelors students who assisted during the initial phase of the project, in July and August. In addition to financial support, the Ministry of Water Resources has provided statistics, professional staff and other infrastructure resources.

1.5. STRUCTURE OF THE REPORT

In addition to this introductory and background chapter on the project, this report contains a number of chapters. Chapter 2 is a review of the literature on water resources with a focus of economics, planning, management, regulations and water policies in the Middle East and other regions. Chapter 3 is a comparative regional study of water resources. A number of water resource indicators provided by the World Bank as part of the World Development Indicators database are used to compare the performance of Iraq and its neighboring countries with those of MENA and world averages. Chapter 4 is about Kurdistan Region's water resources in historical and regional perspectives. We attempt to quantify the different aspects of water resources in the region. Chapters 5 and 6 are on the current state of water resources in Kurdistan Region. The emphasis is on a large number of factors such as: the water sources and quantities available; the current allocation of water by sub-sectors; the optimal allocation by sub-sectors; an estimation of in-optimal use of water by different sub-sectors; the estimated disequilibrium in supply and demand for water; characteristics of the main consumers of water resources; development of agriculture, industry, recreation and tourism, and the population and its concentration. Chapter 7 presents a new water management resources plan and policies. Here the focus is on: public infrastructure and investments; water laws and regulations; statistics and quality monitoring activities; publications of annual reports and forecasts for supply and demand; training, education, health and technology resources; self-sufficiency and vulnerability; proposal for a new water resources plan and policies; and an estimation of resources needed and the cost of implementing the new water resources policies. In Chapter 8 a summary is presented. Chapter 9 is a brief introduction by the Ministry of Water Resources in Kurdistan Region, covering its organizational structure and activities.

Chapter 2

REVIEW OF THE LITERATURE ON ECONOMICS AND MANAGEMENT OF WATER RESOURCES

ABSTRACT

This chapter is a review of research on the economics of water resources. The main focus is on the management of water resources. The state of water resources at the regional level and the water management policies applied are investigated. The EU water and landscape policy and efforts for a global agenda are reviewed and experiences gained are used in the design of water policies for Kurdistan Region. Through studies of legal and common pool aspects, water policies and management, we wish to identify the determinants of water management and effective policies. Particular attention is paid to policies targeting major sources and users of water resources. A number of areas such as the hydro-politics and water sharing conflict resolution, urban water management price and investment policies, irrigation externalities and control mechanisms, and the economic and environmental advantages of waste water reuse are studied. Alternative policies are suggested to remedy problems facing the region. The structure of the region's economy, major changes in the population structure, negligence of water resources, the deteriorated water sanitation facilities, and increased water pollutants are causal factors to the deteriorated environment. Improvements to the old and inadequate water resource regulations and their implementation are proposed. Finally, models and methods used in the evaluation of policies, pricing and forecasts are discussed.

2.1. INTRODUCTION

Robert B. Zoellick, President of the World Bank, states that "it is the vision of the World Bank Group[2] to contribute to an inclusive and sustainable globalization - to overcome poverty, enhance growth with care for the environment, and create individual opportunity and hope". The World Bank Group lists six strategic themes to meet the global challenges. The first theme is the poorest countries overcoming poverty and spurring growth. The top priority is to build infrastructure that will support higher economic growth. The second theme addresses special problems of post-conflict and fragile states. Here the focus is on security, political frameworks, and capacity-rebuilding integrated with quick support, reintegration of refugees, and more flexible development assistance. The third theme is to offer competitive development solutions to the middle income countries. This strategic theme aims at each nation's specific needs, whether they are loans, guarantees, other financial products, or advice, they must be tailored to the circumstances. In the fourth theme global public good that benefits developing countries is provided. For instance, climate change solutions should promote low-carbon growth that does not penalize poor countries. The fifth theme supports good governance, social services and private sector growth in the Arab world. The objective is for a broader-based growth to ease social tensions and create opportunities for the many young jobless people. The final theme is enhancing knowledge and learning by using banking experience for better development outcomes. Here the banks are expected to deliver, test, and expand their most important product.

One of the most challenging problems linked to the strategic themes listed above - inclusive and sustainable globalization - to face in the near future in most parts of the world is the shortage of supplies of water. Supplying clean drinking water is already a critical issue in many parts of the world. The increasing demand for water usage in irrigation to produce enough food to feed the growing population is critical for our survival. Thus, effective and fair allocation of existing water sources reduces the inequality in access to water and also the risk of intra-national and international conflicts. Kurdistan, with few waterways that are sources of multiple water uses and which span a number of national borders could be a place where conflicts erupt. This chapter, by reviewing the literature, looks at possible solutions for alleviating water crises, conflicts and political tension arising from the management of common pool water sources.

The EU water initiative (EU, 2002)[3] is increasingly considered as a global standard for water resources management. The worldwide challenges of the EU water initiative leading global water problems are: (i) over 1.1 billion people have no access to safe drinking water, (ii) over 2.4 billion people have no access to improved sanitation, (iii) more than 5 million people die every year from preventable water-related diseases, and (iv) 2 billion people are affected by water shortages. The European Union Water Framework Directive (WFD) from 2000 (EU, 2000), the World Summit on Sustainable Development (WSSD) from 2002 and the Millennium Development Goals (MDGs) are all attempts to address the future problems including scarce and critical water resources to achieve sustainable economic development.

This study is a review of research on water resources. The main focus is on management of water resources in the Middle East region, but is not necessarily limited to this particular region. The objective is to investigate the state of water resources at the regional level and the water management policies applied. The EU water and landscape policy and efforts for a global agenda are reviewed and experiences gained are used in the design of water policies for Kurdistan Region in Chapter 7. Through studies of legal and common pool aspects, water policies and management, we wish to identify the determinants of water management and effective policies. Attention will be put on policies targeting major sources and users of water resources such as population, agriculture, industry and services.

In this report a number of areas such as hydro-politics and water sharing conflicts, urban water management price and investment policies, irrigation externalities and control

---

[2] http://www.worldbank.org/
[3] For a description of goals, background and different approaches to the initiative, see http://www.euwi.net/

mechanisms, and the economic and environmental advantages of waste water reuse are studied. Alternative policies are suggested to remedy a number of problems facing the region in the aftermath of decades of war, sanctions and invasions. The structure of the region's economy, major changes in the population structure, negligence of water resources and in particular the deteriorated water sanitation facilities and water pollutants are among causal factors to the deteriorated environmental and living conditions. Improvements to the old and inadequate water resource regulation and their implementation are proposed.

The rest of the chapter is organized as follows. After the introduction the readers are introduced to the EU water framework directive in Section 2. Section 3 is on hydro-politics and water sharing conflicts. Measures for dealing with water resource disputes which concern only the rights and responsibilities of states are discussed. Pricing and other policies used in the management of urban water are discussed in Section 4, while externalities and control mechanisms associated with irrigation are discussed in Section 5. The economic and environmental advantages of waste water and its re-use as a source of water are discussed in Section 6. Discussion of policy evaluation methods, forecast and summary and conclusions follows in Sections 7 and 8.

2.2. THE EU WATER FRAMEWORK DIRECTIVE

The Water Framework Directive (WFD, 2000)[4] is European legislation designed to preserve, restore and improve the water environment in Europe. It establishes a framework for managing the water environment by taking into account environmental, social and economic aspects. The directive was introduced on October 2000 and published by the European Commission (EC).[5] The Commission is the executive body of the European Union (EU) that proposes legislation, implements the policies and enforces the EU laws by requiring the member states to implement the legislation and achieve the objectives set by the Directive. An integrated multi-disciplinary approach is used by the Commission that is based on geography, ecology, economics and sociology disciplines.

Unlike the case of the developing world, access to clean drinking and good sanitation facilities are taken for granted in the EU. Thus, the EU water initiative is designed as a regional model for the Union but also to serve as a global model for future actions to contribute to meeting the millennium development goals (MDGs)[6] for drinking water and sanitation within the context of an integrated approach to global water resource management. The environmental objectives of the EU Directive to be met by 2015 include: (i) all surface water bodies within the union to achieve good ecological status, (ii) all groundwater bodies to achieve good quantitative and chemical status, (iii) modified and artificial water bodies to achieve good ecological potential and chemical status, (iv) no water bodies to experience deterioration in status, and (v) protected areas to achieve requirements in relation to the water environment.

---

[4] http://www.euwfd.com/

[5] The Directive was published in the Official Journal of the European Communities L327 43, 1-71. See also http://www.euwfd.com/html/water_framework_directive.html.

[6] For a detailed description of the goals and continuous reports on progress in achieving the goals see, http://www.un.org/millenniumgoals/2008highlevel/

The challenges posed by the management of water resources across the EU are the convergence of existing national policies with the stipulations of the WFD. Giupponi et al. (2002) suggest research can support the transition by identifying compatibility and sources of conflicts between legislative instruments, encouraging cooperative relationships and providing criteria and tools for conflict resolution. The complexity in planning decisions is addressed by the MULINO project.[7] It is a 3-year research program that aims at the creation of decision support systems to assist water managers in responding to the evolution of complex policies and management methodologies.

The WDF was followed by the World Summit on Sustainable Development (WSSD) held in Johannesburg in September 2002 where the EU launched the EU water initiative. In the water initiative, addressing the water challenge is considered a key to sustainable development. This and reducing poverty are the two key elements of the MDGs. Thus, any sustainable development policies must address the need for equitable and sustainable management of water resources in the interest of society as a whole. Water is a cross-sectored challenge where its provision, sanitation, health, livelihoods, economic development, peace and security are closely interrelated. Increasing urbanization and the neglect of rural areas are particularly important. They imply the need for integrated water resources management at all levels including natural rivers, lakes or groundwater basins to ensure a balance between human water needs and those of the environment.

The MDGs and the WSSD targets on water are: (i) to halve the proportion of people without access to safe drinking water by 2015, (ii) to halve the proportion of people who do not have access to basic sanitation by 2015, and (iii) to develop integrated water resources management and efficiency plans by 2005. The general objectives of the EU water initiative are to reinforce political commitments, to promote better water governance arrangements, to improve co-ordination and co-operation, to encourage regional and sub-regional cooperation on water management issues and to catalyze additional funding. The general approach is based on partnership by mobilization of partners ranging from governments, donors, civil society organizations' water users, and the water industry. The existing regional components include Africa, Eastern Europe, the Caucasus, Central Asia, the Mediterranean and Latin America. Achievement of the goals requires financial and research resources as well as monitoring, reporting and communications and information systems.

Giupponi et al. (2002) in their evaluation of EU water policy conclude that the implementation of the WFD in EU member states and in accession countries will be a great challenge facing the Union in the coming decade. The attempt to introduce a coherent legislative framework for the protection and improvement of water resources within the context of achieving sustainable development is a crucial step in the application of policy measures. The WFD establishes new requirements for planning, decision-making, public participation and conceptualizing the spatial aspects of water management and achievement of common pool objectives. It is an example of EU policies emphasizing multi-disciplinary management in a balanced and sustainable development. The water management sector will lead in environmental planning and decision-making. The research project MULINO will provide insights into problems dealing with water policy and its implementation. Success in

---

[7] Giupponi et al. (2002) addresses the challenges and innovations in the second phase of the research to develop the software to operate specific decision situations.

implementation of WFD will also have implications for the future development of the EU as a whole.

Four policy dossiers are reviewed by van Rheenen et al. (2005) in putting nature and landscape goals on the EU political agenda. The dossiers refer to reform of the common agricultural policy and the dairy sector, the common fishery policy, the Natura 2000, and the water framework directive. Nature and landscape are scarce resources, but nations have to co-operate to achieve these goals. Major parts of the EU member states environment and nature policies are laid down in Brussels. Thus, international and interregional agreements influence national policy-making processes increasingly. The Van Rheenen et al. study reveals that the Netherlands has been very effective in Europe, but the country could improve its impact on policy at the EU level. The results suggest that the Dutch influence on EU nature and landscape polices can be considered as moderate to good with room for improvement such as in technical scientific arguments and political sensitivity.

2.3. HYDRO-POLITICS AND WATER SHARING CONFLICTS RESOLUTION

In looking towards 2020, Wolf (1996) examines the past division of a few great waterways, the Nile, the Jordan and the Tigris-Euphrates, as major sources of water in the Middle East and the north-east of Africa. Starr and Stoll (1988) studied the politics of scarcity with reference to water in the Middle East. Water plays a pre-eminent role in survival, ranging from an individual biological to a nation's economy. Therefore, political conflicts over international and common pool water resources can be contentious. The intensity of the conflicts can be exacerbated by the region's geographic, geopolitics or hydro-politic landscape in particular in cases where demand surpasses the supply of water. Wolf, in his examination, also looks at the possible solutions for alleviating a water crisis and the subsequent political tensions it arouses. Boutros-Boutros Ghali, the former Secretary General of the United Nations suggested that a possible future war in the Middle East may be fought over water (Starr, 1991).[8]

Along the lines discussed above, Wolf (1996) explores how critical water shortage came about, the political intentions linked with the scarcity of water and what the involved nations can or will do to help alleviate both the crisis and the political pressures. The focus here is on the Dead Sea in 1978. In this year, the lake was subject to disequilibrium and both Arab and Jewish nationalisms were locked in a demographic race for numerical superiority leading to a drop in the level of water. He describes the hydro-political history of the MENA basins of the Nile, Jordan and Tigris-Euphrates. Some technical and policy options for increasing water supply and decreasing water demands are suggested. The role of water resources in the ongoing multi-lateral peace negotiations is emphasized. The paradigms used in defining

---

[8] For more reading on water resources and conflicts see: Giordano et al. (2002) on the geography of water conflicts and cooperation, Giupponi et al. (2006) on participatory approaches in decision-making processes for water resources, Gleick (1993) on water and conflict, Goldfarb and Kislev (2002) on water management in Israel, Haddadin (2002) on water in the Middle East peace process, He et al. (2005) on strategic water policy options in Egypt and Morocco, Lipchin (2006) on a future for the Dead Sea Basin, Ron (1986) on water resources in the Holy Land, Starr (1991) on water wars, and Starr and Stolt (1988) on the politics of scarcity of water in the Middle East.

equity in sharing water resources are presented. Finally, a summary of principles for cooperative regional water management are given.

Wolf describes the hydro-political tensions surrounding the basins. Concerning the Euphrates basin, he writes about various degrees of hydro-political tensions between Turkey, Syria and Iraq in the 1960s, which in the 1975 unilateral water developments almost led to warfare along the river. The sources of tensions were unilateral developments such as the Keban Dam (1965-73) in Turkey and the Tabqa Dam (1968-73) in Syria which were built to face demands from population pressures. The dams began to fill without any formal agreement and resulted in decreased flow downstream. The Soviet Union was involved in meetings to reduce the tensions. The Turkish Southeast Anatolia Development Project (GAP) is another ongoing source of conflict. The project is a massive undertaking for energy and agricultural development and when completed it will include the construction of 21 dams and 19 hydro-power plans on both the Tigris and Euphrates.[9] A series of talks between the three countries has been held in 1986, 1987, 1990, 1992 and 1993 to regulate the minimum flows of water without any significant breakthrough in the negotiations.

Regarding technical and policy options as solutions to water resource limits, these range from agricultural to technological to economic and public policy measures. Concerning water shortages they fall under two basic categories, namely increasing supply and decreasing demand and a third category of co-operative options (see Wolf, 1996). Water management options to decrease demand unilaterally include: population control, rationing, public awareness, to allow the price of water to reflect true costs, various public policies,, and efficient use of water[10] in agriculture through drip irrigation, use of greenhouse technology and genetic engineering. The unilateral measures to increase supply include: new natural sources, new sources through technology, wastewater reclamation, increased catchment and storage, cloud seeding, desalination, and fossil aquifer development. A third category of co-operative options include: shared information and technology, international water markets to increase distributive efficiency, inter-basin water transfers, and joint regional planning.

2.3.1. Measures in Water Resource Disputes

Equity is crucial in water conflict management particularly in cases where international water law is ambiguous, contradictory and no mechanism for enforcement of agreements exists. Wolf (1996) describes some existing measures of water-sharing equity and their strengths and weaknesses in the context of Middle East hydro-politics. The measures in water resource disputes are divided into: (i) international water law, (ii) needs-based equity, and (iii) economic equity. [11] Each of these is described below.

---

[9] Turkey has been criticized for drowning the Kurdish historical and artistic heritage (Izady, 1996). After Israel, Turkey is another country in the Middle East which has been active in research in the water area. A few such studies are: Moran (2004) on environmental and socio-economic impacts of hydroelectric dams in Turkish Kurdistan, Cankurt et al. (2008) on awareness of environmental pollution in Turkey, and Bilgic et al. (2008) about the willingness to pay for potable water in south-eastern Turkey.

[10] There is a literature on efficiency in production of goods and provision of services. It can be used in evaluation of water policy effects (Giannoccaro et al., 2008; Schmidtz, 2002; Grove and Maluleke, 2006).

[11] A comprehensive list of water economics publications 1961-2003 is provided by Johnson and Schwartz (2004). It covers journal articles, books, chapters in books, technical bulletins and reports, technical articles, published proceedings, abstracts, other papers presented, and M.Sc. thesis and Ph.D. dissertations.

International water law started to be formulated first after the WWI. The concept of drainage basin was accepted by the International Law Association in the Helsinki Rules of 1966. It provides guidelines for 'reasonable and equitable' sharing of common waterways and factors to be taken into account in defining what is 'reasonable and equitable'. The International Law Commission, a UN body, in 1970 was directed to study 'codification of the law on water courses for purposes other than navigation'. The general principles being codified include that: common water resources are to be shared equitably between the states entitled to use them and states are responsible for substantial trans-boundary injury originating in their respective territories. Details about the laws discussed here are found in Wolf (1996) and references there including Cano (1989), Caponera (1985) and Housen-Couriel (1992). However, the laws only concern themselves with the rights and responsibilities of states. Political entities with water right claims like Kurds and Palestinians are not represented in the international water law. Furthermore, the International Court of Justice is with no practical enforcement mechanism to back up its findings. States can therefore easily disclaim the Court's jurisdiction and findings (Caponera, 1985; Cano 1989).

Rogers (1991) explains that the claims for water rights for sharing are often based on geography where rivers originate from territory controlled by a state or on chronology based on having used the water longest. The extreme positions are referred to as the 'doctrine of absolute sovereignty' where the state has the absolute right to water flowing through its territory, and 'prior appropriation' suggesting first in time, first in right. Wolf (1996) finds that these two doctrines of geography and chronology are conflicting and clash regarding all rivers in the Middle East. The upstream riparian like Turkey take the doctrine of absolute sovereignty, while downstream riparian, like Iraq with low rainfall, the position of prior appropriation. In many disputes, like Egypt and Sudan over the Nile, the agreements are not rights-based but rather needs-based. The success of a needs-based solution in the case of the Nile has encouraged the application of this method to water disputes over the Jordan, as well as those where Palestinian water rights claims are partially taken into account.

Economic equity is the third principle employed in water conflict resolution, which is the allocation of water resources based on their economic value. The different uses and users along a waterway value the resource differently. This leads to increased overall efficiency (reallocation) and equity (satisfaction) of water utilization by accounting for economic equity in the water sharing principle. Two approaches are used to achieve efficient allocation of scarce water resources among competing uses. These are central planning and water market solutions where social planners' preferences and market mechanisms are used as instruments. In a game theoretical approach with a small number of participants, in addition to economic value the political aspects of water sharing are taken into consideration. Water resource planning and development encourage co-operation between owners of riparian. The subfield of alternative dispute resolution (ADR) is a process of integrating potential for ADR into public institutions which deal with water conflicts (see Ury et al., 1988).

The economic and political consideration in regional co-operation models is developed further by Dinar and Wolf (1997). Cooperation requires benefit to all players and meeting efficiency requirements through economically-driven allocations. However, in the case of political players that are hostile to each other or to an entity like Kurds, these conditions may not be met and their ignorance in economic analysis for political reason hinders possible arrangements. Dinar and Wolf propose an economic-political framework for evaluating transfers or trade of scarce resources. It is applied to a potential water and water-efficient technology transfer in the western Middle East. The results suggest that economic efficiency alone is not sufficient as water conflict resolution and accounting for political considerations stabilizes the regional economic-based solutions.

2.4. URBAN WATER MANAGEMENT PRICE AND INVESTMENT POLICIES

Urban water supply is often provided by a public monopoly supplier and the demand for the service is often inelastic to price level and changes. It means the price must increase significantly to bring about a small reduction in the quantity consumed. If the water price covers both costs and markups, this characteristic of the market may encourage profit maximization by the utility, resulting in inefficient allocation of water. In practice, public provision and government regulations including price control prevents monopolistic rent seeking. The regulator or social planner maximizes the social welfare by water availability constraints. The policy tools available to the social planner in the case of water are demand management and supply augmentation. The demand management involves price, rationing, awareness campaigns and incentives to improve water use efficiency policies. These policies aim at restricting or reducing water use in times of scarcity, while supply augmentation policies are concerned with the nature and timing of additions to water inflows and storage capacity supply infrastructure like dams and desalination plans. In certain cases, like electric utilities, education, health, transportation and communication services, privatization as a common measure to enhance competition and efficiency in provision of public services is considered.

It should be noted that in the short run the supply infrastructure is fixed which, in the event of a large reduction in inflows or demand increase, it necessitates a rationing of demand. However, water consumption has an essential and a nonessential component. The former refers to the minimum amount of water required to meet basic sanitation, drinking, bathing and food preparation needs. This component is non-responsive to price changes and must be supplied at all times to maintain good public health, but the non-essential component of water consumption can be subject to various optimal policy measures especially in times of scarcity. In the long run, the supply infrastructures can be altered and there are possibilities to determine simultaneously both demand management and supply augmentation policies to balance the non-essential use of water and the production and social costs of supply augmentation.

Water restrictions are initially a short run management of water demand, but they are increasingly used to achieve long-term reductions in demand and in certain cases they remain as permanent restrictions-imposed demand. The measure involves rules and regulations for outdoor use of urban water ranging from complete ban on water uses to various degrees of limitation in the form of inconvenient times and costs to discourage consumption such as limits on hours or taxes on water use, as well as marketing campaign and subsidies for water saving equipment whose benefits exceed their costs. The water use restrictions may lead to allocative inefficiency in water use and they do not directly limit inside residential water use and industrial water use (Edwards, 2006). In addition the transaction costs and the allocative efficiency costs, the implementation and enforcement costs of water restrictions are substantial (Grafton and Ward, 2007). Since the pricing regime is regulated by the government, the regulatory agencies use the long-run marginal cost in their price determination. The method has the disadvantage that it does not consider the uncertainty over dam inflows and short run fluctuation in storage levels. Australian water utilities use a two-part tariff system combining a consumption based price component and a residual fixed access charge designed to recover total and long-term infrastructure investments costs (Hughes, et al. 2008).

The supply augmentation to meet the growing demand for water is often undertaken by construction of new dams. The lack of suitable sites and adverse environmental impacts and potential for climate changes and water conflicts reduce the attractiveness of this policy measure. Two alternative measures to new dam construction to provide a stable source of water are water recycling and desalination. However, despite positive environmental impacts, both sources require significant capital and operating costs. In general, decisions on alternative supply augmentation projects should be based on comprehensive cost benefit analysis of such public projects, accounting for trends, financial, social, economic, political, security and environmental considerations. As will be discussed later, in the Middle East water diversion and construction of dams has increased with positive effects but also negative externalities. The capacity to conduct professional evaluation of effects is still low and investigations are often biased towards certain positive expected effects.

Most countries in the Middle East and in particular their urban water utilities face a significant challenge in designing appropriate demand management and supply augmentation water policies. The challenge is severe under the conditions of water scarcity and uncertainty over rainfall and dam inflows. In general there are some negative trends that deteriorate the water conditions. The increasing population combined with high rate of urbanization and potential for climate change have further reduced water availability and its increased level variability over time and across locations. These factors have increased pressure on public urban water utilities to implement more efficient water demand management policies and to invest in optimal supply augmentation decisions. The imposition of water restrictions and rationing during the times of scarcity are among two common water policy measures, each with their benefits and limitations. Scarcity pricing is a potential alternative in demand management policy of water restrictions. Grafton and Ward (2007) and Grafton and Kompas (2006) compare the scarcity pricing of urban water versus rationing of water and discuss the positive and negative effects of such alternative policies.

Recent drought conditions across Australia have depleted urban water storages, resulting in the implementation of water restrictions in most capital cities of the country. Gradual long-term decline in inflows, increasing population and urbanization together with minimal additions to supply capacity are negative trends in the development in the water area. The issue of uncertain optimal price and investment policies in the urban water management in Australia is studied by Hughes et al. (2008). The authors have developed a stochastic dynamic programming model of an urban water market. It is based on the capital territory. The model considers uncertainty by investigating the probability distribution over dam inflows. Given specifications of demand and supply for water, optimal price and investment policies are estimated. The results illustrate how water price is inversely related to storage level and the basic factors governing the timing of investment differs according to the dependency on rain augmentation options. Dwyer et al. (2005) discuss the integral rural and urban water markets in south-east Australia.

Surface water transfer or diversions of water from agriculture to urban users is one alternative way of managing water concerning the augmentation of the water supply. The economic impact of exported surface and groundwater to metropolitan areas is assessed by Sperow (2004). A non-linear two stage optimization model is developed for major hydrologic features of water and cropping patterns in the Colorado's San Luis Valley. Through simulations the doctrine of prior appropriation in Colorado and producers response to restricted water supplies is evaluated. The negative effects in the form of intervention in the water market are that in addition to reduced crop production, it prevents an efficient allocation of water resources, leads to inefficiency in irrigation technologies and under the condition of access to groundwater it does not encourage water conservation in times of scarcity of water. The net return from crop production is declined but unaffected by declining river flows. Only agricultural areas without groundwater rights are affected by the water transfer measure. The policies discussed above are examples of policies easily adapted to the Middle East water market and conditions.

2.5. IRRIGATION EXTERNALITIES AND CONTROL MECHANISMS

Irrigated agriculture represents a large share of land used in agriculture as well as a large share of gross value of agriculture-related production. Irrigation serves as a supplement to rainfall in a field-based agricultural production system. The rainfall varies greatly by location in the Middle East and active conditions for catchment of rain differ across the region. In total, agriculture accounts for a large share of total water use. There is large heterogeneity in the quantity and timing of use by regional location and their farming specializations.

The literature on irrigation is vast and diverse. To mention a few examples, Banerjee and Martin (2008) compare the econometric and engineering predictions of water demand and value for irrigation. Bartolini et al (205) analyze the water policy and sustainability of the irrigated water system in Italy. The issue of water regulation and irrigated agriculture under the EU Water Framework Directive is investigated in Bazzani et al. (2002). The irrigation water pricing policy in rural China (Huang et al., 2008) is another recent irrigation study. Stijn et al. (2008) estimate the effect of water charge introduction to small scale irrigation in South Africa. Finally, Taylor et al. (2007) conduct economic analysis of water conservation policies in Texas.

Irrigation has several externalities which change the environment. Therefore, many different environmental changes are associated with the supply of water for irrigation and intensive use of water in agriculture. These are distinguished by changes to hydrological conditions, habitat, water quality and ecological conditions. The changes occur at each stage of irrigation water supply and use chains including harvesting, extraction, storage, diversion, delivery and use. These environmental externalities may exist but without any human reaction, they may not be clearly considered as economic externalities.

Dwyer et al. (2006) developed a framework for analyzing the characteristics of externalities incorporating three salient elements of an externality: its sources; how it is transmitted; and its effects. These characteristics of externalities affect the choice of solutions, their successfulness and effectiveness of policy instruments employed. The possible water supply externalities include alterations to river flows, cold water releases from dams and obstructions to fish passages. The water use externalities include water logging, land salinisation and downstream salinity. Many of the externalities are complex and it is very difficult to understand the link between effects and resulting changes in environmental conditions. The changes can affect productivity of industries, it can have an impact on the health of users, and also individuals can be affected indirectly if they value water and land for different purposes.

The framework for analyzing the characteristics of externalities developed by Dwyer et al. (2006) looks at the observability, spatial variation, temporal variation and knowledge and uncertainty about processes in respect to sources, transmission and effects. Government actions are needed to address such externalities. Such actions are costly in the form of policy development, administration, monitoring, enforcement and compliance with regulations. However, governments should intervene in the market only when the monetary and non-monetary benefits from intervention outweigh the costs. The options for intervention include using or creating markets, regulations and education, information, price instruments such as taxes, charges and subsidies, and regulations to restrict the level of produced outputs and uses of inputs. The choice of instruments depends on a number of factors. Appropriateness of the instrument, effectiveness, efficiency and equity are important selection principles. Internalization of external costs from changing environmental conditions should be given a high priority and accounted for in production and consumption decisions.

Externality charges or taxes are used to ensure the costs of negative externalities as well as to reduce the magnitude of externalities. The method is transparent and it provides incentives to the users of water to address environmental externalities from water harvest, storage, delivery and use. An optimal Pigouvian tax schedule that is equal to the marginal cost of external damages caused at each level of water use activity can improve efficiency in water use and provide sufficient incentives to undertake water abatement activities. Taxes combined with quantity regulations or progressive taxes are more helpful in achieving social, economic and environmental targets. In order for the tax to be effective, a number of conditions must be fulfilled. There must be a direct link between the externality and water use, the rate should be continuously overviewed, the tax revenue should not crowd out expenditures on environmental problems and the tax should not present legal uncertainties.

There are a number of factors that are to be taken into account in implementing externality tax on water use. Dwyer et al. (2006) suggests that the tax effects depends on many factors including the tax size, the price effect, the price responsiveness of demand for irrigation water, the initial water allocation, seasonal conditions, trade possibility, and existence of mechanisms to address externalities. Tax is more effective when there is water trade. Other issues in designing an externality tax are the appropriateness of the tax, variation in efficiency benefits, the possibility of interactive externalities, determination of the tax rate, use of the tax revenue and legal feasibility of externality tax. In practice the responses to an externality tax differ across irrigators, districts, seasons, and over time. For instance the decreasing effect of an externality tax on water use can be outweighed by the increase in supply at the market. In the presence of scarcity rents, a tax has no effect, but over time it improves the efficiency in water use.

2.6. Economic and Environmental Advantages of Wastewater Re-Use

One alternative source of additional water is the re-use of wastewater. In situations with scare water sources, the sustainability of agriculture is linked with effectiveness in use of water. The use of fresh water in agriculture is becoming increasingly less economically justified and at the same time the supply of reclaimed sewage and other alternative sources from urban consumption with a high priority of access to fresh water is increasing. Agriculture as a main user of water is subject to competition with other users such as urban, industrial and environmental consumers. Therefore, farmers have to rely on marginal water sources like recycled and saline water. With some health-agriculture-environmental restrictions the urban wastewater can be utilized for agricultural irrigation and river rehabilitation. Devi et al. (2007) investigate the conceptual issues related to the economics of wastewater treatment and recycling.

In regard to the existence of such an environmentally-friendly new wastewater market, Axelrad and Feinerman (2007) aimed at developing and implementing regional planning models which describe the economic, environmental and organizational aspects of sharing fresh and recycled wastewater among entities that co-operate. The potential consumers are the agricultural sector for irrigation and the environmental sector for river rehabilitation. The planning model determines the optimal crop mix and the optimal allocation of limited water and land resources among users. The objective is to maximize regional social welfare which is composed of the net benefits from the two (agriculture and environmental) sectors in the region. The model further determines the total net benefits that should follow certain procedures to be allocated among the economic entities. The model is an extension of optimization models previously introduced by Dinar and Yaron (1986) and Haruvy (1998).

The empirical results in Axelrad and Feinerman are based on the Sharon region in central Israel with two cities operating one wastewater plant, the River Authority and two farmer groups. The objective is to maximize social welfare composed of the sum of agricultural and environmental net benefits in the Sharon region. The maximization is subject to a given supply of wastewater, environmental and health regulations, and the farmers' capability and willingness to utilize the recycled wastewater for crop irrigation accounting for negative environmental damage associated with the use of wastewater. In addition to direct monetary incentives, the model has benefits in the form of a more effective reallocation of fresh water from agriculture to urban areas and cultivation of new land. The model is sensitive to co-operation and acceptable allocation schemes mutually agreed upon. The model is expected to serve as a building block for extended regional analysis under uncertain conditions to provide a basis for policy decisions. For details about the structure of the optimization model and its application see Axelrad and Feinerman (2007).

2.7. Models and Methods Used in Evaluation of Policies, Pricing and Forecasts

The models and methods are formulated and designed to solve problems related to the environment, biology, technology, economics and policies of alternative water resources and their uses. The research is often of multi-disciplinary characters covering several disciplines such as agriculture, biology, technology, politics, economics, sociology, mathematics, statistics, and, in most recent decades, information technology. The alternative sources are in general ground, surface and wastewater while their uses are for household, agriculture, environment and industrial consumption. The players at the market are mainly municipalities, consumers, farmers, business and regulators. There are a number of areas that the water economics literature emphasizes. These are briefly described below without many technical details about the models and methods employed there. The literature on irrigation is a main component. It elaborates on several sub-areas such as: irrigation technology and biotechnology, technology adoption and groundwater conservation, drip irrigation technology, windmills and solar watering systems, and tillage and cropping and irrigation. Another branch of sub-areas include forecasting use of irrigation, costs of land retirement, agricultural sustainability and irrigation, estimation of potential to reduce water demand for irrigation, effects of soil-water-pest-disease relationship on spatial and temporal variability of crops and their outcomes.

Among irrigation incentives and policies to mention are subsidized irrigation water programs and loans, linear dynamic programming approach to irrigation system management, water management and water conservation policies, regional water planning and water management strategies, sewer surcharges and pollution control, nature effects of sewer and wastewater charges and the assessment of methods of maintaining soil productivity to reduce water use for irrigation. The optimal mix of policies and incentives may differ by different background characteristics of sources, users, resources allocated and the environment.

The economic evaluation of different aspects of water, technology adoption and effects of policy measures are intensively studied. These include for instance the electric power deregulation and effects on crop irrigated production and effects of electricity and gas prices on irrigation in agriculture. In particular, the design of models to estimate the optimal use of irrigation water, optimal use of groundwater, optimal use of irrigation and nitrogen use in different production, optimal and priority-based allocation of water sources to alternative uses of water and economic and environmental evaluation of precision farming practices in irrigated cotton production are among areas studied. Several of the studies listed above elaborate these evaluations.

In addition the economic evaluation concerns applications to crop and cotton production and an assessment of their profitability in general, long-term profitability of alternative irrigation loan programs, cost and benefit analysis of water distribution, economics of water pollution control, economic returns from alternative water conservation, economic impact of precision farming and its technology development, water rights, estimation of per capita use and cost of water-based recreation areas, environment economic analysis of municipal waste water irrigation, economic analysis of municipal sewer water and industrial wastewater surcharges and economic analysis of the different water supply alternatives. The economic analysis is further extended to the analysis of investment in alternative irrigation systems, alternative water diversion and distribution systems. Due to space limitation we are unable to go into detailed theories, models, methods and outcomes of such policies and evaluation of their outcomes.

One example of such studies employed in different environments is Farolfi et al. (2007) who use contingence valuation analysis to estimate domestic water use and values in Swaziland. Duda (2003) evaluate integrated management of land and water resources based on a collective approach to fragmented international conventions. There are several country cases studies such as Fang et al. (2006), who study water shortage, water allocation and economic growth in China, and Othe et al. (2003), who study the water utilization of natural and planted trees in Chinese Mongolia, while Jowett (1986) studies the water crisis of Tianjin. Rockstrom (2003) also looks at water for food and nature in drought-prone tropics. Water studies of more global characters include Jackson et al. (2001) on water in changing world and Lundqvist et al. (2003) who focus on dimensions and approaches for third world city water scarcity.

2.8. Summary and Conclusions

This study was aimed at reviewing research on water resources. It investigated the state of water resources at the regional level and the water management policies applied in the Middle East region. The EU water and landscape policy and efforts for a global agenda are reviewed and experiences gained are to be used in the design of water policies for Kurdistan Region. Through studies of legal and common pool aspects and water policies employed in different environments and under different conditions, the determinants of water management and effective policies are to be identified. Special attention is paid to policies targeting major sources and users of water resources such as urban population, agriculture and industry. The areas studied are hydro-politics and water sharing conflicts resolution, urban water management price and investment policies, irrigation externalities and control mechanisms, and economic and environmental advantages of waste water re-use. This review can help with alternative policies to be suggested to remedy a number of problems facing the region.

The Water Framework Directive, which is European legislation designed to preserve, restore and improve the water environment, establishes a framework for managing the water environment by taking into account environmental, social and economic aspects. The directive uses an integrated multi-disciplinary approach based on geography, ecology, economics and sociology. The water initiative is designed as a model for future actions to contribute to meeting the MDGs for drinking water and sanitation within the context of an integrated approach to water resource management. The complexity in EU water planning decisions is addressed by MULINO project. The WFD was followed by the WSSD where the EU launched its water initiative. Addressing the water challenge is seen as a key to sustainable development and reducing poverty.

The politics of water scarcity in relation with the few great waterways, the Nile, the Jordan and the Tigris-Euphrates, as major sources of water in the Middle East and North West Africa, is vast. The water plays a pre-eminent role in survival and can be contentious. The intensity of the conflicts can be further exacerbated by the region's geographic, geopolitics or hydro-political landscape in particular in cases with shortages. The review showed possible solutions to alleviate a water crisis and subsequent political tensions. The role of water resources in the region's ongoing multilateral peace negotiations is emphasized and equity in sharing water resources and principles for co-operative regional water management are discussed. The hydro-political tensions surrounding the Euphrates basin between Turkey, Syria and Iraq in the 1960s and 1970s and Turkish GAP project has been high. The measures in water resource disputes are divided into international water law, needs-based equity, and economic equity. However, the water laws only concern themselves with the rights and responsibilities of states. Political entities with water right claims like Kurds and Palestinians are not represented. In practice, claims for water rights for sharing are often based on geography or on chronology.

The urban water supply is often provided by a public supplier and the demand for the service is inelastic to price level and changes in it. This characteristic of the market may encourage profit maximization and inefficient allocation of water. Government regulations including price control prevent monopolistic rent seeking. The regulator or social planner maximizes the social welfare by water availability constraints. The policy tools available are demand management and supply augmentation. The former involves price, rationing, awareness campaign and incentives to improve water use efficiency by restricting or reducing water use in times of scarcity. The latter policies are concerned with the nature and timing of additions to water inflows and storage capacity supply infrastructure. In the short-run the supply infrastructure is fixed and water consumption has an essential and a non-essential component. In the long run, the supply infrastructures can be altered and there are possibilities to determine simultaneously both demand management and supply augmentation policies.

Agriculture accounts for a large share of total water use. There is large heterogeneity in the quantity and timing of use by location and production specialization. Irrigation has several externalities which change the environment. Many of the changes are associated with the supply and intensive use of water in agriculture. These are distinguished by changes to hydrological, habitat, water quality and ecological conditions. The changes occur at each stage of irrigation water supply and use chain. Frameworks are developed for analyzing the characteristics of externalities incorporating their sources, how they are transmitted and their effects. These characteristics affect the solutions and the effectiveness of their policy instruments. Government actions are needed to address externalities. Such actions are costly in the form of policy development, administration, monitoring, enforcement and compliance with regulations. Governments should intervene in the market only when the benefits from intervention outweigh the costs. The options for intervention include using or creating new water markets, regulations and education, information, price instruments such as taxes, charges and subsidies.

One possible source of additional water is the use of wastewater. The use of fresh water in agriculture is becoming restricted and at the same time the supply of reclaimed sewage and other alternative sources from urban consumption is increasing. Agriculture as a main user of water is subject to competition with other users such as urban, industrial and environmental consumers. Therefore, farmers have to rely on marginal water sources like recycled and saline water. With minor environmental restrictions urban wastewater can be utilized for agricultural irrigation and river rehabilitation. Regional planning models are developed to describe the economic, environmental and organizational aspects of sharing fresh and recycled wastewater among entities. The planning model determines the optimal crop mix and the optimal allocation of limited water and land resources among users. The objective is to maximize regional social welfare.

Models and methods are designed to solve problems related to the environment, technology, economics and policies of alternative water resources and their uses. The research is often of multi-disciplinary characters covering several disciplines such as agriculture, biology, technology, politics, economics, sociology, statistics and information technology.

The alternative sources are in general ground, surface and wastewater while their uses are for household, agriculture and industrial consumption. The players in the market are mainly municipalities, consumers, farmers, businesses and regulators. Regulators maximize social welfare by effective use of water resources. There are a number of areas that the literature emphasizes. The literature on irrigation is a main component. It elaborates on several sub-areas such as irrigation technology adoption, groundwater conservation, drip irrigation, forecasting irrigation, agricultural sustainability, and potential reductions in water demand.

The incentives and policies used include subsidized irrigation programs, linear dynamic programming approach to irrigation system management, water management and water conservation policies, sewer surcharges and pollution control. The economic evaluation of different aspects of water, technology adoption and effects of policy measures are intensively studied. Models are designed to estimate the optimal use of irrigation water, groundwater, irrigation and nitrogen, optimal and priority based allocation of water sources to alternative uses. In addition, the economic evaluation concerns analysis of investment in alternative irrigation systems, alternative water diversion and distribution systems.

Chapter 3

A COMPARATIVE REGIONAL STUDY OF WATER RESOURCES

ABSTRACT

This study presents a comparative partial Middle East regional study of water resources. The objective is to investigate the state of water resources in Kurdistan Region. Due to the lack of separate statistics, Kurdistan Region's water resources will be studied indirectly by aspects of its linkages to the water resources in Iraq and its neighboring countries. The links are in respect to statistics, legal and common pool aspects, water policies and management. The state of water in Iraq and its neighbors is further compared with the average for the Middle East and North Africa and the World. The World Bank's world development indicators database for the period 1981-2005 are used to extract a large number of water resource indicators for the purpose of comparison. These cover major sources and users of water resources such as population, agriculture, industry and services. We find significant heterogeneity among the sample countries and their economic and social conditions change over time. The heterogeneity is related to the land and population sizes of the countries and their agriculture, industrial and population structures. Results suggest that the Iraqi economy is different from other economies in the region due to decades of war, sanctions and destruction. Under such conditions, it is reasonable to expect a significant deterioration in Iraq's living standards and water resource conditions in recent years. The general changes in the structure of the economy, major changes in the population structure, negligence of water resources and in particular the deteriorated water sanitation facilities and water pollutants are among causal factors to the deteriorated environmental and living conditions. Out of date and a lack of regulations and their inappropriate implementation has worsened the situation.

3.1. INTRODUCTION

A study of water resources in Kurdistan Region cannot be conducted without a linkage to the water resources in (the rest of) Iraq and neighboring countries. Nearly the entire water resources of Iraq originate from Kurdistan Region. Even though Kurdistan Region has to release a sizable amount of its water to the rest of Iraq, the greatest impact on the water resources of Kurdistan Region in fact comes from Iran and Turkey. Another link to the rest of Iraq is in respect of the lack of separate statistics, legal aspects, common pool aspects and interrelated water policies and management. However, the inter-relationship should not be limited only to the rest of Iraq, but mostly to the neighboring countries which in the capacity of upstream can dramatically change the water condition downstream in Kurdistan Region. For this reason in this chapter we conduct a comprehensive analysis of the state of water resources in Iraq, its neighboring countries with common pool water resources and also compare it with the average for the Middle East and further with the average of the world. In this way we put Kurdistan Region's and Iraq's water resources and their utilization in a comparative perspective with those of the Middle East and North Africa[12] and the world averages.

The data used in this chapter are there to illustrate the water resource conditions in the Middle East and the world. The information obtained is available in the World Development Indicators (WDI) Data 2006[13] which is compiled and provided by the World Bank. The data covers the period 1960-2005 and it contains 695 economic and social indicators covering agriculture, manufacturing, industry, services, population, governance, finances, trade, etc. Of these we have identified 39 indicators or variables with direct linkage to or strong impact on water resources and environment. These, in the form of descriptive statistics, are used as basis for the general comparative water resources analysis in this chapter.

The indicators are grouped into eight distinct but complementary groups. The first group is related to the agriculture, industry, manufacturing and services share of GDP (Gross Domestic Product). The second group is land area, arable land, irrigated land, forest area, and livestock production index. The third group is the population and its distribution between urban and rural areas. The fourth aspect is the electricity production and consumption. The fifth group involves tourism. The sixth group of indicators is associated with investment in water and improved sanitation facilities and sources defined as the share of the population with access to improved sanitation and treated water. The seventh group is related to emissions and pollution at the aggregate national level, while the eighth group covers the different industries' water pollution measured as their share of the total BOD emissions.[14] Each of these groups of indicators is studied below.

Distribution of the data for Iraq and its neighbors including Iran, Jordan, Kuwait, Saudi Arabia, Syria and Turkey and averages for the Middle East and North African (MENA) and the World's is reported here but can be obtained from the author upon request. Here, as part of the summary statistics, we report the number of observations, number missing values, mean, standard deviation, minimum and maximum values of each indicator.

The indicators measured in percentages (agriculture value added as percentage of GDP) or in per capita or other units (CO2, carbon dioxide, emissions in metric tons per capita)[15] are directly comparable for analysis of distribution, while other indicators measured in quantities (land area and population) are not useful as the scales differ among the countries depending

---

[12] Middle East and North Africa is in the World Development Indicator database is reported together as a group.

[13] For more information about this World Development Indicators Database and its access please see http://www.worldbank.org/

[14] BOD is a measure of industrial organic pollutants per available freshwater measured in metric tons of BOD emissions per cubic km (t/km^3) of water.

[15] Total Emissions (excluding land-use) Units measured as thousand metric tones of carbon dioxide per capita figures are expressed in per 1,000 persons.

on their size of land and the population of the countries. This makes the distribution skewed. Each measure has its own benefits and limitations. The per capita measures neglect levels, while the quantity level intensity in per capita and comparability. Due to the high frequency of missing unit values, we have limited the period of study to 1981-2005. The total number of observations is 225.[16] The period is further divided into 5 sub-periods of 1981-85, 1986-90, 1991-95, 1996-00 and 2001-05. In the latter case the number of observations is 45.[17] The use of average values of indicators per sub-period instead of consecutive years will help to reduce the complexity of tables and reduces the frequency of missing values

3.2. INDICATORS OF WATER RESOURCES

A. Different Sectors Share of GDP

The main sectors of an economy are in general divided into agriculture, industry and services. In addition to this division the data allows for a further separation of manufacturing from the industry sector. Ideally, it should be possible to divide the service sector into private household and public sector recreation and tourism service. Regardless of division and levels, the focus will be on Iraq's position concerning those indicators compared with the neighboring countries. Agriculture is a main sector considering the use of water and as a source of contamination of water from animal husbandry and aquaculture production and the leakages from fertilizer and pesticides used in farming to groundwater. Table 3.1 shows that the world share of agriculture value-added as a share of GDP declined from 6.4% in 1981-85 to 2.6% in 2001-05. The MENA region's share is higher 15.4% than the world (5.0%) during the period 1981-2005. Syria has the highest share at 25.3%, followed by Iran (18.8%) and Turkey (17.4%). Kuwait and Saudi Arabia have the lowest shares, 0.5 and 4.8%, respectively. In general we observe a declining trend in the agriculture share of GDP at all three national, regional and global levels. This is part of process along transformation of societies from agricultural societies to industrial and societies.

The speed of declining agriculture share of GDP is slower in the case of Saudi Arabia and Syria. Saudi Arabia has made comprehensive investment in agriculture with successful outcomes in particular in the area of animal production, but at the same time export of oil and GDP has increased, reducing the relative share of agriculture. The annual growth rate in agriculture value-added was above 10% in 1981-1990.

Table 3.2 shows that the annual growth rate in agriculture valued-added declined to 1.1% post 2000. The highest annual growth rates are attributed to Kuwait in 2001-05 which reached 14.9% and Jordan which attained 10.3%. Among the sample countries we find that Kuwait, Saudi Arabia, Jordan, Iran and Syria have a higher growth rate than average MENA and the world countries average. Iraq shows the lowest annual growth rate.

---

[16] Iraq, 6 neighboring countries, MENA and the World each observed 25 years, 9x25=225 observations.
[17] Iraq, 6 neighboring countries, MENA and the World each observed 5 periods, 9x5=45 observations.

Table 3.1. Agricultural value added (in % of GDP)

Rank	Country	1981-85	1986-90	1991-95	1996-00	2001-05	Average
1	Syria	20.1	26.2	29.5	25.9	24.5	25.3
2	Iran	20.0	24.3	20.3	16.4	11.6	18.8
3	Turkey	22.1	18.4	15.9	16.5	13.0	17.4
4	MENA	15.3	18.3	16.6	14.0	12.3	15.4
5	Iraq	.	.	.	8.3	8.6	8.4
6	Jordan	6.0	7.0	6.4	3.0	2.6	5.1
7	World	6.4	5.7	4.8	4.1	3.5	5.0
8	Saudi	2.3	5.8	5.9	5.5	4.7	4.8
9	Kuwait	0.4	0.6	0.3	0.4	0.5	0.5

Table 3.2. Agricultural value added (in annual % growth)

Rank	Country	1981-85	1986-90	1991-95	1996-00	2001-05	Average
1	Kuwait	.	.	.	1.6	14.9	6.6
2	Saudi	11.6	10.4	2.2	2.0	1.1	5.6
3	Jordan	1.3	12.8	3.6	-3.2	10.3	4.7
4	Iran	5.8	3.2	4.5	2.6	4.6	4.1
5	Syria	-0.6	3.1	6.9	5.6	3.6	3.8
6	MENA	3.2	3.4	2.1	3.6	5.0	3.4
7	World	3.3	2.3	0.8	2.7	2.2	2.3
8	Turkey	0.2	2.3	0.7	2.0	0.3	1.1
9	Iraq	.	.	.	4.2	-3.6	0.3

Table 3.3. Industry value added (in % of GDP)

Rank	Country	1981-85	1986-90	1991-95	1996-00	2001-05	Average
1	Iraq	.	.	.	76.9	74.0	75.7
2	Kuwait	59.0	50.0	44.0	55.3	55.7	52.6
3	Saudi	53.6	41.5	48.8	49.5	54.0	49.3
4	MENA	38.6	31.2	34.7	38.8	41.3	36.7
5	World	36.0	34.0	31.5	29.7	28.2	32.2
6	Iran	32.5	23.5	33.6	31.8	39.7	31.9
7	Turkey	25.3	31.8	30.3	26.2	23.5	27.6
8	Jordan	28.8	25.2	27.8	25.9	27.3	27.0
9	Syria	23.4	22.1	18.7	27.9	28.6	23.9

The positive growth rate (4.2%) in 1996-00 was turned to negative growth rate (-3.6) in 2001-2005. There are no statistics available prior to 1996 for Iraq. The low growth rate and lacking statistics are attributed to the UN imposed sanctions, oil for food program[18] and intervention and invasion conflicts.

---

[18] The Oil for Food Program had the single most damaging effects on agriculture in Iraq due to the free distribution of imported food as part of the program. This made it impossible for local producers to survive under such market conditions. However, the Iraqi Central and Kurdistan Regional Governments are to be blamed for their failure due to their lack of policy or insights into the UN programs. The policy showed that the UN intervened for humanitarian reasons, it facilitated the dumping of the western excess supply of food on the Iraqi market, and finally it made Iraq dependent on imports of food to such an extent that its imported food supply can be achieved only by securing a supply of oil.

The industry share of GDP is increasing and with it, its use of water as input in different production processes. The nature and concentration of industry differs in the Middle East compared to a normal industrialized economy. In the Middle East, the industry sector consists mainly of the Oil and Gas sector. The picture is evidenced in Table 3.3 where the oil producing countries like Iraq, Saudi Arabia and Kuwait, with oil as a significant share of their GDP, dominate, while Turkey, Jordan and Syria are ranked lowest in their industry share of GDP. The sample countries show different development patterns over time. There is a decline in the industry value-added share of GDP post 1981-85, but it recovers in the 90s and 2000s. The average share varies in the average interval maximum of 75.7% (Iraq) and minimum of 23.9% (Syria), keeping in mind the differences in industry structure among oil and non-oil producing countries.

In terms of annual growth rates of industry value-added (see Table 3.4), the non-oil producing countries like Jordan, Syria and Turkey show higher annual growth rates, on average from 5.2% to 5.8% during 1981-2005. The corresponding rates for the oil producers are 1.1% to 4.9%. The lowest rates are attributed to Kuwait and Saudi Arabia, 1.4% and 1.1% respectively. The industry sector value-added growth rates are fluctuating largely and negatively for Saudi Arabia (-12.6% in 1981-85), Syria (10.3% in 1986-90), Iraq (25.7% in 1996-99 and -15.9% in 2001-05). The volatility in the growth rate of industry share of value-added in the case of Iraq is attributed to the 2003 invasion and pre-war sanctions and terrorist actions against the oil infrastructure after the invasion, as well as the country's desire to increase its production capacity to reconstruct and develop its public development infrastructure.

Table 3.4. Industry value added (in annual % growth)

Rank	Country	1981-85	1986-90	1991-95	1996-00	2001-05	Average
1	Jordan	10.5	-1.1	8.3	2.6	9.7	5.8
2	Syria	5.8	10.3	9.5	5.0	-5.0	5.6
3	Turkey	7.5	7.1	4.3	3.5	3.1	5.2
4	Iraq	.	.	.	25.7	-15.9	4.9
5	Iran	8.3	4.1	1.4	-0.5	7.9	4.1
6	MENA	5.7	2.7	2.5	3.7	2.1	3.4
7	World	1.6	3.7	1.6	3.1	1.4	2.4
8	Kuwait	.	.	.	0.3	3.1	1.4
9	Saudi	-12.6	8.7	4.6	1.9	3.6	1.1

Table 3.5. Manufacturing value added (in % of GDP)

Rank	Country	1981-85	1986-90	1991-95	1996-00	2001-05	Average
1	World	.	22.8	21.0	19.5	17.7	20.4
2	Turkey	17.0	20.6	19.5	16.5	14.3	17.7
3	Syria	.	20.4	14.6	21.6	.	16.4
4	Jordan	13.3	11.8	14.4	15.0	17.2	14.2
5	MENA	11.1	13.4	14.6	13.1	12.8	13.0
6	Iran	9.2	10.4	13.9	13.6	12.3	11.9
7	Saudi	6.4	8.7	9.1	10.1	10.3	8.9
8	Kuwait	5.5	12.7	7.4	3.3	2.8	6.7
9	Iraq	.	.	.	0.8	1.6	1.1

None of the countries, neither the MENA average exceeds the World average concerning the manufacturing value-added share of GDP (Table 3.5). Unlike industry, which incorporates the oil and gas industries, manufacturing represents pure technology and the degree of industrialization of the countries' economies. After the world average, Turkey (17.7%), Syria (16.4%) and Jordan (14.2%) are ranked higher than average MENA (13.0%), while Iran, Saudi Arabia, Kuwait and Iraq (only 1.1%) are ranked lower than the MENA region's average. It seems that there is a negative relationship between oil production and the development of manufacturing. It is a reflection of the development policies failure in taking advantage of the oil sector to promote industrial development. It is also evident that more attention is devoted to the development of gas and oil at the cost of manufacturing and location production.

The annual growth rate of the manufacturing value-added share of GDP is in general positive but irregular and non-systematic. Exceptions according to Table 3.6 are the case of Kuwait in relation to the Iraqi invasion of the country in the early 90s and Iraq in the post 2000 period. The rank of the countries changes and it is less linked to the oil producing characteristics of the sample countries. The highest positive growth rate is that of the Jordanian manufacturing in 2001-05. It is a result of the increased insecurity in Iraq and negative development of its manufacturing which is compensated for by increased capacity building in the neighboring country of Jordan.

Table 3.6. Manufacturing value added (in annual % growth)

Rank	Country	1981-85	1986-90	1991-95	1996-00	2001-05	Average
1	Iran	5.1	6.3	6.0	5.4	10.7	6.5
2	Turkey	8.3	7.6	5.2	4.0	4.7	6.0
3	Saudi	10.0	2.7	4.0	6.0	5.5	5.7
4	Jordan	1.8	2.8	6.7	5.3	11.7	5.4
5	MENA	.	5.1	3.2	5.0	5.3	4.6
6	World	.	.	.	4.9	1.0	2.5
7	Kuwait	.	.	.	-0.4	2.5	0.7
8	Iraq	.	.	.	0.8	-11.3	-5.2
9	Syria	.	.	.	.	.	.

Table 3.7. Services value added (in % of GDP)

Rank	Country	1981-85	1986-90	1991-95	1996-00	2001-05	Average
1	Jordan	65.2	67.8	65.8	71.0	70.2	67.9
2	World	57.6	60.4	63.7	66.1	68.2	62.8
3	Turkey	52.6	49.8	53.7	57.3	63.5	55.1
4	Syria	56.5	51.7	51.9	46.2	46.9	50.8
5	Iran	47.5	52.2	46.1	51.7	48.7	49.3
6	MENA	46.2	50.5	48.8	47.1	46.4	47.9
7	Kuwait	40.5	49.4	55.6	44.3	43.8	47.0
8	Saudi	44.2	52.7	45.4	45.0	41.3	45.9
9	Iraq	.	.	.	14.8	17.4	15.9

The evolution of societies from agriculture to basic industry/manufacturing, industry/manufacturing with quality advancement and then to a service and knowledge-based society has led to a deceleration pattern in the agricultural society but an acceleration pattern in the industrial society. The development is towards an industry society combined with a strongly developing service sector. The degree of acceleration increases with advancement of quality and the accelerating progress of the service and knowledge-based society. The growth in economies as a result of technology advancement, improved labor productivity and increased use of production inputs generates a bigger gap in the share of manufacturing and services and an accelerating tradeoff between the two over time as the knowledge-based society emerges and develops.

Jordan is the country that has a higher share of services (67.9%) than the world average (62.8%). It is a result of the insecurity in Iraq, where the majority of international and some Iraqi national organizations have moved their headquarters and operations to Jordan (see Table 3.7). Similar developments are found in the case of Iraq's other neighbors, Turkey (55.1%), Syria (50.8%) and Iran (49.3%), which in part can be attributed to service demand from Iraq. This is confirmed by the fact that all the countries above exceed that of the average MENA region. The average services share of GDP for the period 1996-2005 in Iraq is only 15.9%. The declining annual growth rate in Iraq's services is matched by similar expansions in services in its neighbors Jordan, Turkey, Syria and Iran, in the interval 4.0% to 9.2% (see Table 3.8).

Table 3.8. Services value added (in annual % growth)

Rank	Country	1981-85	1986-90	1991-95	1996-00	2001-05	Average
1	Turkey	5.2	4.7	3.4	4.3	4.0	4.3
2	Iran	3.2	-3.3	9.4	7.1	4.9	4.2
3	MENA	5.3	1.4	4.7	4.2	4.7	4.0
4	Syria	4.0	-1.1	7.7	-1.2	9.2	3.5
5	Jordan	4.4	-1.9	5.7	4.1	4.5	3.3
6	Kuwait	.	.	.	2.6	3.9	3.1
7	World	2.9	3.6	2.6	3.6	2.3	3.1
8	Saudi	4.0	-0.7	1.4	3.5	3.6	2.3
9	Iraq	.	.	.	-14.7	10.9	-1.9

B. Land, Irrigation, Forest, Livestock Production and Fertilizer Consumption

The sample countries differ in their land size measured in squared km (see Table 3.9). The land size is constant over time. The world's land size was largely changed in 1992. It has not been possible to find any explanations for the change. The MENA share is 7.52% of the world's land size. Saudi Arabia, the largest among MENA countries occupies 20% of MENA's land size. Iran is the second largest country in our sample and geographically it does not belong to MENA. The same applies to Turkey, which has a desire to become and considers itself to be part of Europe. Due to the fact that they border Iraq, we have added them to the sample. Kuwait is the smallest with only 17.8 thousand squared km of land size.

Only a small fraction of the world's land is used for agriculture. The share of the arable land varies between 10.5% and 10.8% of the total land size during the study period. Table 3.10 shows that there is a slowly increasing trend in the size of arable land. The corresponding share for the MENA region is 5.7% but with a small decline in the growth rate over time. Among the sample countries Turkey (31.8%) and Syria (25.1%) have the highest shares, while Kuwait (0.8%), Saudi Arabia (1.7%) and Jordan (3.1%) had the lowest in 2001-05. The Iraqi share is around 12.0% and is mainly concentrated in the north. However, in recent years in relation to urbanization, the UN-managed Oil for Food Program, and mismanagement of the agricultural policy, it might have declined significantly.

Water is a scarce resource which is used foremost in the irrigation of land. Only 18.0% of the world's arable land was irrigated in 2001-2005 (See Table 3.11). The corresponding proportion for the MENA region is 29.1%. The share is highest for Kuwait, Iraq, Saudi Arabia and Iran, but lowest for Jordan, Syria and Turkey. The irrigated land share in Iraq increased from 32.0% in 1981-85 to 63.3% 10 years later, but it declined again to 58.6% in 2001-05. The change might be attributed to exclusion of non-irrigated land from statistics, changes in structure of the rural population, a bi-product of the production of electricity for urban areas where water is used for agriculture as well, changes in priorities in allocation of resources, inability to develop agriculture and mismanagement of agriculture and water resources.

A total of 30.5% of the world's land area is forest (see Table 3.12). The corresponding proportion for the MENA region is only 2.3%. Turkey (13.0%) and Iran (6.8%) have a higher rate than the average for MENA but remaining sample countries have much lower rates, 0.3%-2.3%. The low rate of forestation is a result of mismanagement of the land, in particular the heights which are often used for grazing in the northern part of the MENA region. It should be noted that the forest areas in the MENA and Iran are not often productive forest for industrial use. It is just recently that the countries' environmental agencies have been able to prevent deforestation for cooking and heating purposes in the rural areas. The low rate of forestation makes the land vulnerable to erosion.

The development and heterogeneity in livestock production among the sample countries and in relation to the world and MENA average is large (see Table 3.13). The livestock production index for the world has increased from 61.3 in1981 to 109.0 in 2005. The index base 1999-2001=100. It reflects the increased world population and its food demand. The corresponding rate for MENA is much faster by an increase from 49.9 to 109.8 and a reflection of its larger population growth. The Turkey's livestock production index is higher than the world's. Syria is the highest among the MENA countries but the lowest rates are those of Saudi Arabia and Kuwait. However, the latter countries have been investing much in food production and thereby the livestock production has increased significantly. There are no statistics available for Iraq concerning livestock production during the entire period of the study. In Kurdistan Region, with a strong tradition in agriculture and livestock production, there is marked decline in animal husbandry. It is a result of unbalanced economic development where priorities are given to the construction of public infrastructure and the drought in recent years. The drought resulting in a lack of water and grazing led to the slaughter of animals and it will take a long time to build up the stock again.

The world's fertilizer consumption measured in 100 grams per hectare of arable land increased from 850 to 1009 during 1981-2005. The corresponding rate for the MENA region is an increase from 460 to over 860 (see Table 3.14). Kuwait and Saudi Arabia are use a higher rate than the world, followed by Turkey, Iran and Jordan which in turn use a higher rate than the world, while Syria's and Iraq's usage rates are the lowest. The low rate of Iraq is due to its extremely low usage rate in the past. The consumption rate increased from 146 in 1981 to over 1111 in 2002.

Table 3.9. Land area (in 1000 sq km)

Rank	Country	1981-85	1986-90	1991-95	1996-00	2001-05	Average
1	World	106637.8	106648.8	124770.8	129648.4	129662.3	119049.1
2	MENA	8954.9	8954.9	8954.9	8954.9	8954.9	8954.9
3	Saudi	2149.7	2149.7	2149.7	2149.7	2149.7	2149.7
4	Iran	1636.2	1636.2	1636.2	1636.2	1636.2	1636.2
5	Turkey	769.6	769.6	769.6	769.6	769.6	769.6
6	Iraq	437.4	437.4	437.4	437.4	437.4	437.4
7	Syria	183.8	183.8	183.8	183.8	183.8	183.8
8	Jordan	88.2	88.2	88.2	88.2	88.2	88.2
9	Kuwait	17.8	17.8	17.8	17.8	17.8	17.8

Table 3.10. Arable land (in % of total land area)

Rank	Country	1981-85	1986-90	1991-95	1996-00	2001-05	Average
1	Turkey	31.8	32.2	32.0	31.6	30.8	31.7
2	Syria	28.1	26.7	26.1	25.5	25.1	26.4
3	Iraq	12.0	12.1	12.0	12.0	13.1	12.2
4	World	10.5	10.7	10.8	10.8	10.8	10.7
5	Iran	8.8	9.4	10.5	9.9	9.3	9.6
6	MENA	5.4	5.6	5.9	5.9	5.7	5.7
7	Jordan	3.4	3.4	3.1	2.8	3.1	3.2
8	Saudi	1.0	1.4	1.7	1.7	1.7	1.5
9	Kuwait	0.1	0.2	0.3	0.4	0.8	0.3

Table 3.11. Irrigated land (in % of total cropland)

Rank	Country	1981-85	1986-90	1991-95	1996-00	2001-05	Average
1	Kuwait	.	53.3	67.3	82.7	77.0	71.3
2	Iraq	32.0	43.5	63.3	63.0	58.6	51.5
3	Saudi	38.5	46.2	42.9	43.5	42.7	42.8
4	Iran	39.7	42.3	38.3	41.5	44.1	40.9
5	MENA	24.9	27.5	30.0	31.5	32.9	29.1
6	World	16.5	16.8	17.0	17.8	18.0	17.2
7	Jordan	12.4	16.3	18.3	19.3	18.8	16.9
8	Syria	10.4	11.9	17.7	21.6	24.1	16.6
9	Turkey	11.3	13.6	15.1	16.4	19.5	14.8

Table 3.12. Forest area (in % of total land area)

Rank	Country	1981-85	1986-90	1991-95	1996-00	2001-05	Average
1	World	.	30.0	.	30.8	30.5	30.4
2	Turkey	.	12.6	.	13.1	13.2	13.0
3	Iran	.	6.8	.	6.8	6.8	6.8
4	MENA	.	2.2	.	2.3	2.4	2.3
5	Syria	.	2.0	.	2.4	2.5	2.3
6	Iraq	.	1.8	.	1.9	1.9	1.9
7	Saudi	.	1.3	.	1.3	1.3	1.3
8	Jordan	.	0.9	.	0.9	0.9	0.9
9	Kuwait	.	0.2	.	0.3	0.3	0.3

Table 3.13. Livestock production index (1999-2001=100)

Rank	Country	1981-85	1986-90	1991-95	1996-00	2001-05	Average
1	Turkey	81.4	91.6	94.3	100.3	100.2	93.3
2	World	64.2	75.5	86.2	95.7	105.7	84.6
3	Syria	63.2	68.4	73.1	95.0	111.1	81.0
4	MENA	53.2	64.8	74.8	93.6	106.4	77.4
5	Jordan	41.6	53.8	89.2	100.7	95.8	75.4
6	Iran	48.9	58.7	76.9	93.7	103.5	75.2
7	Kuwait	58.8	82.2	37.3	86.6	114.6	74.3
8	Saudi	37.8	59.7	70.7	89.7	105.2	71.3
9	Iraq	.	.	.	.	.	.

Table 3.14. Fertilizer consumption (in 100 grams per hectare of arable land)

Rank	Country	1981-85	1986-90	1991-95	1996-00	2001-05	Average
1	Kuwait	2300.0	1005.0	1600.0	1840.1	752.3	1601.4
2	Saudi	851.7	1506.2	1178.6	954.7	1062.6	1117.3
3	World	883.2	976.4	907.8	981.8	995.8	942.6
4	Turkey	604.7	694.1	741.1	831.6	714.2	717.5
5	Iran	619.9	692.8	633.7	781.0	894.5	701.2
6	Jordan	455.5	568.5	608.7	901.3	1039.1	670.4
7	MENA	545.5	658.1	622.8	735.3	852.1	659.6
8	Syria	358.5	551.5	678.6	764.4	674.3	596.1
9	Iraq	221.0	406.8	538.8	706.2	1111.4	526.7

No statistics are available for the recent years of fertilizer consumption in Iraq. The fast growing rate is also found in the case of Jordan. Leakage from fertilizer and pesticides to ground and surface sources of water are among the two major sources of water pollution.

C. Urban Population

The population of the world has been steadily growing from 4.51 billion in 1991 to 6.37 billion in 2004. Table 3.15 shows that the development of the sample, MENA and the world population from 1981 to 2005. The MENA population in the same period increased from 173.4 to 300.3 million. Despite a positive net flow of migration from the region, the region's population has been developed faster than the world's. However, the growth rate has been declining. Turkey and Iran have higher populations, 71.7 and 67.0 million, than Iraq with 24.4 million in 1999. There are no population statistics available post-1999, but only population projections. Kuwait with 2.5 million and Jordan with 5.5 million are the smallest sample countries. The two countries' population movements have fluctuated highly due to war and immigration.

There are positive changes in the urbanization of the population structure at the global level. The Table 3.16 shows that more than 48% of the world's population lives in urban areas. The most recent figure for the MENA shows a higher level, 56.3% in 2005. In general there is an increasing trend in urbanization across the world and MENA, including all of our sample countries. However, the condition in Iraq's case is somewhat different with periodical fluctuations. The degree and fluctuation of the patterns differ among the countries. For instance, the highest urban share of the population is that of Kuwait with more than 96% and the lowest is that of Syria with close to 52% and lower than the MENA average. The Iraqi urban population increased from 66.2% in 1981 to 69.7% in 1990. In the period since 1990 it has been declining, reaching 67.1% in 2004. The reverse urbanization for Iraq might be attributed to the war and increasing violence and insecurity in the urban areas.

The increased urbanization is confirmed by looking at Table 3.17. The annual growth rate of the urban population is 2.4% in the world, while the corresponding figure for the MENA region is 3.2%. It should be noted that the growth rate is positive but declines over time. Saudi Arabia, Jordan, Turkey, Iran and Syria show a higher annual growth rate than the average for MENA, while Iraq and Kuwait have lower rates. A significant change in the urban population growth rate is found in the case of Kuwait. It declined with 44.3% in 1990 in relation to the Iraqi invasion of Kuwait. The invasion and subsequent refugee flows led to an increased growth rate in the urban population in Jordan from 5.3% to 12.8% in the same year. Changes in the structure of urban-rural populations and the urban population's positive and high growth rate have strong implications for the management of water demand and supply across the region. Thus, changes in population should be monitored better and on a regular basis for the purpose of planning and water management.

Table 3.15. Total population (in 1,000,000)

Rank	Country	1981-85	1986-90	1991-95	1996-00	2001-05	Average
1	World	4666.7	5081.1	5504.2	5905.6	6251.5	5449.7
2	MENA	184.5	213.1	241.9	268.3	291.8	237.7
3	Turkey	47.9	53.8	59.5	65.2	70.1	58.8
4	Iran	43.7	51.8	57.1	62.0	65.9	55.7
5	Iraq	15.4	17.6	20.3	23.3	.	18.9
6	Saudi	11.5	15.0	17.8	20.3	23.0	17.3
7	Syria	10.1	12.0	14.0	16.0	17.9	13.8
8	Jordan	2.5	3.0	3.9	4.6	5.2	3.8
9	Kuwait	1.6	2.0	1.6	2.0	2.4	1.9

Table 3.16. Urban population (in % of total population)

Rank	Country	1981-85	1986-90	1991-95	1996-00	2001-05	Average
1	Kuwait	92.8	94.6	95.3	95.8	96.2	94.9
2	Saudi	69.9	76.0	81.0	84.8	87.3	79.5
3	Jordan	63.9	69.9	75.8	78.5	79.0	73.2
4	Iraq	67.5	69.3	69.2	68.2	67.4	68.4
5	Turkey	49.0	56.5	61.0	63.7	66.1	59.0
6	Iran	51.9	55.2	58.7	62.7	66.2	58.6
7	MENA	48.5	50.9	52.8	54.5	55.9	52.4
8	Syria	47.4	48.5	49.5	50.0	50.2	49.1
9	World	40.3	42.3	44.3	46.3	48.1	44.1

Table 3.17. Urban population growth (in annual %)

Rank	Country	1981-85	1986-90	1991-95	1996-00	2001-05	Average
1	Saudi	7.8	6.3	3.8	3.6	3.3	5.0
2	Jordan	5.8	5.3	7.2	3.2	2.9	5.0
3	Turkey	6.1	4.6	2.9	2.6	2.3	3.8
4	Iran	5.2	4.0	2.9	2.9	2.4	3.5
5	Syria	4.3	3.9	3.1	2.7	2.6	3.3
6	MENA	4.3	3.5	3.0	2.5	2.5	3.2
7	Iraq	3.9	2.8	2.8	2.7	2.5	3.0
8	World	2.7	2.7	2.4	2.2	2.1	2.4
9	Kuwait	5.1	4.5	-44.3	4.0	3.0	1.8

D. Electricity Production

There is a negative trend in the share of electricity production from hydro-electric sources. It declined from 19.0% in 1983 to 15.8% in 2003 (see Table 3.18). The corresponding decline in the MENA region was much sharper and fell from 24.5% in 1981 to 7.4% in 2003. The decline in the share does not reflect the true production level changes. The production of electricity at the global level has increased significantly, but is diversified and mainly based on non-hydro sources of production such as oil, gas, and wind, solar power and other sources.

Turkey (38.3%) and Syria (25.2%) have the highest shares of total electricity consumption, which is generated from hydro power, while Iran (11.9%), Iraq (4.1%) and Jordan (0.4%) have the lowest shares. There are no statistics available for Saudi Arabia and Kuwait. These countries use fuel-based electricity production. Iraq increased its production share from 2.7% in 1986 to 11.6% in 1987. However, the share declined gradually to 1.5% in 2003. The statistics for Iraq are not reliable and are volatile due to frequent interruptions in production, mainly for various technical reasons.

In recent years the oil-based production is the main source, while imports from Iran and Turkey have also been significant components. Hydro-power electricity production has strong implications for the management of water and strong impacts on the second and third parties' water consumption, as well as on nature and rural life.

Table 3.18. Electricity production from hydro-electric sources (% of total production)

Rank	Country	1981-85	1986-90	1991-95	1996-00	2001-05	Average
1	Turkey	45.0	41.4	40.7	34.7	23.6	38.3
2	Syria	46.5	30.2	19.1	12.9	11.6	25.2
3	World	18.5	16.6	18.1	17.8	16.2	17.6
4	MENA	18.9	14.0	10.6	8.2	7.1	12.1
5	Iran	19.2	15.3	11.1	5.9	5.6	11.9
6	Iraq	3.9	9.4	2.7	1.9	1.8	4.1
7	Jordan	.	0.4	0.3	0.3	0.6	0.4
8	Kuwait	.	.	.	.	.	.
9	Saudi	.	.	.	.	.	.

Thus, the crowding out effects of hydropower electricity generation is strong and economically not sustainable. Maneta et al. (2007) present a hydro-economic model for assessing the effects of surface water and groundwater policies.

E. Tourism and Private Investment in Water

At the global level, the tourism share of total imports is 9.6% (Table 3.19). The MENA average share is less, 7.3%. Kuwait, Syria, Jordan and Saudi Arabia have the highest shares, 9.6% to 22.0% and Iran the lowest rate, 2.4%. No statistics from Turkey and Iraq are available. Turkey is a main destination for many European, Middle Eastern and Russian tourists. The flow is to Turkey and not the other way round. Thus, the tourism share of imports might be very low. Iraqi non-official citizens face visa and financial restrictions in their international movements.

Table 3.19. International tourism, expenditures (in % of total imports)

Rank	Country	1981-85	1986-90	1991-95	1996-00	2001-05	Average
1	Kuwait	.	.	19.9	22.0	23.9	22.6
2	Syria	.	.	.	.	10.3	10.3
3	Jordan	.	.	14.7	10.7	7.1	9.7
4	Saudi	.	.	.	.	9.6	9.6
5	World	.	.	7.9	7.5	7.0	7.3
6	MENA	.	.	4.3	4.9	6.5	5.5
7	Iran	.	.	1.6	2.5	.	2.4
8	Iraq	.	.	.	.	.	.
9	Turkey	.	.	.	.	.	.

Table 3.20. International tourism, receipts (in % of total exports)

Rank	Country	1981-85	1986-90	1991-95	1996-00	2001-05	Average
1	Jordan	.	.	28.0	28.6	26.1	27.5
2	Syria	.	.	.	.	17.8	17.8
3	MENA	.	.	12.3	13.4	16.7	14.6
4	World	.	.	8.0	7.7	6.9	7.4
5	Saudi	.	.	.	.	4.7	4.7
6	Kuwait	.	.	2.2	2.7	1.5	2.2
7	Iran	.	.	1.1	2.2	.	2.0
8	Iraq	.	.	.	.	.	.
9	Turkey	.	.	.	.	.	.

Concerning the receipts of international tourists, the MENA average (14.6%) is twice the world's average (7.4%) of total exports. Table 3.20 shows that Jordan and Syria top the list with their share, 27.5 and 17.8%. This might be due to the concentration of NGOs and air transport between Iraq and these two countries. The lowest rates are associated with Iran (2.0%), Kuwait (2.2%) and Saudi Arabia (4.7%). No such statistics are available for Turkey and Iraq. As mentioned previously, Turkey is a main destination for the inflow of international tourists. The country has been successful in developing its tourism industry. The north and south-west coastal parts and major historical sites play a key role in the attraction of tourists to the country. The service industry share of GDP and its annual growth rates was 64.7% and 8.3% in 2004, respectively.

Table 3.20. International tourism, receipts (in % of total exports)

Rank	Country	1981-85	1986-90	1991-95	1996-00	2001-05	Average
1	Jordan	.	.	28.0	28.6	26.1	27.5
2	Syria	.	.	.	.	17.8	17.8
3	MENA	.	.	12.3	13.4	16.7	14.6
4	World	.	.	8.0	7.7	6.9	7.4
5	Saudi	.	.	.	.	4.7	4.7
6	Kuwait	.	.	2.2	2.7	1.5	2.2
7	Iran	.	.	1.1	2.2	.	2.0
8	Iraq	.	.	.	.	.	.
9	Turkey	.	.	.	.	.	.

F. Improved Sanitation Facilities and Water Resources

The private investment in water and sanitation resources is measured in current values and per $1,000,000 reported in table 3.21. The information is available only since 1991. Limited information is available for average MENA region and a few of the sample countries in recent years, but this are non-systematic and only available on an irregular basis. The few statistics show that in the Middle East, despite no or low income tax, little private effort ($197) is made to improve sanitation facilities and water resources. The effort is far below the world average ($3028).

A number of measures related to improved sanitation facilities are used. The estimated data collections cover only 1990 and 2002. These include percentage share of total, rural and urban components of the total population with access to improved sanitation. We report these three measures in tables 3.22, 3.23 and 3.24, respectively. There is a marked increase in the share of the population with access to improved sanitation facilities. The world average increased from 43.2% to 54.3% (see Table 3.22). The share in the MENA region increased from 69.2% to 74.7%. Jordan tops the list with 93.0% followed by Iran (84.0%), Turkey (83.0%), Iraq (80.0%) and Syria (77.0%). No statistics have been collected covering Saudi Arabia and Kuwait.

The ranking of the countries in improvement of sanitation facilities differs when population is decomposed into urban and rural areas. As expected, there is a significant inequality among the two population sub-groups with access to public investment in infrastructure. The rural population's share at the global and MENA levels is 34.8% and 53.5%, respectively (see Table 3.23). Other countries' rural share varies in the interval 56.0 and 85.0%. The share of the Iraqi rural population is only 48.0% with a larger gap compared to the level of the neighboring countries and to the urban population. Iraq was ranked as 178 out of 180 countries as one of the most corrupt countries in the world in 2006.[19] The gap in provision of finances to improve sanitation facilities must have deteriorated in the past few

---

[19] See The 2006 Transparency International Corruption Perceptions Index, an annual survey conducted by the Berlin-based organization Transparency International, viewed on September 22, 2008 at: http://www.infoplease.com/ipa/A0781359.html

years and in particular for the disadvantaged rural areas. Finland, Denmark, and New Zealand are perceived to be the world's least corrupt countries, and Iraq, Somalia and Myanmar are perceived to be the most corrupt countries.

Table 3.21. Private investment in water and sanitation (current in 1000,000 US$)

Rank	Country	1981-85	1986-90	1991-95	1996-00	2001-05	Average
1	World	.	.	2012.8	4939.4	1907.6	3028.0
2	Turkey	.	.	.	471.0	.	471.0
3	MENA	.	.	6.0	336.5	84.5	197.4
4	Jordan	.	.	.	0.0	169.0	84.5
5	Saudi	.	.	.	.	26.0	26.0
6	Iran	.	.	.	.	.	.
7	Iraq	.	.	.	.	.	.
8	Kuwait	.	.	.	.	.	.
9	Syria	.	.	.	.	.	.

Table 3.22. Improved sanitation facilities (in % of population with access)

Rank	Country	1981-85	1986-90	1991-95	1996-00	2001-05	Average
1	Jordan	.	.	.	.	93.0	93.0
2	Iran	.	83.0	.	.	84.0	83.5
3	Turkey	.	84.0	.	.	83.0	83.5
4	Iraq	.	81.0	.	.	80.0	80.5
5	Syria	.	76.0	.	.	77.0	76.5
6	MENA	.	69.2	.	.	74.7	72.0
7	World	.	43.2	.	.	54.3	48.8
8	Kuwait	.	.	.	.	.	.
9	Saudi	.	.	.	.	.	.

Table 3.23. Improved sanitation facilities, rural (in % of population with access)

Rank	Country	1981-85	1986-90	1991-95	1996-00	2001-05	Average
1	Jordan	.	.	.	.	85.0	85.0
2	Iran	.	78.0	.	.	78.0	78.0
3	Turkey	.	67.0	.	.	62.0	64.5
4	Syria	.	56.0	.	.	56.0	56.0
5	MENA	.	51.4	.	.	55.6	53.5
6	Iraq	.	48.0	.	.	48.0	48.0
7	World	.	21.8	.	.	34.8	28.3
8	Kuwait	.	.	.	.	.	.
9	Saudi	.	.	.	.	.	.

The urban population with access to improved sanitation facilities at the global level is 78.6% which is below the MENA level (87.8%) and the remaining sample countries (95.0-100.0%), Iran being an exception (87.8%). Table 3.24 shows that Saudi Arabia reports 100% access rate. Iraq reports 95.0% access rate which is based on statistics collected in 2002. The situation in general has deteriorated since the invasion of 2003. Kurdistan Region is an exemption where significant investments in public infrastructures have been made, but yet no standards have been established concerning private households' obligations.

Similar to sanitation facilities, access to improved water sources is reported for the entire population and is also decomposed into rural and urban sub-populations. These data are reported in table 3.25, 3.26 and 3.27, respectively. Again the data is estimated and it covers only two years, 1990 and 2002. The world share of total population with improved water sources in 2002 (81.7%) is much lower than the average MENA country (87.8%). From Table 3.25 it can be seen that the access rate for other sample countries varies somewhat and in the interval 79.0% (Syria) and 91.0% (Jordan). The access rate for Iraq in 2002 is 81.0% - somewhat lower than in 1990 (83.0%). Again we observe differences in the access rate to improved water sources by the rural and urban sub-populations (see Table 3.26 and 3.27).

Table 3.24. Improved urban sanitation facilities (in % of population with access)

Rank	Country	1981-85	1986-90	1991-95	1996-00	2001-05	Average
1	Saudi	.	100.0	.	.	100.0	100.0
2	Syria	.	97.0	.	.	97.0	97.0
3	Jordan	.	97.0	.	.	94.0	95.5
4	Iraq	.	95.0	.	.	95.0	95.0
5	Turkey	.	96.0	.	.	94.0	95.0
6	MENA	.	86.4	.	.	89.1	87.8
7	Iran	.	86.0	.	.	86.0	86.0
8	World	.	76.3	.	.	78.6	77.5
9	Kuwait	.	.	.	.	.	.

Table 3.25. Improved water source (in % of population with access)

Rank	Country	1981-85	1986-90	1991-95	1996-00	2001-05	Average
1	Jordan	.	98.0	.	.	91.0	94.5
2	Iran	.	91.0	.	.	93.0	92.0
3	Saudi	.	90.0	.	.	.	90.0
4	MENA	.	87.1	.	.	87.8	87.5
5	Turkey	.	81.0	.	.	93.0	87.0
6	Iraq	.	83.0	.	.	81.0	82.0
7	Syria	.	79.0	.	.	79.0	79.0
8	World	.	75.0	.	.	81.7	78.4
9	Kuwait	.	.	.	.	.	.

Table 3.26. Improved rural water source (in % of rural population with access)

Rank	Country	1981-85	1986-90	1991-95	1996-00	2001-05	Average
1	Jordan	.	91.0	.	.	91.0	91.0
2	Iran	.	83.0	.	.	83.0	83.0
3	MENA	.	78.7	.	.	78.6	78.7
4	Turkey	.	65.0	.	.	87.0	76.0
5	World	.	61.9	.	.	71.3	66.6
6	Syria	.	64.0	.	.	64.0	64.0
7	Saudi	.	63.0	.	.	.	63.0
8	Iraq	.	50.0	.	.	50.0	50.0
9	Kuwait	.	.	.	.	.	.

Table 3.27. Improved water urban source (in % of urban population with access)

Rank	Country	1981-85	1986-90	1991-95	1996-00	2001-05	Average
1	Iran	.	98.0	.	.	98.0	98.0
2	Iraq	.	97.0	.	.	97.0	97.0
3	Saudi	.	97.0	.	.	97.0	97.0
4	Jordan	.	100.0	.	.	91.0	95.5
5	MENA	.	95.5	.	.	95.4	95.5
6	World	.	95.1	.	.	94.4	94.8
7	Syria	.	94.0	.	.	94.0	94.0
8	Turkey	.	92.0	.	.	96.0	94.0
9	Kuwait	.	.	.	.	.	.

The difference, however, is much smaller compared to the access rate for sanitation facilities. The access rate for the world's rural and urban populations in 2002 was 71.3% and 94.4%, respectively. The corresponding number for the average MENA country was higher and reached 78.6% and 95.4%. The remaining countries rural and urban population's percentage access rates are in the interval 50.0-91.0 and 96.0-98.0. The total access rate for the Iraqi population is 81.0% and for the rural and urban sub-groups 50.0% and 97.0%, respectively, indicating as previously mentioned significant inequality in access to water sources. Great inequality in opportunities and differences in the intensity of war at different locations in Iraq suggest the presence of enormous variations within the rural population at different places.

G. Emissions and Organic Water Pollutants

The CO_2 emissions measured in annual metric tons per capita are reported in table 3.28. There is a positive trend in the quantity of emissions across all country series. The Kuwait (21.2), Saudi Arabia (13.4) and Iran (4.2) levels are higher than the average world level (3.9) which in turn is much higher than the average MENA level (2.7). The remaining country levels are in the interval 2.6-3.1 tons, where Turkey has the lowest rate. Kuwait is the country with the highest emissions rate. The level increased from 18.6 in 1990 to 30.0 in 1995 and then declined to 26.5 tons in 2002. We do not identify the causing factor behind Kuwait's emission rate which is more than eight times that of Turkey which has a higher developed industry sector. The development and level patterns of combustible renewable and waste as percentage of total energy is opposite to that of emissions reported above. These are reported in table 3.29. The average study periods rate for Turkey (14.3%) is much higher than the world average (11.0%), MENA (1.8%) and Iran (1.0%). The remaining countries' share of the total energy is negligible and close to zero. The aggregate organic water pollutant (BOD) emissions measured in 1000 kg per day is reported in Table 3.30. Turkey (172.8) and Iran (110.8) are ranked as the highest pollutants. The rate for Iraq is 28.2 kg per day. There is a positive association between the size of the population and possibly the agriculture share of GDP and the organic water pollutants. This is confirmed by the low rate of Kuwait (9.2 kg per day). The population adjusted measure in kg per day and per worker is reported in table 3.31. The rate differs a little by country and over time. No information on aggregate or per capita levels for the MENA and World averages are reported in the WDI database.

Table 3.28. CO2 emissions (in metric tons per capita)

Rank	Country	1981-85	1986-90	1991-95	1996-00	2001-05	Average
1	Kuwait	16.8	19.3	19.3	26.8	25.0	21.2
2	Saudi	12.5	12.0	15.0	13.8	14.2	13.4
3	Iran	3.1	3.3	4.4	5.3	5.5	4.2
4	World	3.8	3.9	3.9	3.9	3.9	3.9
5	Jordan	3.0	3.2	3.2	3.2	3.2	3.1
6	Syria	2.5	2.7	3.2	3.0	2.8	2.9
7	Iraq	2.3	3.1	3.0	2.9	3.1	2.9
8	MENA	2.1	2.4	2.8	3.0	3.2	2.7
9	Turkey	2.0	2.5	2.6	3.1	3.0	2.6

Table 3.29. Combustible renewable and waste (in % of total energy)

Rank	Country	1981-85	1986-90	1991-95	1996-00	2001-05	Average
1	Turkey	22.3	16.4	12.7	9.6	8.0	14.3
2	World	11.7	11.1	10.7	10.6	10.5	11.0
3	MENA	2.2	2.0	1.7	1.4	1.3	1.8
4	Iran	1.3	1.1	0.9	0.7	0.6	1.0
5	Iraq	0.1	0.1	0.1	0.1	0.1	0.1
6	Jordan	0.1	0.1	0.1	0.1	0.1	0.1
7	Kuwait	0.0	0.0	0.0	0.0	.	0.0
8	Syria	0.0	0.0	0.0	0.0	0.0	0.0
9	Saudi	0.0	0.0	0.0	0.0	0.0	0.0

Table 3.30. Organic water pollutant (BOD) emissions (in 1000 kg per day)

Rank	Country	1981-85	1986-90	1991-95	1996-00	2001-05	Average
1	Turkey	159.7	173.4	170.9	187.3	.	172.8
2	Iran	86.2	101.4	113.2	136.1	142.0	110.8
3	Iraq	30.9	29.7	20.0	.	.	28.2
4	Syria	27.9	21.6	19.3	15.0	.	21.6
5	Saudi	18.2	18.5	24.4	.	.	20.4
6	Jordan	5.5	7.5	12.5	17.3	18.9	11.5
7	Kuwait	7.6	9.2	8.6	10.9	11.9	9.2
8	MENA	.	.	.	.	.	.
9	World	.	.	.	.	.	.

Table 3.31. Organic water pollutant (BOD) emissions (in kg/day/worker)

Rank	Country	1981-85	1986-90	1991-95	1996-00	2001-05	Average
1	Jordan	0.2	0.2	0.2	0.2	0.2	0.2
2	Syria	0.2	0.2	0.2	0.2	.	0.2
3	Iran	0.2	0.2	0.2	0.2	0.2	0.2
4	Kuwait	0.2	0.2	0.2	0.2	0.2	0.2
5	Turkey	0.2	0.2	0.2	0.2	.	0.2
6	Iraq	0.2	0.2	0.2	.	.	0.2
7	Saudi	0.1	0.2	0.1	.	.	0.1
8	MENA	.	.	.	.	.	.
9	World	.	.	.	.	.	.

H. Industrial Sub-Sector Water Pollution

The water pollutant as a percentage share of the total organic water pollutant (BOD) for different industries contributing to the total emissions is reported in tables 3.32 to 3.39. The industries include chemical, clay and glass, food, metal, paper and pulp, textile, wood and other industries.

The food, textile, paper and pulp and chemical industries are the main water-polluting industries when ranked in a list of the highest to the lowest polluters. The least pollutant industries are metal, clay and glass and wood and other industries. In addition to the high degree of heterogeneity across the countries and industries, we find large changes for individual industries over time as well. It should be noted that the share of organic water pollutants is simply proportional to the size of the industry and it does not necessarily reflect the pollution intensity of the industry sector. Countries are differently industrialized and specialized in different industries. In none of the cases do we have any statistics on the world and MENA levels to compare the performance of countries at the regional or global levels.

Saudi Arabia, Kuwait and Iran seem to be ranked as the most organic water-polluting countries. Turkey, which has relatively well-developed industrial sectors, is ranked at the middle level among the sample countries. Iraq's emission rates for different industries ranked from high to low levels are the following: food (52.2%), textile (14.0%), chemical (12.5%), paper and pulp (12.4%), metal (4.7%), other (3.1%), clay and glass (0.7%), and wood (0.7). None of these industries are concentrated or located in parts in Kurdistan Region.

Table 3.32. Water pollution from chemical industry (in % of total BOD emissions)

Rank	Country	1981-85	1986-90	1991-95	1996-00	2001-05	Average
1	Saudi	5.8	19.0	21.1	.	.	15.3
2	Jordan	16.2	16.2	15.2	13.4	11.5	14.9
3	Kuwait	14.3	14.3	12.0	11.3	11.1	12.9
4	Iraq	11.1	13.3	15.2	.	.	12.5
5	Iran	7.5	8.2	8.7	10.5	10.8	8.8
6	Syria	8.4	8.2	6.5	4.4	.	7.1
7	Turkey	6.3	6.9	7.0	7.5	.	6.9
8	MENA	.	.	.	.	.	.
9	World	.	.	.	.	.	.

Table 3.33. Water pollution from clay and glass industry (in % of total BOD emissions)

Rank	Country	1981-85	1986-90	1991-95	1996-00	2001-05	Average
1	Saudi	1.4	1.0	1.0	.	.	1.1
2	Iraq	0.8	0.6	0.7	.	.	0.7
3	Iran	0.8	0.7	0.6	0.7	0.6	0.7
4	Jordan	0.8	0.6	0.6	0.5	0.5	0.6
5	Syria	0.4	0.4	0.6	0.9	.	0.5
6	Kuwait	0.5	0.4	0.3	0.4	0.4	0.4
7	Turkey	0.3	0.3	0.3	0.3	.	0.3
8	MENA	.	.	.	.	.	.
9	World	.	.	.	.	.	.

Table 3.34. Water pollution from food industry (in % of total BOD emissions)

Rank	Country	1981-85	1986-90	1991-95	1996-00	2001-05	Average
1	Syria	62.9	66.9	69.6	70.2	.	67.1
2	Iraq	56.5	53.9	39.8	.	.	52.2
3	Jordan	47.7	50.6	50.7	51.5	53.4	50.4
4	Turkey	49.7	46.3	46.0	43.2	.	46.3
5	Kuwait	47.1	45.0	42.4	47.4	50.2	45.7
6	Saudi	41.3	50.2	45.1	.	.	45.5
7	Iran	45.0	42.5	39.7	42.9	43.8	42.6
8	MENA	.	.	.	.	.	.
9	World	.	.	.	.	.	.

Table 3.35. Water pollution from metal industry (in % of total BOD emissions)

Rank	Country	1981-85	1986-90	1991-95	1996-00	2001-05	Average
1	Iran	13.4	16.9	19.8	17.2	17.2	16.9
2	Turkey	16.5	16.4	13.9	11.4	.	14.5
3	Saudi	4.7	6.0	4.4	.	.	5.0
4	Iraq	4.3	2.4	8.2	.	.	4.7
5	Jordan	5.2	5.1	4.2	4.4	4.7	4.7
6	Syria	2.5	2.9	3.5	4.1	.	3.2
7	Kuwait	2.7	2.7	2.4	2.5	2.1	2.6
8	MENA	.	.	.	.	.	.
9	World	.	.	.	.	.	.

Table 3.36. Water pollution from paper& pulp industry (in % of total BOD emissions)

Rank	Country	1981-85	1986-90	1991-95	1996-00	2001-05	Average
1	Kuwait	17.9	18.5	18.1	16.7	16.6	17.8
2	Saudi	17.2	14.7	15.9	.	.	15.9
3	Jordan	16.3	15.5	15.7	15.0	16.2	15.7
4	Iraq	11.3	13.2	14.5	.	.	12.4
5	Turkey	7.5	7.7	7.9	7.4	.	7.6
6	Iran	7.2	6.5	7.9	7.2	7.1	7.2
7	Syria	3.3	1.8	1.7	1.5	.	2.2
8	MENA	.	.	.	.	.	.
9	World	.	.	.	.	.	.

Table 3.37. Water pollution from textile industry (in % of total BOD emissions)

Rank	Country	1981-85	1986-90	1991-95	1996-00	2001-05	Average
1	Turkey	14.9	17.3	19.6	24.2	.	19.0
2	Syria	19.4	18.3	17.2	18.4	.	18.3
3	Iran	19.5	19.0	17.1	14.5	12.5	17.3
4	Iraq	12.8	14.1	16.8	.	.	14.0
5	Kuwait	9.9	11.9	15.3	13.3	11.6	12.6
6	Jordan	7.9	6.5	7.4	8.8	10.4	7.9
7	Saudi	14.4	1.7	3.8	.	.	6.6
8	MENA	.	.	.	.	.	.
9	World	.	.	.	.	.	.

Table 3.38. Water pollution from wood industry (in % of total BOD emissions)

Rank	Country	1981-85	1986-90	1991-95	1996-00	2001-05	Average
1	Kuwait	3.0	2.9	3.4	2.9	2.8	3.0
2	Jordan	2.9	2.6	3.1	3.3	0.5	2.7
3	Saudi	4.3	1.6	2.0	.	.	2.6
4	Iran	1.1	1.1	0.8	0.8	0.8	0.9
5	Turkey	0.7	0.7	0.8	1.2	.	0.8
6	Syria	1.6	0.3	0.3	0.2	.	0.7
7	Iraq	0.4	0.4	0.3	.	.	0.4
8	MENA	.	.	.	.	.	.
9	World	.	.	.	.	.	.

Table 3.39. Water pollution from other industry (in % of total BOD emissions)

Rank	Country	1981-85	1986-90	1991-95	1996-00	2001-05	Average
1	Saudi	10.8	5.8	6.8	.	.	7.8
2	Iran	5.6	5.1	5.5	6.2	7.1	5.7
3	Kuwait	4.4	4.3	5.9	5.4	5.2	5.0
4	Turkey	4.2	4.3	4.6	5.0	.	4.5
5	Iraq	2.8	2.3	4.6	.	.	3.1
6	Jordan	3.1	2.9	3.0	3.0	3.1	3.0
7	Syria	1.4	1.1	0.7	0.2	.	0.9
8	MENA	.	.	.	.	.	.
9	World	.	.	.	.	.	.

3.3. SUMMARY OF THE COMPARATIVE REGIONAL STUDY

Due to the fact that a study of water resources in Kurdistan Region cannot be easily conducted without a link to the water resources in Iraq and its neighboring countries, a comparative study of the Iraqi and its neighbors' water resources was undertaken. The links to the rest of Iraq and neighboring countries are in respect to statistics, legal and common pool aspects, water policies, as well as water management in general. The state of water in Iraq and among the neighbors (Turkey, Iran, Syria, Jordan, Kuwait and Saudi Arabia) is further compared with the averages for the Middle East and the world.

The data used to illustrate the water resources conditions were obtained from the World Bank's database, the World Development Indicators Database 2006. The data covers the period 1960-2005 and it contains 695, mainly economic, indicators. A total of 39 indicators mostly directly but also a few indirectly linked with water resources and environment are used for the general comparative water resources analysis during the period 1981-2005. The indicators are grouped into eight groups. These include: the major sectors share of GDP, arable land area and its utilization, population structure and its distribution, hydro-based electricity generation, international tourism, improved water sanitation and water resources, CO_2 emissions and organic water pollutant, and different industrial sub-sectors water pollution.

The results suggest the presence of significant heterogeneity among the sample countries and changes over time. The heterogeneity is related to the land and population sizes of the countries and their agricultural, industrial and population structures. In order to compress the amount of information to a reasonable level, to smooth non-systematic variations in the data and to eliminate the effects of missing units in the data it is divided into five 5-year periods.

The countries' economies differ by the combination of population, agriculture, industry and services – the main sectoral users of water resources. Each of these sectors requires access to water resources differently. Agriculture uses water mainly for irrigation, industry for different production processes, while services are mainly for public service provision such as tourism and recreational activities. Turkey and Iran have economies based on a better balanced combination of industry and agriculture. The Saudi Arabia and Kuwait agriculture sector are negligent in comparison with the oil-related industries. The service sector in Turkey and Jordan are different from those of Saudi Arabia and Kuwait with strong domestic consumption orientation. Ideally one should create a composite index to rank countries by one single way, using methods such as principal component analysis. This is not possible because frequent units miss data points.

The Iraqi economy is different from other economies in the region due to the decades of war, sanctions and invasion conditions, as well as the lack of statistics. The data for Iraq, when available, covers the period before 2002. For most indicators no data is available for the post-2003 invasion period. It is reasonable to expect a significant deterioration in the living and water resource conditions in recent years. The general changes in the structure of the economy, major changes in the population structure, negligence of water resources and in particular the deteriorated water sanitation facilities and water pollutants are among causal factors to the deteriorated environmental and living conditions. Old and lacking regulations and their implementation have worsened the situation.

The available statistics indicate that neighbors are ranked higher than the average MENA region countries, and that the MENA region is in turn better ranked than the world average. Several of the sample countries are major oil-producing countries with agriculture and industries that have access to unlimited investment and human resources. This can be both positive in terms of improvements of processes but also negative in the form of intensity in the use of agriculture. The balance is determined by the long-term oil prices and the international market demand for oil and gas products.

In order to reduce heterogeneity and to enhance cooperation among the MENA countries in the region, they should take advantage of the general objectives of the EU water initiative[20]. The objectives include: to reinforce political commitment, to promote better water governance arrangements, and to improve co-ordination and co-operation on water management issues. The general approach is based on partnership by mobilization of partners. However, achievement of the goals require joint financial and research resources as well as monitoring, reporting and communication and information systems. In this chapter we did not discuss interstate cooperation in the areas of water resources. The issues of cooperation and interstate institutional infrastructure will be discussed in Chapter 7. Given the high oil prices and accumulation of wealth in the Middle East financing such cooperation and its resource requirements should not be a problem.

---

[20] For a description of the initiative see, http://www.euwi.net/

Chapter 4

KURDISTAN REGION WATER RESOURCES IN AN HISTORICAL AND REGIONAL PERSPECTIVE[*]

ABSTRACT

This chapter discusses different types of water resources in the Kurdistan Region. They are groundwater, surface water, dams and treated waste water. Groundwater is the main source of drinking water and to a limited extent a source of irrigation. The benefits and limitations of this type water from consumer, producer and environmental points of views are discussed. Surface water is quantitatively the main source of water in Kurdistan. It includes rivers, spring and stream sources and rain water. These sources are reported geographically by the governorates. The minimum and maximum discharge rates of rivers and springs are discussed in detail. Data is also collected and presented about the average rainfall and snowfall by governorates. The dams, as the third source, are categorized according to the completeness of construction and their location in the respective governorates. The characteristics of each category of completed, under construction and planned dams are presented. Treated waste water is the fourth source of water discussed here.

4.1. INTRODUCTION

When studying the management of water resources information on the water infrastructure and the overall conditions in the past is of great value and needs to be taken into account in plans and decisions concerning the future of the sector. There are a number of reports covering the water resources in Kurdistan Region.[21] These are mainly of geologic character and conducted by foreign contractors in the form of feasibility studies in relation to the construction of dams mainly by the former Soviet Union or by FAO in relation to the implementation of the Oil for Food program in Iraq in the late 90s and at the beginning of the new millennium. Since these reports are technical and of geologic character and not necessarily directly related to the management of water resources, we utilize them only in

---

[*] Contributions from Binar Jawhar, Aumed Muhammed, Nabaz T. Abdullah and Zozan Othman to earlier versions of sections 4.2-4.5 is acknowledged.

limited form. Thus, we have completed the background information by collecting new data which is rather difficult retroactively.

This chapter, as the title indicates, discusses different types of water resources in the Kurdistan Region in historical and regional perspectives. The sources are groundwater, surface water, dams and treated waste water. Groundwater is the main source of drinking water and used in irrigation to a limited extent. The benefits and limitations of this type of water from consumer, provider and environmental point of views are discussed. Surface water is quantitatively the main source of water supply and it includes rivers, spring and stream sources as well as rain water. These sources are reported geographically by the governorates. The dams which are growing in number are grouped according to the completeness of construction and their location in the respective governorates. The characteristics of each category of completed, under construction and planned dams are presented. Treated waste water is the fourth source of water which is negligible as treatment plants are rare in the region.

As mentioned above, this chapter illustrates the historical background and regional perspective of water resource in the Kurdistan region. It describes the topography, aquifer and the formation of the land of Iraq which is classified into four parts. Each part has its own characteristics concerning the availability of water. One of Iraqi's richest parts is the northern part, represented by the Kurdistan Region. This chapter attempts to provide a picture of the climatic conditions of the region. The chapter describes the four essential sources of the water supply. To each source a section is devoted where various sources and types of data are used to provide a full picture of the actual conditions.

The first source of water is groundwater. Wells represent the main component of groundwater, besides some streams and seasonal springs. These wells, their properties and density differ from one location to another. The differences are attributed to the geological nature of fold, layer and landscape. Many factors point to the beneficial characteristics of this resource in different sectors. In many locations the degree of dependency on groundwater for various aspects of life is quite high, for instance its usage for drinking. Therefore there will be limitations in groundwater access associated with a series of problems arising because of population increase and drought. The increasing trend in effects of pollution on groundwater is a result of neglecting agricultural waste, household waste in urban and rural areas, and the increased magnitude of industry waste material.

The second resource is surface water. It is important to clarify that there are only two main rivers in Iraq with national coverage as a whole, namely the Tigris and Euphrates. They are both main sources of water. Some other tributaries have their origin from these two rivers. The region is not a passage for the Euphrates River. Here, we examine the major tributaries of the Tigris in the region's three governorates; Hawler, Sulaimanyah and Duhok. In addition, we investigate the streams and springs in the region again by their governorate's location. It attempts to measure the rate of water in rivers and springs through three different methods. Furthermore, maximum and minimum discharges of rivers and springs are mentioned with the average rate of rain and snowfall in the three governorates.

The third resource of water is the water collected in dams. A study of the historical background of the dams in the Kurdistan Region explains their importance as a source of

---

[21] For comprehensive reports on water resources, land and hydropower plant development in Iraq and Kurdistan Region see TEPCO (2004) and SBEC (1982).

water. Basins and reservoirs have been used intensively and with a long tradition. They are used for different purposes such as drinking and irrigation. In the past there was little dependency on dams because of the excess supply of various sources of water and the simplicity of community life and undeveloped technology. The importance of dams is further emphasized by presenting some basic statistics about the current dams in the region. In addition, we discuss dams under construction. The neighboring countries water policies concerning water originating in those countries are elaborated. The negative and positive impact of dams and basins on the environment and economy are shown. Here the focus is on the role of the management of water resources and the problems that are associated with management of water, particularly in relation to the neighboring countries. Finally, the look at the current state of the large dams not completed and planned dams in the region as a whole. These are supported with necessary statistics obtained from related official sites in the region.

The fourth resource of water is treated wastewater. There are several resources of wastewater in the region that can be used following treatment. Residential and industrial water uses, and rainfall if it has been merged with the sanitation network are among wastewater sources. This section studies possible methods to purify these wastewater sources. The treated water after the process of sanitation can be re-used in the agriculture sector, industry and for the purpose of groundwater recharges.

4.2. GROUNDWATER IN THE KURDISTAN REGION

A. History and Landscape of Iraq

Iraq occupies land that historians regard as the location of the earliest civilizations of the Middle East. Because of its fertile land and vegetation and sufficient water supply, ancient Mesopotamia (where the land between the rivers, now the Tigris and Euphrates, flowed) attracted settlers in 6,000 B.C. Elements of early urban culture developed in response to the unpredictable natural measure of the rivers are still found nowadays.

Iraq has four main geographical regions. The desert zone of Iraq's west and southwest as the first region is part of the Syrian Desert, dominated by wide, flat, sandy areas. The second region is the alluvial plain that extends from north of Baghdad southward to the Persian Gulf, following the lower Tigris and Euphrates rivers. The area, which is a large delta, includes lakes and marshlands. The extent of marshland in the alluvial plain varies according to the volume of water carried by the rivers in the flood season. The marshlands were subject to massive changes aiming to depopulate the region. There are attempts to recreate the culture of the marshland under the supervision of the UN and World Heritage Fund. In their lower reaches, the two main rivers break into several channels. The uplands region is the third region, which occupies most of Iraq's northern part, beginning about 120 kilometers north of Baghdad and including the watersheds of the Tigris and Euphrates rivers to the Syrian border in the second region. The uplands region, which is also called the primarily desert region, is characterized by a deep river basin. The fourth region is the Northern highlands, Kurdistan Region, which includes all of Iraq's north eastern territory and expands into other parts of Kurdistan in the neighboring countries of Turkey and Iran. A series of heights mixed with plains gives way to mountains as high as 4,000 meters near the Iranian and Turkish borders.

The four regions differ greatly in the length of their seasons and also in the level of temperature and rainfall. Most of Iraq has a desert climate, with mild winters and long, hot dry, summer seasons. The north eastern uplands have cold winters with irregular heavy snowfall. In the western desert and the north eastern foothills, average winter temperatures range from a low of 0°C to a high of 15°C, and average summer temperatures range from a low of 22°C to a high of 38°C. In the alluvial plain, the winter range is 4°C to 17°C, and the summer range is 29°C to 43°C. About 90 percent of Iraq's rainfall occurs between November and April. In recent years significant changes in temperature have been observed. For instance on the Hawler plain in the northern highlands region a temperature of around 45°C has also been measured frequently during the warm summer season.

In 1950 only a modest number of wells had been drilled in the northern, western and central parts of Iraq. In 1953–1957, on the basis of the data which were then available, both deep (up to 150m depth) and shallow hand-dug wells were used. The number of wells increased due to the increased concentration of population in urban areas far from water basins, increased farm land and irrigation, increased population and wealth, diversion of common pool water sources prior to arrival in this region as well as increasing income, access to electricity and technological advancement.

B. Groundwater in Kurdistan

Kurdistan relies on groundwater as a major source of drinking water, and for other urban and rural uses. The landscape and the formation of the land's layers in Kurdistan have led to large variation in well discharge levels. For instance, wells in the plain areas are different from others in the mountainous areas in both quantity and quality. Therefore the formation of the aquifer plays an important role in the kind of wells in each governorate in the north. These well's potential water supply varies by governorates.

There is another source of groundwater which is streams and springs. Previously the rural population relied mainly on springs for its daily water. This was due to difficulties in digging wells as mechanical technologies were expensive and not available in the remote parts of Kurdistan. In the vent springs discharges were low the population moved to new locations with springs. This source cannot be reliable as a source of water especially because of the unstable climate conditions. This indicates that springs are a seasonal source of water and not very reliable as a source of water for uses that require continuity and security in water flows[22]. The central government's systematic deportation of the rural population to concentration camps and the destruction of springs added further to increased instability in their flows.

C. Benefits and Limitations of Groundwater

The region uses mainly wells as a source of water for almost all applications. For instance, it is used in industrial, agricultural, commercial sectors and for human applications such as drinking, cooking and washing. The number of wells is sustainably increasing for

---

[22] Springs are originally coming from undergrounds then strengthened form surface water.

many reasons such as the increasing size of the population, periodic shortage in rainfall which causes drought, and for economic growth. Approximately five million people inhabiting the region are the origin Kurdish people. In addition, thousands of non-residents in recent years have arrived from other regions of Iraq and from abroad seeking refuge in the region. There are limited data and the quality of data is low. Groundwater is nearly the only source of water in the Kurdistan Region based on the limited statistics that are provided by the KRG's ministries. Due to the low population and industrial density untreated groundwater might be of an acceptable quality as drinking water.

In respect to the importance of groundwater, limitations on access to it will have disastrous implications for the region. Currently the region suffers from water shortages, which is one of the principal problems faced by the region. The Kurdistan Regional Government has made serious efforts to resolve this issue. It has given a priority to water security. This problem is the result of the past 15 years of neglect of groundwater resources. The level of groundwater has lowered compared to previous years and many of these wells have been dry or with a very low flow. Currently the region is seeking a solution to the problem. In case of the failure of mastering the public provision problem, the probabilities are: to eliminate the shortage through diversion of surface water sources; the use of other sources and reallocation of water from agriculture to household and industry; or allowing for private solutions which will have damaging consequences resulting from contamination and mismanagement of water. Cholera, typhoid and other waterborne diseases can erupt as a result of public mismanagement of water.

Modern and similar technology is used to dig wells with different depth levels in different regions and for different purposes. According to the statistics published by the Ministry of Water Resources, the number of deep wells in Duhok governorate is 2,020. The Hawler governorate has around 6,800 deep wells, but the corresponding number is 30,776 in the Sulaimanyah governorate. The available statistics are incomplete in respect to the type and depth of the wells. These wells are the second major water resource that is used to a large extent for drinking and in a variety of other fields of use. Groundwater and its quantity relies strongly on the amount of rainfall, snowfall, the kind of soil, vegetation and the groundwater responsiveness.

Economically groundwater puts a great deal of pressure on the government financially and environmentally. It costs too much since the number of wells has reached to more than 39,000 legal deep wells in the entire region. Advanced instruments, equipment, skill and financial resources are needed to drill and complete such wells. The period of time that each well takes to lead to a flow of water differs by a number of factors such as the number of workers, the water networks, access to and the power of engines or generators for pumping water and electric power. In addition to the company's requirements for achieving this objective, other services such as housing and other requirements are to be supplied. Furthermore, material for purifying polluted water is also needed. The attached table (Table 4.1) shows the most recent statistics regarding the number of wells in each of the three primary governorates of Hawler, Sulaimanyah and Duhok.

It is worth mentioning that wells are divided into a number of groups such as those for drinking water, for agriculture, for industry and for other purposes. Wells for drinking water are the largest category of wells, while agriculture is not a very exploited area and industry has yet not developed well as a consumer of well water. It should be noted that the number of illegal wells (19,760) is estimated to be larger than the number of legal or authorized (19,448) ones.

Wells are of different depths and supply capacity. The wells' range of production of water by governorates is reported in table 4.1. The largest range, the difference between maximum and minimum production, is attributed to Hawler groundwater basins, which is in the interval between 50 and 220 gallons per minute. The wells' production of water in cubic meters per day (m^3/day) is reported in table 4.2 by the governorate. The table is incomplete but it provides an estimation of the magnitude of legal and illegal water supply or water use by different categories of users.

Table 4.1. Well production of water in Kurdistan Region by governorates, in gallons

Governorates	Number of wells for drinking water		Number of agricultural wells		Number of industrial wells		Number of educational wells		Suggested wells product according to governorates (by gallons) Min –Max
	legal	illegal	legal	illegal	Legal	illegal	legal	illegal	
Hawler	2370	300	1800	2200	85	-	55	-	50-220
Duhok	1122	-	235	30	235	-	-	-	65-180
Sulaimanyah	12022	17230	1524	-	-	-	-	-	30-150
Total	15514	17530	3559	2230	320	-	55		-
Total legal Wells in Kurdistan Region					19448				
Total illegal Wells in Kurdistan Region					19760				
Total legal+ illegal Wells in Kurdistan Region					39208				

Sources: Ministry of Water Resources, Annual Report.

Table 4.2. Well production of water in Kurdistan Region in m^3 per day

governorates	Production of drinking water M^3/day		Production of agricultural wells M^3/day		Production of industrial wells M^3/day		Production of educational wells M^3/day	
	legal	illegal	legal	illegal	Legal	illegal	legal	Illegal
Hawler	1151820	145800	874800	1069200	1069200	-	26730	-
Duhok	492558	-	103165	13170	13170	-	-	-
Sulaimanyah	344600	6480	493776	-	-	-	-	-

Sources: Ministry of Water Resources, Annual Report.

D. The Effect of Pollution on Groundwater

Groundwater can be polluted by land block, infected tanks, leaky underground gas tanks, lack of water treatment and waste water management, and from overuse of fertilizers and pesticides in agriculture. Inefficiency in waste water management resulted in polluting the upstream of Darbandikhan Dam which is the main source of drinking water in this area. These sources of pollutions pose a great risk to public health since the majority of the fresh water supplies are obtained from groundwater. Many of the groundwater pollutants are colorless, neutral, and tasteless and not caused by external factors. The alarming conditions of groundwater supplies also occur as a result of poor land management. In the case of the Kurdistan Region the polluted groundwater results from some other different causes besides the traditional reasons mentioned above. For instance, some of these factors include the effects of many decades of war, destruction and neglect, agriculture, households and industrial dumps. These factors are each briefly described below.

D.1. Decades of Wars, Destruction and Neglect

Iraq has witnessed two destructive wars with two of its neighboring countries, Iran and Kuwait. The first war against Iran lasted more than eight years, from 1980 to 1988. It can be characterized as a full-scale war between the two countries. During this period different kinds of heavy weapons were used, in particular those related to terrestrial, marine and airpower. In some of the battles Iraq used chemical weapons against its opponents and civilians. The second war was with Kuwait. In fact, Iraq invaded Kuwait in 1990. The international coalition forces led by the USA stood against Iraq. Hundreds of airplanes, battleships, tanks, a variety of war trucks and more discharged on Iraq and invaded Iraq from both air and land. Millions of tons of advanced weapons have contaminated the soil, vegetation water and have subsequently affected the health of the population of the country. Even rainfall was not normal anymore because of the polluted and smoky air. For example as happened when Iraq in retaliation set on fire the oil wells and the oil deposits in Kuwait. The pollution lasted for duration of several months because even the professional teams were not able to put out the fires or to control them. The sky was covered by huge black clouds which were followed with black rain and subsequent contamination.

The Iraqi people, atmosphere and environment were exposed to all the above shocks and their negative effects. In addition the groundwater was affected to a great extent. These dumps were absorbed by the soil and penetrated the depths through to the groundwater. These two wars combined with the continued internal conflicts, which have left behind tons of harmful weapons, the results of which both the region and the entire country are still suffering from. Millions of tons of mines are spread over large areas. As a result of this war Iraq witnessed crucial periods of unrest and harmful environmental damage. In the recent 28 years and for the reasons mentioned above, food, water and air was became unfit for human use. In addition, the economic sanctions made the situation worse over time. People were forced to consume polluted food and water. The rates of cancer patients and dangerous diseases linked to pollution have become highly significant. Innate deformation increased to a great extent in this period and that following it. All these were the consequence of polluted air, land, food and water.

The successive regimes in Iraq have imposed wars on the Kurds and their territories in Kurdistan and this has had an impact on water resources and the environment. For example during the 80s the Iraqi regime used chemical weapons against the civilian Kurdish population of the city of Halabja. Thousands of people were killed and injured. It is obvious that the impact of these weapon remains for a very long time. The entire environment in the city is damaged, poisoned and contaminated. This was the most damaging event for the air and land in the region. These areas could not regain their normal life until a long time after the gas attack and are not safe even in our time. Those exposed to the bombs are still suffering and receive intensive medical treatment. They are still suffering psychologically and physically from different kinds of cancers and diseases after being subject to the gas attack. The agricultural products and water sources are still highly harmful for human use. Surface and groundwater are certainly unhealthy for human usage.

D.2. Agriculture Waste and Pollution

Another main source of pollution is agriculture. It is clear that fertilizers and pesticides are common and widely used in agricultural production. Fertilizer is mainly in a non-organic form and traditional NPK combination. The use of organic fertilizer in not very common in the region but in some parts agriculture utilizes sewage wastewater and black water for both irrigation and fertilizing purposes. Regardless of the degree or intensity in their utilization, leakage to the water and air is certain. Many of these chemical resources are absorbed by soil and into the groundwater and in the agriculture-based products consumed by people. The negative externalities to the environment and their effects on food and water cause diseases and have severe negative health effects on the population.

D.3. Household Waste in Both Urban and Rural Areas

As a result of the daily production and consumption activities by the population of various items, a significant quantity of dumps are left behind. Different institutions, households, parks and manufacturing areas and markets produce waste material on a daily basis. There are municipality services that care about cleaning and processing the waste material. In the absence of proper sanitation the region's household's waste material pollutes the housing environment. This pollution gradually leaks into the air and land. Consequently the groundwater will be affected. In addition there are shallow wells close to sewerage water which leads to a high contamination. This practice of waste and water management has certainly major negative impacts on people's health and it may cause epidemic diseases such as malaria, cholera, and many others negative health effects. A limited outbreak of cholera has been observed in a few cases.

D.4. Industrial Waste Material

Industry is one of the most significant causes of air, water and land pollution. In Kurdistan there are not many plants and factories. Despite this a lack of regulations and environmental and water laws increases the negative effects of industry on the environment. Each industry functions in its domain. All plants and equipment are highly dependent on water to function. In other words and as is explained below, water is a crucial factor for production at these plants. It is interesting that almost all these plants and factories rely heavily on groundwater in the form of wells for their main source of water. Groundwater is the sole source used for their production activities.

Based on some statistics obtained from the Ministry of Industry at the KRG (2007) plants and factories differ in their use of water based on the type of their production. Some production activities require high quantities of water while others are less demanding. To be more specific, some industries use well water, where part of it is used for production processes and they waste the remaining part. Others take benefit from the residual part by re-using the used water in their production. For example, metal production needs a high quantity of water, and it uses the residual of used water. The waste and un-cleaned water here is not absorbed by the land. It is evaporated by the high temperature. In brick, pipe and metal industries water is largely used and evaporates, but in some other cases the waste water created by industries contaminates the land through pollutants in the groundwater.

4.3. SURFACE WATER IN KURDISTAN

A. Historical Background

Geographically Iraq is located in a part of the Middle East which has great water resources. Both of the large transnational rivers of the Tigris and Euphrates are a symbol of prosperity in Iraq. These two rivers enter Iraq from Syria and Turkey respectively. The Tigris River is further enlarged by several tributaries in Iraq, the most important tributaries are Khabur, Greater Zab, Lesser Zab, Sirwan and Awa spy (Uzaym), all of which join the Tigris before reaching Baghdad. The Tigris River flows into the Euphrates through the Shat al Arab in the South East of Iraq. A number of channels are distributed through the Tigris and the Euphrates rivers, diverting parts of its mass of water. See Map 4.1.

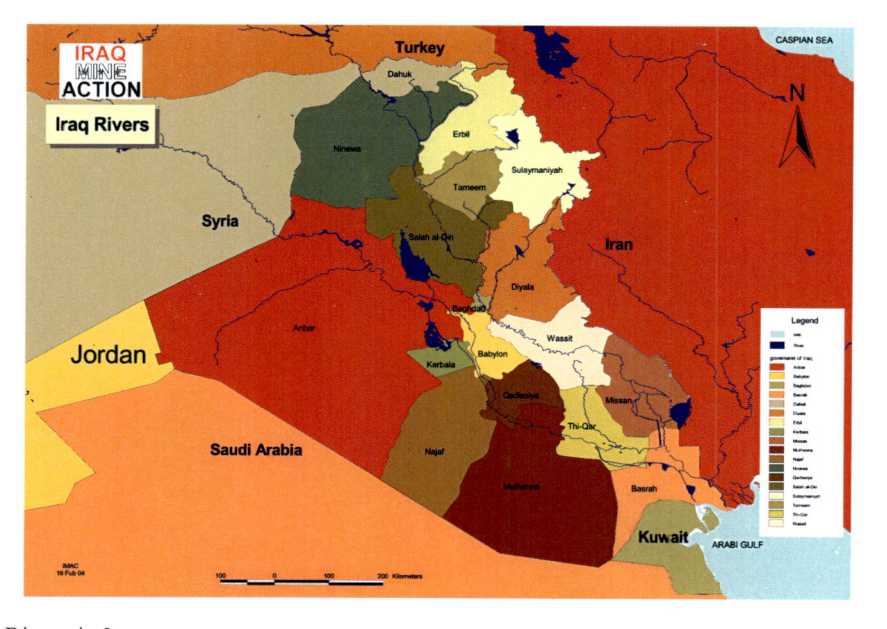

Map 4.1. Rivers in Iraq.

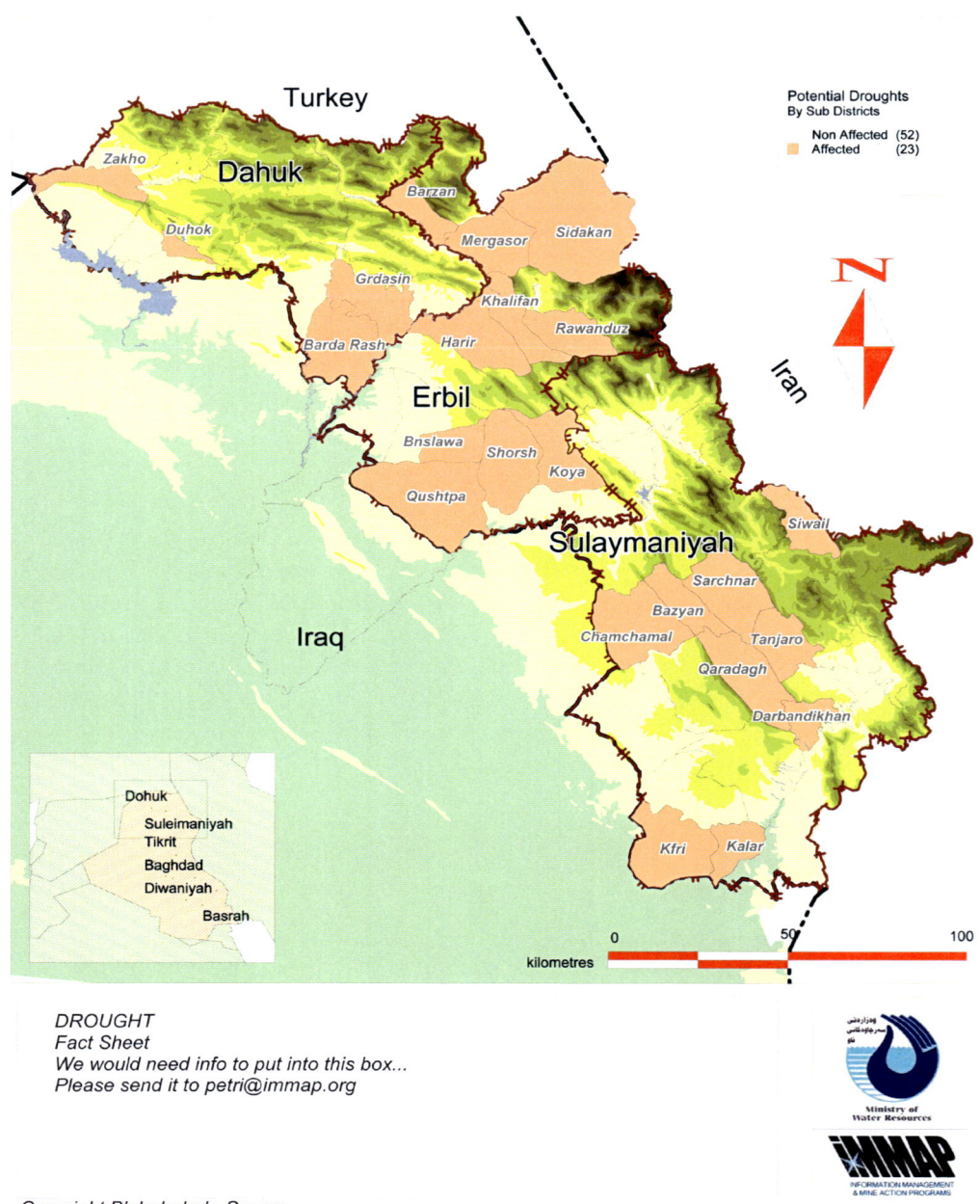

Map 4.2. Effected area by draught in Kurdistan Region of Iraq.

Meanwhile, the flow of the two rivers is largely reduced gradually until they unite at Al Qurnah. The Karun River, which originates from Iran, is located below Basra and it contains large quantities of polluting material which cause a health and environmental problem for the

Kurdistan Region. In addition the suspended materials in turn have become a major obstacle to the rivers smooth flow.

Many among the Iraqi population satisfy their basic needs for water through these two rivers. However, both rivers have also negative effects on the life in Iraq. The rate of the water is often reduced in September and October while there is flood in March, April, and May that may carry forty times more water than the low levels of water in the fall. The flow of water and flooding have both decreased since Syria built a dam on the Euphrates.

The Kurdistan Region is rich in water resources that are beneficial concerning irrigation in agriculture and living in rural areas. The main sources of water in the Kurdistan Region are snow and rainfall. This is why a lack of rain or snow is the main reason behind drought in Kurdistan. The city of Hawler seems to have a better situation due to the availability of groundwater and Ifraz water (a project that has been completed recently to satisfy the water demands of the Hawler governorate). On the other hand, Sulaimanyah which is the second largest city faces a lack of groundwater and rivers subject to drought pass through the governorate. The population in Sulaimanyah governorate cannot access water in sufficient quantities to satisfy their basic needs.

The drought periods have a negative impact in particular on the mountainous areas. Lack of rain and snowfall has decreased the rate of water in the rivers and springs. This type of water shortage has been observed since 2001-2004. (See Map 4.2) On the other hand, an increasing rate of rain and snowfall leads to increases in the rate of water accessible. This will also increase the rate of groundwater. Part of the groundwater again flows in the form of springs in the fissures of mountains.

B. Major Tigris Tributaries in Kurdistan

The Tigris river passes through the Kurdistan Region. Tributaries of the river are distributed across several regions. The North of Iraq (Kurdistan) has several rivers that are distributed across the Hawler, Sulaimanyah, and Duhok governorates. The path of the Tigris and its branches in these main governorates of Kurdistan Region are described below. See Map 4.3.

B.1. Greater Zab Tributary in Hawler

The Hawler governorate, the capital city of Kurdistan, has one major tributary of the Tigris which is the greater Zab that flow into the Tigris. The Greater Zab originates mainly in the Wan Lake in Turkey. Then the river flows across the Iraqi border at Alamadieh. Furthermore, the river continues flowing to the Iraqi-Turkey borders. Then it unites with the Rawandouz River that is near the Bekhme cleft. The length of the Greater Zab is 392 km. In addition, the Greater Zab has five sub-tributaries and they are Shamzenan, Rwo Kochek, Rawandouz, Bastourah, and Khazir. The Greater Zab's annual mean water flow is 4,190 MCM (million cubic meters) at Bekhme, while the annual mean of the Tigris River is 17,173 MCM at Mosul.

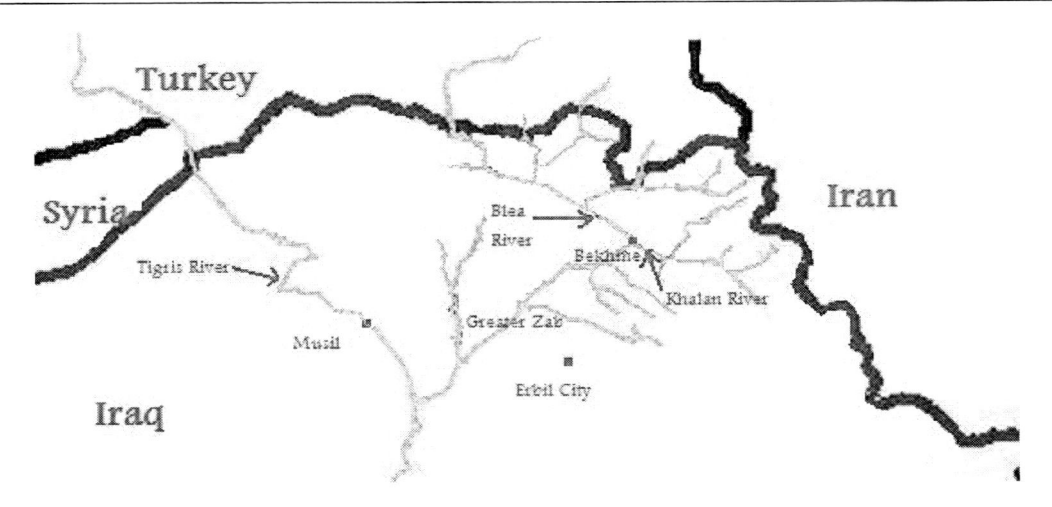

Map. 4.3. Tigris river tributaries.

B.2. Lesser Zab Tributary

The Lesser Zab is an international tributary originating from the Iranian mountains and which passes through the Sulaimanyah governorate. This river flows from Qandil Mountain in the west of Iran which is 3200m above sea level. The river flows from the east to the southwest across Bedrazhour near the Iraqi-Iranian border. Afterwards, it continues flowing to the south into the cleft of Dukan where the Dukan dam is constructed. Then it flows to the west across Taqtaq, Altun Kopry Dibis. The catchment area of the Lesser Zab is 22,250 km^2 and its length is 400 km.

B.3. Khabur Tributary

The Khabur is also an international river originating from Turkey which enters into the Kurdistan Region through the Duhok governorate from the Zakho district. The length of the Khabur River is 160 km. It flows from the high mountains on the Iraq-Turkey border where it originates. The catchment area is estimated to be 6,268 km^2. This catchment area can further be divided into 1,663 km^2 of hilly areas and the remaining 4605 km^2 of mountainous areas.

B.4. Sirwan Tributary

The Sirwan, a **trans**national river, originates in Iran with a catchment area of 17,850 km^2, of which 70% is permanently in Iran and 30%, which is seasonal, is in the Kurdistan Region. The length of the river is 385 km. Its minimum annual discharge in year 2007 was measured at 21 m^3/sec. The annual product of the river reaches 5.86 BCM (billion cubic meters), which is 13.57% of Tigris River. It rises near Senah, in the Zagros Mountains of Iran.

B.5. Awa Spy (Udhem)

The river originates in the Kurdistan Region and its length is about 230 km. The catchment area is 1,100 km^2 with an annual water flow of 790 MCM. Awe Spy River enters the Tigris River near the city of Balad. Its main branches are the Khasa stream in Kirkuk, the Daquq stream in western Kirkuk and the Awe Spy river which originates in the Qaradagh mountains.

C. Springs in Kurdistan

There are a large number of springs providing fresh water in the Kurdistan Region in the north of Iraq. Although the number of the springs is not known, the springs can be divided according to the basins. The spring lines in Kurdistan Region can be classified according to the following geographic lines: (i) Imadiah, Raniah and Sulaimanyah line; (ii) Hawler, Shaqlawa, Koya, Doly Alanah and Darbandikhan line; (iii) Doly Hiran-Shaqlawa line, and (iv) Doly Alanah line. A description of the condition in each governorate in a more detailed form is found below.

C.1. Springs in Hawler Governorate

The Hawler governorate has many springs that are the main source of attraction for local tourists. There are two different opinions about whether springs are groundwater or sub-surface water. The source of water for the springs comes from rain and snowfall. This indicates that a lack of rain and snow are the main reasons behind the drought. Hawler has many large springs such as Hasan Bag, Betrma, Hiran, Bekhal, Jundian and Haji Omeran with different discharges in different seasons.

C.2. Springs in Sulaimanyah Governorate

Springs are seasonal sources of fresh water supply. This means that an increase in rain and snow will increase the rate of water flow in the springs. On the other hand, in dry seasons, the water will dry out. The Sulaimanyah governorate has many spring lines. The spring lines are classified according to the following geographic lines: (i) Halabja-Sharbazher line, (ii) Khalakan- Sulaimanyah-Sharazur line, (iii) Aghjalar-Sangau-Darbandikhan line, and (iv) Qadir Karam-Kalar line. The main springs in the Sulaimanyah governorate are: Zalm, Sarchinar, Sargalu, Shekh Mansuryan, Kani Watman, Banikhelan and Sangau. These springs originate from deep groundwater with different discharges in different seasons.

C.3. Springs in Duhok Governorate

In similarity with the previous two governorates, the spring lines in Duhok governorate are also classified according to a number of lines as follows: (i) Imadiah line, (ii) Duhok line, and (iii) Sarsang and Zawita line. Duhok has many large springs whose water flows are also sensitive to seasonal variations. These springs originate from groundwater sources. The biggest spring is Gely spring with variable discharges in different seasons.

D. Measuring the Flow of Water in Rivers and Springs

Discharge of rivers and springs of Kurdistan are measured by several methods. In this section we introduce the readers to three such common methods: current meter, V-notch, volumetric and rating curve. Each of these is described briefly below.

The first method of measurement is *Current meter*. This method is used by measuring the rate of the total speed of wastewater and measuring its area. Then by multiplying both measurements the quantity of waste water is computed. The formula for the measurement is written as:

$$Q = A \times V$$

where Q is the quantity of water flow (measured in m^3/sec, or liter/sec), A is the area (measured in m^2), and V is the velocity water flow. Generally, the water flow is measured in m3/second.

Another method used for measurement of water is called V-notch. This method is used for the type of water that is measured in liter/second. It is an easy way in which the tool can be transferred easily. The formula is written as:

$$Q = 0.0147 \times H^{5/2} \times \tan \Phi / 2$$

where Q is discharge m3/second measured in liter/sec, H is the depth in meters through V-notch, and Φ is the angle of V-notch.

A third method is Volumetric which is used to measure those spring waters that have a low flow range of water and it is measured in liter/second.

There are many other ways to measure water in the rivers and springs. A rating curve is another important method of water measurement in rivers and springs. This method is used after the current meter is used. It can produce a graph between the discharge and water depth for analysis.

E. Maximum and Minimum Discharge of Rivers and Springs in Kurdistan

There are statistics available to us covering the state of water level and flow conditions of 13 rivers and 3 springs in the Kurdistan Region. The maximum and minimum discharges from years 2003 to 2005 are presented in table 4.3 for these rivers and springs.

As expected the distribution and level of discharges differ from one place to another and from one time to another. The minimum is stable but the maximum is more volatile. It can be noticed that the discharge of the rivers and springs increased to a high level in 2005. This increase in rainfall led to flooding in some areas. It also led to financial losses in many cities and rural areas of the Kurdistan Region. Meanwhile, the lowest rate of discharge in the rivers and the springs is attributed to 2004. Increases and decreases in the discharge are due to the increase and decrease in the rate of rain and snowfall in the region. The rate of rain decreased at a high rate during 2001-2004 which led to the drying up of many springs.

F. Average Rate of Rain and Snowfall in the Kurdistan Region Governorates

Rain and snow in the region varies significantly from one year to another. According to the geographical location of the region, especially surrounding the city centers, the amount of rain and snow are the main factors behind the changing variability of water levels in the rivers and springs. In recent years, the snow rate was very low. In addition, the rate of rain also decreased in all parts of the region. These are the causal factors behind the lack of sufficient irrigation water facing agriculture in the region. Table 4.4 below shows the average rate of rain and snow.

Table 4.3. The summary of maximum and minimum discharges for (13) Rivers and (3) Springs

River/ Spring Name	2003		2004		2005	
	Maximum Discharge (m^3/sec)	Minimum Discharge (m^3/sec)	Maximum Discharge (m^3/sec)	Minimum Discharge (m^3/sec)	Maximum Discharge (m^3/sec)	Minimum Discharge (m^3/sec)
Alana	4.8970	0.6170	2.6800	0.6100	2.8880	0.6340
Balakian	93.2640	1.6630	100.4200	1.0270	104.0890	1.0890
Basan	4.7120	2.0040	6.3320	2.2370	6.2610	2.2540
Bekhal	5.8300	2.7250	6.4150	2.6590	8.5540	2.4090
Darban Gomasapan	1.5570	0.0170	1.1490	0.0010	1.1600	0.0070
Greater Zab	88.6420	17.2460	1452.3540	71.8650	1033.0730	72.0790
Greater Zab	663.1240	116.2420	1423.2450	79.1560	1101.2140	77.5090
Greater Zab	603.9870	106.8280	652.0490	67.1790	997.0880	66.4490
Hujran	0.4030	0.1560	0.4190	0.1010	0.4580	0.0900
Jundian	45.3140	12.0200	50.1150	6.5590	50.6000	6.3430
Jundian Saru Kani	0.1410	Drought	0.4050	0.0251	395.2490	Drought
Khalan	122.5460	18.0310	62.9930	1.9100	58.3660	11.0500
Razga	2.9870	0.0510	2.6350	0.0200	3.0590	0.0270
Rezan	60.9060	31.7190	58.1200	16.5360	5601.0000	16.0550
Ruste	6.8890	1.3800	5.3610	0.1980	7.2090	0.2170
Sabat (Nawprdan)	0.0047	0.0020	0.0014	0.0012	0.0013	0.0012
Khanaqah	14.1100	1.0760	-	-	-	-
Average	101.1361	19.4861	239.0433	15.6303	585.6418	17.0809

Source: Ministry of Water Resources, Annual Report.

Table 4.4. Average rainfall in Kurdistan Region[23]

Period	Hawler	Sulaimanyah	Duhok
2000-2001	4,039	4,200	4,445
2001-2002	2,645	2,800	1,205
2002-2003	530	1,100	1,100
2003-2004	4,037	4,900	4,700
2004-2005	2,947	3,600	3,200
2005-2006	1,452	1,700	1,050

Source: Ministry of Water Resources, Annual Report.

---

[23] Note that in some years the rate is very low because some countryside is not included.

4.4. Dams and Reserviors

A. Historical Background of Dams in Iraq

Iraq has more water than most Middle Eastern nations, which led to the establishment of one of the world's earliest and most advanced civilizations. Strong, centralized governments - a phenomenon known as "hydraulic despotism" - emerged because of the need for organization and for technology in order to exploit the Tigris and Euphrates rivers. Archaeologists believe that the highest point in the development of the irrigation system occurred about 500 A.D., when a network of irrigation canals permitted widespread cultivation that made the river basin into a regional granary. However, having been poorly maintained the irrigation and drainage canals had deteriorated badly by the twelfth and thirteenth centuries, when the Mongols destroyed what remained of the system.

About one-fifth of Iraq's territory consists of farmland. About half of this total cultivated area is in the northeastern plains and mountain valleys, where sufficient rain falls to sustain agriculture. The remainder of the cultivated land is in the valleys of the Euphrates and Tigris rivers, which receive scant rainfall and rely instead on water from the rivers. Both rivers are fed by the snowpack and rainfall in eastern Turkey and in the northwest of Iran. The rivers' discharge peaks in March and in May, too late for winter crops and too early for summer crops. The flow of the rivers varies considerably every year. Destructive flooding, particularly of the Tigris, is not uncommon, and some scholars have placed numerous great flood legends, including the biblical story of Noah and the Ark, in this area. Conversely, years of low flow make irrigation and agriculture difficult.

Not until the twentieth century did Iraq make a concerted effort to restore its irrigation and drainage network and to control seasonal flooding. Various regimes constructed several large dams and implemented river control projects, rehabilitated old canals, and built new irrigation systems. Barrages were constructed on both the Tigris and the Euphrates to channel water into natural depressions so that floods could be controlled. It was also hoped that the water could be used for irrigation after the rivers peaked in the spring, but the combination of high evaporation from the reservoirs and the absorption of salt residues in the depressions made some of the water too brackish for agricultural use. Some dams that created large reservoirs were built in the valleys of the tributaries of the Tigris, a measure that diminished spring flooding and evened out the supply of water over the cropping season. When the Euphrates was flowing at an exceptionally low level in 1984, the government was able to release water stored in reservoirs to sustain farmers.

In 1988 barrages or dam reservoirs existed at Samarra, Dukan, and Darbandikhan, on the Tigris and Habbaniyah on the Euphrates. Two new dams on the Tigris at Mosul and Al Hadithah, named respectively the Saddam and Al Qadisiyah, were on the verge of completion in 1988. Furthermore, a Chinese-Brazilian joint venture was constructing a US$2.0 billion dam on the Upper Zab River. Additional dams were planned for Badush and Fathah, both on the Tigris River. In Hindiyah on the Euphrates and in Ash Shinafiyah on the Euphrates, Chinese contractors were building a series of barrages.

Geographic factors contributed to Iraq's water problems. Like all rivers, the Tigris and the Euphrates carry large amounts of silt downstream. This silt is deposited in river channels, in canals, and on the flood plains. In Iraq, the soil has a high saline content. As the water table rises through flooding or through irrigation, salt rises into the topsoil, rendering agricultural land sterile. In addition, the alluvial silt is highly saline. Drainage thus becomes very important; however, Iraq's terrain is very flat. For example, Baghdad, although 550 kilometers from the Persian Gulf, is only 34 meters above sea level. This slight gradient makes the plains susceptible to flooding and, although it facilitates irrigation, it also hampers drainage. The flat terrain also provides relatively few sites for dams. Most important, Iraq lies downstream from both Syria and Turkey on the Euphrates River and downstream from Turkey on the Tigris River. In the early 1970s, both Syria and Turkey completed large dams on the Euphrates and filled vast reservoirs. Iraqi officials protested against the sharp decrease in the river's flow, claiming that irrigated areas along the Euphrates in Iraq dropped from 136,000 hectares to 10,000 hectares in just one year from 1974 to 1975.

Despite cordial relations between Iraq and Turkey in the late 1980s, the issue of water allocation continued to cause friction between the two governments. In 1986 Turkey completed tunnels to divert an estimated one-fifth of the water from the Euphrates into the Ataturk Dam reservoir. The Turkish government reassured Iraq that in the long run downstream flows would revert to normal. Iraqi protests were muted, because Iraq had not yet exploited the Euphrates River water fully for irrigation, and the government did not wish to complicate its relationship with Turkey in the midst of the Iran-Iraq War.

B. Dams and Reservoirs in Kurdistan Region

As most of the civilizations thought about water saving, the people in Kurdistan thought of this issue as well. There are water basins and reservoirs created according to the population requirements and capability available to them. These water basins and reservoirs have been made by people since years ago and still exist and are used. They are used for domestic drinking water, irrigation in agriculture and livestock and mills as well as saving water for the seasons when there are shortages of water. Depending on conditions and needs, the dams and reservoirs are made from rocks, soil and tree branches on rivers, streams and springs.

One of the most important usages of these basins and small dams which are not used nowadays was water mills. Mills could work for a longer time in the summer, which is the season which lacks water. In the Kurdistan Region, through these basins and small dams, it was possible to control the flow of water and use it regularly in periods of water shortages and water abundant seasons. This is the main idea behind the creation of large dams nowadays, flood prevention and usage in dry seasons.

In the plain areas in the Kurdistan Region where there are no rivers, streams and water springs close to the villages, people used to make big pools by excavating the lowest location close to them and they used the excavated soil for surrounding the pool to serve as a wall. Then in the winter and spring seasons rainwater was gathered into these pools and used for domestic use and water for livestock but not for irrigation. These pools were sufficient to provide water for one or two months after the rainy season ended. This kind of pool was called 'Hawrr' in the Hawler plain area.

The idea of dam creation was not developed in Kurdistan for several reasons. First, people usually lived separately and in smaller societies like villages, where dams cannot be made by a few people and no tools had been developed which means that building a dam was beyond their ability. Second, people were easily able to relocate from where they faced water scarcity to places with good water resources. Due to rich water resources people could easily find places with plenty of water because Kurdistan was rich in water. This made them less prone to thinking about solving their water supply problem in the long term.

C. The Socioeconomic Impacts of Dams

Dams have become an important means to increase the gross domestic product (GDP) in most countries, as they are an important basis of the water supply to the following areas: agriculture, industry, domestic use, forestry, fishery, tourism, groundwater recharge and power generation. In addition to enhancing the water supply, dams allow the effective control of floods and regulate the optimal discharge of water.

In the last century more than 48,000 large dams were built worldwide. The International Commission on Large Dams (ICOLD) defines a large dam as being over 15 m high. The definition also includes dams between 5-15 m high with a reservoir exceeding 3 million cubic meters. 30-40% of the irrigated lands and 19% of the total energy supply are from dams at the worldwide level. Thus dams, despite their negative environmental impacts on the landscape, are a main contributor to sources of water and its effective utilization for different purposes.

The nature of the Kurdistan Region, which is mostly mountainous, is suited to building dams to control the water supply to the entire region in all aspects. Until the mid 20th century there was no dam in Kurdistan. The Iraqi government constructed the first one in Dukan in 1959, and two years later, in 1961, the Darbandikhan dam was constructed. The two dams have shown the importance of water management in the region and have been found to play a major role in the region's economic development.

Despite greater needs, unfortunately there are only three large dams in Kurdistan which provide water to very limited areas. After the Ba'ath party came to power, the Iraqi government did not implement any significant long term strategic plans in the Kurdistan Region. It neglected rural areas and destroyed more than 4,000 villages, which eventually destroyed Kurdistan's development infrastructure. The three large dams we have now in Kurdistan cannot provide sufficient water for all places. So, most areas in Kurdistan depend on rivers, springs and rain water which have made the region vulnerable and dependent on hostile neighbors. The water shortages and needs have led to threats by neighboring countries to cut water passing across its borders. In such cases, the importance of dams can be emphasized. A dam does not only have economic benefits, but also impacts on politics and security. For example, the Turkish government has 625 dams in the country which control effectively water on the two main rivers in the Middle East, Tigris and Euphrates. The Euphrates is the main source of water in Syria, so the Turkish government, by using hydro-politics, could force the Syrian government to deport opposition parties from Syria by reducing the water flow on the Euphrates.

Iran now has 66 dams and they have many more under construction. Iran is also trying to dry all rivers before they cross its border with Iraq, which has a very negative effect on the Kurdistan Region. For example Alwand River is about to dry out. It is the main water supply to Khanaqeen area in the south east of the Kurdistan Region. If Iran continues to divert water, the city of Khanaqeen will be subjected to evacuation and its population will be displaced by force to other areas. The Iranian government is also planning to dry out the Sirwan River by constructing 4 additional dams on the sources of this river. About 70% of the Sirwan river water originates from sources in Iran. If Iran implements this plan Darbandikhan Dam will lose 70% of its sources which will make the dam useless. Darbandikhan Dam and Sirwan River provide water for many societies and the agricultural land areas in Kurdistan.

Management of water resources is a very important issue because the problems nowadays facing people and countries are greater than what they were in the past for two reasons: first, the growth of the population and their needs for a water supply; second, scarcity of water available because of climate changes and possible global warming in which the Kurdistan Region is a part. To these two factors one should add the cutting off of water sources by neighboring countries. The importance of dams for solving water problems in the Kurdistan Region should urge the KRG to construct the maximum number of dams as soon as possible in the region. The construction of dams is a costly project. Therefore one should evaluate carefully the water sources and neighboring countries water policies. In parallel one should negotiate with the neighboring countries on a fair sharing of the common pool water resources. This is necessary to secure flow of water before decision to construct dams is made.

D. Major Dams in the Kurdistan Region

There are only three large dams in Kurdistan that have been constructed so far. These are the Dukan, Darbandikhan and Duhok dams See map 4.4. The large dams are of different types, build at different time and are of different capacities and are used for different purposes concerning hydropower generation. The details about the characteristics of each of these large dams are given in the Table 4.5.

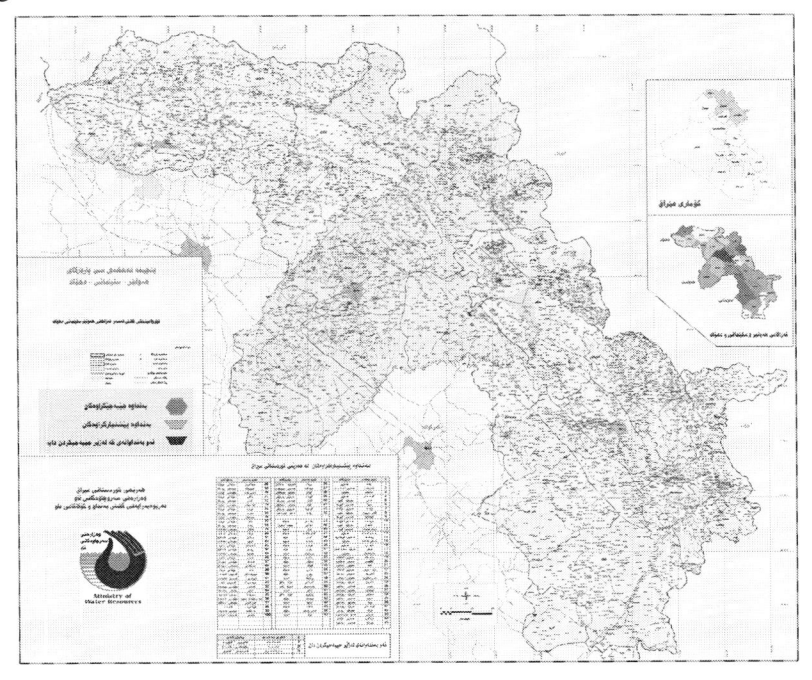

Map 4.4. Dams constructed in Kurdistan Region of Iraq.

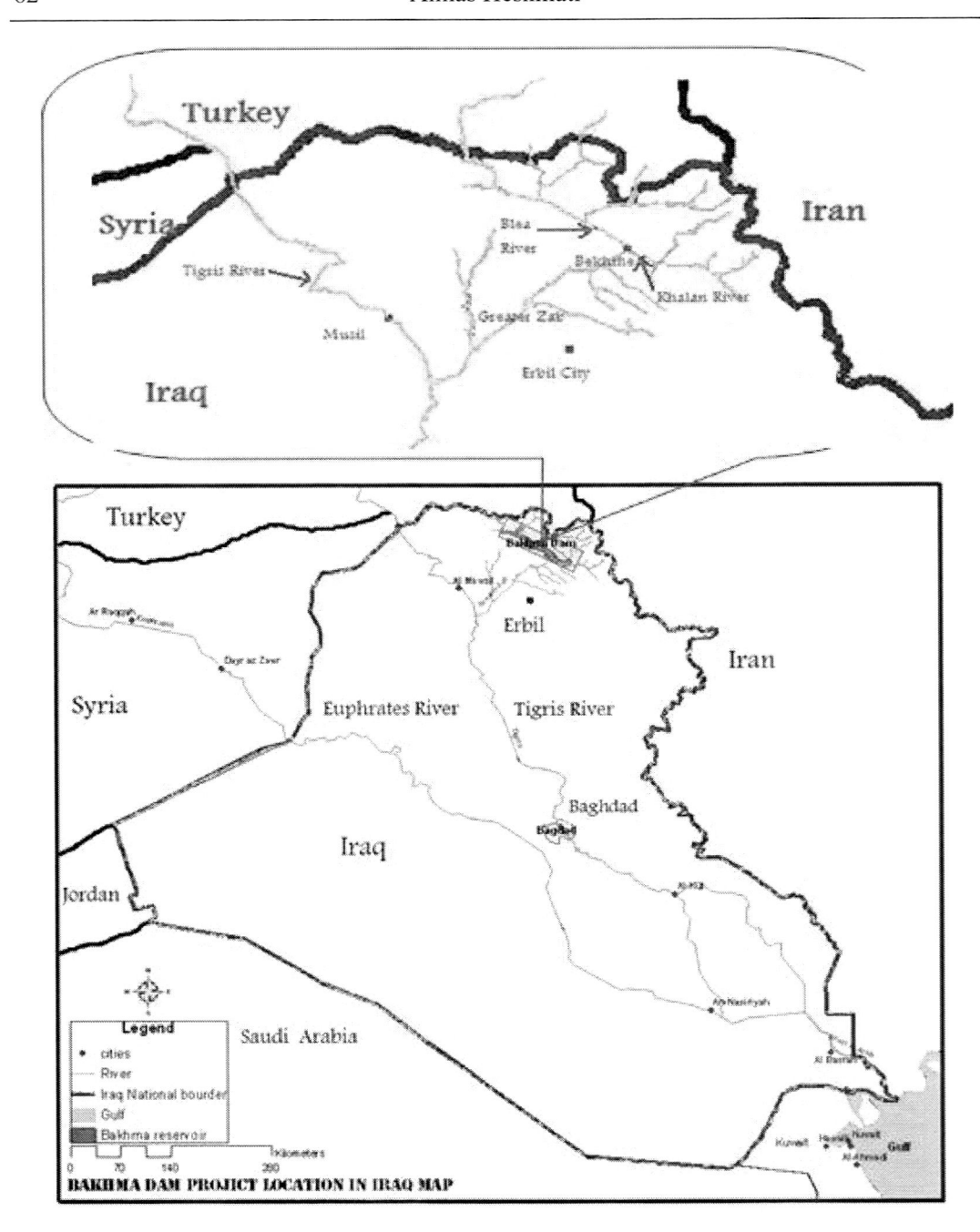

Map 4.5. Location of Bekhmen Dam.

There is an uncompleted dam project in Bekhme village which can be considered as one of the greatest dams in the Middle East. Its construction started in 1984 and in 1990, 37% of the project was finished but because of the Second Gulf war and limited human and financial resources, the project was stopped. See map 4.5.

The Middle East witnessed its best period of dam construction in the1990s, but Iraq did not construct even one single dam in the period when the Kurdistan Region was a part of it because of the Kuwait invasion in August 1990, and the later siege of it. The international sanctions in Iraq destroyed the infrastructure of the country. The Federal Region of Kurdistan as a part of Iraq has gone through a very difficult period. No important project of great national interest and conducive to development was implemented in the region from 1990 until the fall of the Iraqi regime in 2003.

Table 4.5. Characteristics of large dams in Kurdistan Region, 2007

Dam	Completion date	Catchments area (km²)	Dam Type	Length (m)	Height (m)	Storage (BCM)	Power (kW/h)
Dukan	1959	50.00	Arch	325	116.5	6.800	400,000
Darbandikhan	1961	120.00	Rock fill	535	127.0	3.000	240,000
Duhok	1988	2.56	-	-	60.5	0.052	-

Source: Ministry of Water Resources, Federal Region of Kurdistan.

Table 4.6. Characteristics of mini dams in Kurdistan Region, 2007

ID	Dam Name	Year of Construction	Height in m	Length in m	Capacity in m³	Irrigated area by ha
1	Benata	2006	13	120	120,000	40
2	Bilijanke	2005	10	100	45,000	45
3	Ghilishe	2005	18	70	200,000	85
4	Kora	2006	12	40	55,000	35
5	Ghilbok	2002	7	95	35,000	18
6	Bihere	2005	18	87	380,000	200
7	Dilia	2005	10	72	50,000	60
8	Darkar Ajam	2002	20	90	180,000	80
9	Bosali	2005	23	77	350,000	150
10	Beghabar	2004	9	65	50,000	20
11	Levo	2003	9	63	40,000	15
12	Girbir	-	5.5	100	120,000	80

Source: Ministry of Water Resources, Federal Region of Kurdistan.

Since the fall of the former regime, the Kurdistan Region has received 10-17% of the total Iraqi revenue from selling crude oil which is billions of US dollars every year. A lot of projects have been implemented since that time in 2003. In Duhok city 12 small dams have been constructed. Their names are same as the neighboring villages' names where they are located. The small dams' characteristics are shown in table 4.6.

The purpose of establishing these small dams is primarily for the irrigation of agriculture, and more or less they support the groundwater recreation. These dams through learning by doing and observation of economic effects and environmental externalities can be considered as a good step for enhancing local knowledge for starting large dam construction in the near future.

E. Dams under Construction

The 5th cabinet of the KRG has established a ministry (Ministry of Water Resources) for the water resources. This decision is an indication of the concern of the government about water issues. Since the Ministry of Water Resources has started their work, some key projects have already been started including dams. There are some dams that have been started but their implementation process is not finished yet. Table 4.7 shows the characteristics of the dams under construction.

The dams listed in table 7 are funded by the KRG except the Gomaspan dam which is funded by the central government of Iraq. After the construction of these dams is completed, the capacity in irrigation of agricultural land, electricity power generation and groundwater recreation will increase evidently. This will have a great impact on the region's economy.

The importance of the incomplete dam project - Bekhme dam should not be forgotten in this respect. As mentioned before, the building of this dam started in 1984, but construction of the project was interrupted because of the outbreak of the Second Gulf war. Now the federal government of Iraq aims to complete this strategic project because it will solve many of the water problems in Iraq, for example that of electricity generation. Also the groundwater level, which has declined noticeably and to a great extent in the last few years, should recover to the previous higher level.

The project was planned for construction by the EPDC Company. The design is questionable because the Iraqi government at that time wanted to separate the Peshmerga from the cities by submerging a wide area which contains hundreds of villages. By implementing this plan the Iraqi government would have been able to put a security barrier round it and prevent political disputes from spreading to the main cities. Now there are several alternatives to the main EPDC design, suggesting that there are no more fears and need to separate the Peshmerga from the cities. In addition it avoids submerging the entire area which includes hundreds of villages.

Table 4.7. Characteristics of incomplete dams in Kurdistan Region, 2007

ID	Dam Name	Type of dam	Height	Storage (MCM)	Electricity Power in MW/h
1	Basara	Rock fill	50	53.000	4.0
2	Hamamok	Soil	25	0.152	-
3	Bawashaswar	Soil	17	6.492	-
4	Taqtaq	Rock fill with soil core	90	2,850.000	270.0
5	Khewata	Soil	62	300.000	-
6	Gomaspan	Arch concrete	85	215.200	2.8
7	Mandawa	Rock fill with soil core	88	1,850.000	620.0
8	Bakirman	Arch concrete	112	490.000	24.0

Source: Ministry of Water Resources, Federal Region of Kurdistan.

Displacing all these people and compensating them is not an easy task. So, there is a trade off; if the KRG gives priority to a minimum number of impounded villages, the capacity of the dam will also be minimized as a result. Table 4.8 below contains 4 alternatives to the Bekhme dam designs. By looking at the data in the table it is possible to tell much about the importance of the Bekhme dam, thus if the KRG do not agree with the original design, in our view the alternatives 1 or 2 are better choices than alternatives 3 or 4.

Table 4.8. Illustration of four alternatives to the EPDC design, 2007

Description	Units	EPDC	Alternative 1	Alternative 2	Alternative 3	Alternative 4
Reservoir :						
Gross storage capacity	$10^6\,m^3$	17,100	8,105	8,105	4,365	4,365
Effective storage capacity	$10^6\,m^3$	12,600	6,040	6,040	2,300	2,300
Catchments area	Km^2	223	140	140	90	90
Dam:						
Type		Rockfill dam with center core	RCC Dam	Rockfill dam with center core	RCC Dam	Rockfill dam with center core
Height	m	230	170	175	142	140
Power generation						
Maximum output	MW	1,500	840	840	380	380
Irrigation						
Annual average water supply	m^3/s	257	204	204	0	0
Irrigable area	ha	565,000	448,800	448,800	0	0

Source: Ministry of Water Resources, Federal Region of Kurdistan.

F. Future Dams in Kurdistan Region

One of the activities of the Ministry of Water Resources is to study the water resources and locations in the region and to propose the construction of dams in different locations. A team in the Ministry of Water Resources has studied the geographical and geological conditions of most areas in the region with the potential for dam construction and found more than 100 places that are suitable for dams to be constructed. However, in addition to the geographic and geologic investigations, the political, economic, environmental and social aspects also must be studied before a final decision can be made. Their advantages and disadvantages, or cost-benefit analysis for the short and long term must be computed and presented. For example, the construction of dams in fertile areas leads to the displacement of many people. It is quite a costly and difficult task to provide housing, services and jobs for the displaced families. Examples of large impounded areas are found in the cases of dam construction in India and China. In this case professional economists shall decide whether to take this project on or not, considering its social and welfare effects. The next chapter shows the advantages and disadvantages of the dams suggested by the teams in the Ministry of Water Resources, and gives advice on which one should be taken on and which not, as well as setting priorities for the accepted dam construction projects.

4.5. WASTE WATER TREATMENT

The rapid development of the world economy, population growth and high concentration of population in urban areas have resulted in a high demand and a shortage of water in many places. The excess and shortage of water differs from one region to another. The condition is such that, despite some countries having no water shortages because of the variety and availability of normal water resources, the fresh water distribution worldwide is not optimal. This has resulted in an inadequate water supply, and subsequent water demand problems. This has led the planners to think about alternative sources of water, and in this regard, waste water treatment is considered as an additional source of water.

Much of the water used by households, industries, and businesses must be treated before it is released back to nature. Nature has a strong ability to gradually eliminate small amounts of water pollution, but for large amounts of waste water produced every day without active support, nature cannot treat the wastewater. Therefore in the neighborhood of cities treatment plants are established to reduce pollutants in waste water to a level that nature can treat it before releasing it.

The major aim of wastewater treatment is to remove as much of the suspended solids as possible before the remaining water, called effluent, is discharged back to nature. As solid material decays, it uses up oxygen, which is needed by the plants and animals living in the water. Thus without such treatment and in the presence of reduced oxygen the water self-regulatory power is reduced and the environment for survival and expansion of plants and animals is significantly reduced.

The wastewater is usually collected from different sources:

1. Housing and residential areas
2. Industrial water uses
3. Rainfall water in the case that it has been merged with the sanitation network
4. The linkage of water underground

The treated water can be used for the following direct and indirect uses:

1. Agriculture sector
2. Industry
3. Groundwater recharge

There are many advantages associated with using the treated water, for instance using it for agriculture irrigation will reduce the groundwater usage; the treated water contains different items that can be used as fertilizer, which means lower production cost of agriculture products. The treated water can also be used for drinking, recreation and tourism sites it can be also used for treating the salinity of groundwater in the areas that face the lowering of groundwater level by discharging the aquifer with the treated water to maintain the level. In addition concern for nature by cleaning waste water before its discharge has implications for the health and well-being of societies. For instance, an improvement of the sanitation service in urban and rural areas and the treatment of waste water will reduce the negative effects of waterborne diseases.

Prior to the 1991 Gulf War, the population of Kurdistan enjoyed a relatively high level of water supply and relatively good access to sanitation services. The sector operated efficiently by utilizing up-to-date technologies. According to data from MOWR- Baghdad, sanitation services covered about 75% of the urban communities (25% connected to sewerage systems and 50% with on-site septic tanks) and about 40% in rural areas. The number given the economic and technology conditions at the time was relatively better than the average for developing countries.

Since 1991, the water supply and sanitation sector has experienced a steady decline in the quality and accessibility of the water-related services and treatments. Aging infrastructure, poorly maintained equipment, leaking water and sewer networks and low technical capacity are some of the key problems of the sector. Diseases associated with poor sanitation, unsafe water and unhygienic practices have increased to alarming rates. It is estimated that water-related diseases are responsible for about 15% of all deaths of children in Kurdistan (UNICEF, 2001c). Only a small number of the urban population outside Hawler is served by sewerage systems, while the northern and rural areas do not have piped sewerage systems. Moreover, the unavailability of a continuous power supply due to infrastructure damage has crippled the ability of the ministries and water and sanitation authorities to manage and to operate basic services in a satisfactory way.

Like people in so many parts of the world, Kurdistan citizens now face daily challenges in securing safe drinking water. Drinking water and wastewater treatment systems were already degraded before the war. Frequent power outages and a shortage of chlorine to treat water may have serious effects on public health among the Kurdistan Region's five million citizens. A broad-based effort by the United Nations and humanitarian relief organizations during the Oil for Food program has restored parts of the basic water services in many areas, and appears to have headed off widespread outbreaks of cholera and other waterborne diseases. However, establishing a safe and reliable water supply and the establishment of appropriate sewage and waste water treatment remains a long-term task for the regional government.

4.6. SUMMARY

The Kurdistan Region is rich in water resources and highly fertile land. It has several sources of water that are used on a daily basis for various uses and foremost by household and agriculture. The sources are classified according to four categories including groundwater, surface water, dams, and waste water treatment. This section also illustrates the benefits and limitations as well as negative externalities of using these sources. The negative externalities refer to explanations for the pollution of water.

One of the most used water resources is groundwater. Groundwater is the major resource for drinking water, and also for other urban and rural life uses. Groundwater is available in all parts of Kurdistan. One of the most used types of groundwater is water originating from wells. Wells are used by all sectors of the economy in the Kurdistan Region. Sulaimanyah has the largest number of wells compared to Duhok and Hawler. Using wells is environmentally not a good idea but it is an easy and cheap method of providing water. The choice of groundwater is due to easy access to water, generous permission from the state, underdeveloped public water utility systems and its low reliability. The water shortage is one of the main problems faced by the region. Water resources in many places have been polluted by the household and industry sectors, which have caused a great risk to public health and agriculture. Agriculture by itself is also a pollutant.

Surface water is another common source of water in the Kurdistan Region. It is in the form of rivers and springs. The main rivers in the Kurdistan Region are classified according to the river basins. Beside the rivers, there is also a large number of springs in the Kurdistan Region. The springs are classified according to the governorates in Hawler, Sulaimanyah, and Duhok. Rain and snowfall are the main factors behind the variation in the river and spring water levels. It affects the maximum and minimum discharges of the rivers and springs. Lack of rain and snow in recent years has caused serious problems in the form water shortages for the population.

There has been a history of dam-building since early times. People created basins and reservoirs to meet their needs through saving water in one season and using it for another season. Kurdistan is a mountainous region which means that it is suitable for constructing dams to preserve water. This is why the government has built some dams in some places. However, dams have not been constructed in all parts of the Kurdistan Region. Unfortunately there are only three large dams in Kurdistan which provide water to very limited areas. There are about 8 incomplete dams in the region. Dams are important for increasing domestic products and can be used for meeting the needs of different sectors and agriculture. Despite the good effects of dams, they also have negative environmental impacts on the landscape. A well-thought out design of their placement may partially reduce the negative effects.

Waste water treatment is a fourth source of water. This method has not been developed in the Kurdistan Region yet. This includes refreshing waste water and using it again for several uses such as industrial processes, in agriculture and for groundwater recharges.[24] The regional government has a plan for saving wastewater that is used by households and in business and cleaning it to be reused for the second time. In addition, the treated water can be used for different purposes directly or indirectly. Using treated water has some advantages which will reduce the groundwater usage. This method can help the region to solve partially the problems of water shortages.

---

[24] Wallace, Acreman and Sullivan (2003) discuss the co-management or sharing of water between society and ecosystem.

Chapter 5

CURRENT STATE OF WATER RESOURCES IN KURDISTAN REGION[*]

ABSTRACT

This chapter aims to present the current state of water resources in the Kurdistan Region. There are several sources of water in Kurdistan and these are classified as surface water, groundwater and reservoirs. The main reservoirs and their current capacity are mentioned. The surface water includes rivers, springs and rainfall. Rivers are named individually and their discharges discussed. The surface water and rainfall are also studied with the objective of getting a quantitative picture of the current situation. Another objective is to investigate the allocation of water resources by subsectors of agriculture, industry and households. The agriculture sector as a main user is discussed in respect to irrigation. The cultivated area is used as a base for calculating water demand. The industry sector's current status is presented and its water demand calculated. The allocation to the household sector has been studied and data provided to show the current water demand and supply conditions in different governorates. The information is finally used to estimate the water usage perspective optimal conditions for all sub-sectors of the region's economy.

5.1. INTRODUCTION

In the previous chapter we studied the historical and regional perspectives of the sources and users of water resources. This chapter builds on the earlier discussion by illustrating the current state of water resources in the Kurdistan Region. An analysis of the current situation is important for better planning and management of water resources and it has strong policy implications. This is especially important in the light of recent years of increased population, urbanization and public finances. The regional government also increasingly pays attention to building up public development infrastructure and is concerned with health issues as well as reconstruction and renewal of the out-of-date sewage and water supply systems.

---

[*] Contributions by Binar Jawhar, Aumed Muhammed and Zozan Othman to earlier versions of Sections 5.2-5.5 is acknowledged.

In analyzing the current state of water resources this chapter aims to introduce sources and quantities of water resources in the form of surface and groundwater which is represented by rivers, springs, streams, wells, and dams. The first section is concerned with the state of the dams. One view is that dams are not sources of water, but that they are used as a means of storage of water, and are therefore considered to be a resource because they function as reserves of otherwise wasted water. This chapter explains the main rivers in Iraq and those in the Kurdistan Region. The Tigris and Euphrates are the only two rivers in Iraq. There are a number of tributaries but these are also considered technically as rivers. Then springs in Kurdistan Region are mentioned in more detail. Quantities of water resources which consist of surface water and groundwater in the region are estimated. These rivers and springs are explained in further detail by using available statistics.

Another important point regarding water resources is rainfall and snowfall in the region illustrated with the most recent documented data. Rainfall and snowfall affect agricultural irrigation, nurture groundwater and influence dams during crisis periods. The sources and quantities of groundwater available in the form of a number of wells in each governorate are also analyzed. In addition in this chapter the current allocation of water in different sub-sectors of the economy including agriculture is reported and explained and is illustrated graphically as well as numerically.

Having analyzed the sources of water, the second objective is to investigate the current allocation of water by the industry sector and the role of types of production on water usage. There is also the current state of household water usage, which represents the most significant component of the users and is often given the highest priority. This is explained through examining the condition of water in the Hawler governorate. Here the number of wells and the water production quantity is illustrated through the most recent data available. Furthermore, the consumption of water per capita is analyzed. The water supply conditions of the Sulaimanyah and Duhok governorates is studied in the same way, as these cities differ in their initial conditions. The most recent statistics are shown here from related sites. Moreover, this chapter studies the main causes of existing problems linked to management of water resources in the region.

The remaining parts of this chapter cover the third objective, namely the optimal allocation of water to different sub-sectors, including agriculture, industry and households. The optimal allocation of the industry sector has been taken for each unit of production. When it comes to the agriculture sector, the task is more complex, and many estimates are being made in order to determine the optimality for this sector.[25] Included is the optimal allocation of household usage, which consists of determining the explicit quantity of water per capita based on Iraqi standards to cover different needs. An estimation of the optimal water quantity use for each sector separately and its comparison with the current levels will allow us to disenable the possibility of enacting the in-optimality level in these sectors. The information could be important for the planning and management of water resources.

The rest of the chapter is organized as follows. In Section 2 the sources of water resources are discussed. The quantities and qualities of these resources are discussed in Section 3. Current and optimal allocations of water by different subsectors are found in Sections 4 and 5, respectively.

---

[25] Here we discuss optimal allocation of water among users. Ringler (2001) is a good example of optimal river basin allocation.

5.2. SOURCES OF WATER RESOURCES IN THE KURDISTAN REGION

Water resources in the Kurdistan Region are classified according to the surface water and groundwater types. Reservoirs are another important source of water which is used as a source of water storage. These sources are already presented in more detail in the previous chapter. Here we provide only a brief review as background to this chapter to be considered as a separate reading.

As mentioned in the previous chapter, there are several dams which have been constructed in the Kurdistan Region, the major ones being Dukan, Darbandikhan and Duhok. These three dams have a storage capability up to 9.852 MCM (million cubic meters). However, there are several small dams in Duhok, their total capacity being 1.505 MCM. The small dams are: Benata, Bilijanke, Ghilishe, Kora, Ghilbok, Bihere, Darkar ajam, Bosali, Beghabar, Levo and Girbir. All of these dams are named after the villages located in their vicinity. In addition there are several dams under construction or planned to be constructed in the near future. Upon completion they will have the capacity of more than 38.000 MCM. The current quantity of water available and location of the dams is given in table 5.1.

The Kurdistan Region is mountainous and is rich in water resources. The region has many rivers and springs flowing from and running throughout its mountains. They provide apparent images of productive lands, abundant water sources, and marvelous countryside.

Iraq as a whole has two principal rivers which are the Tigris and Euphrates. Both rivers enter Iraq from Syria and Turkey, respectively. The Tigris River is enlarged by several tributaries originating in Iraq. The most important rivers are Khabur, Greater Zab, Lower Zab, Sirwan and Udhaym. These rivers all unite in the Tigris north of Baghdad. The Tigris River flows into the Euphrates through the Shatt al Arab.

Table 5.1. Capacity and locations of main reservoirs in Kurdistan

Dam name	Dukan	Darbandikhan	Duhok
Capacity in MCM	6,800	3,000	52
Location	Sulaimanyah	Sulaimanyah	Duhok

Source: Ministry of water resources, the Directorate of Dams.

A number of channels are dispersed throughout the Tigris and the Euphrates rivers diverting water to other areas. As a result, the flow of the rivers is largely reduced by the time they join at Al Qurnah. The Karun River, which flows from Iran, is located below Basra, and unfortunately contains large quantities of mud which causes severe problems for the region. In addition, these problems have created an immense obstacle for river traffic.

The Tigris River enters into Kurdistan Region north of the Feshkhabuor village in Zakho at the border of Turkey and Syria. All of the Tigris's tributaries are on its left depository. The Kurdistan Region depends primarily on these water resources. This is why irrigation is so important for the region, because it can benefit from the wasted water of the river Tigris and the five rivers integrating into it.

5.3. QUANTITIES AND QUALITIES OF WATER RESOURCES

The Kurdistan Region's water resources appear plentiful, but water availability varies considerably across the region and at given times. In addition to climate-related variations and constraints, a variety of users and the demands for water extraction affect the quantity and the availability of water. It is obvious that a supply of water based on needs in areas with an imbalance between demand and supply will be costly to meet in sufficient quantities and with high security. These issues complicate the protection of nature and the region's waters. Therefore assessing water quantity and water use in the region is necessary for the sustainable management of water resources, which provide many social, economic and environmental services.

Water quality is defined as a measure of the life-sustaining nature of water resources and the potential of that water. It is the physical, chemical and biological condition of the waters, and the link between land and water use. Water quality is the integrator of the effects of catchments management practices. It is also a key indicator of sustainability in economic and health development and practices of water management. The building up of a public infrastructure and skills for monitoring and quality assurance are a major responsibility of related public authorities like the Ministry of Water Resources, Ministry of Health and Ministry of Agriculture.

While there are important relationships and overlaps between aquatic health and water quality, aquatic health is reviewed briefly and is beyond the scope of this report. Water quality in this report is primarily concerned with physical-chemical measurements, while aquatic health is based on biotic measures, which synthesize and present an overarching perspective of river health. Drinking Water Quality is probably the most important challenge facing the providers of water and decision makers. It should be assessed separately, as there are specific measurements and responses for maintaining drinking water quality.

A. Quantity of Water in the Rivers and Springs

The quantity of water in rivers of Kurdistan differs from one river to another according to the area and the usage of any given river. If the Greater Zab is compared with the lesser Zab, one can notice that the water supply of the greater Zab is twice as unstable as that of the lesser Zab. The greater Zab is widely exploited by both the private and public sectors. Hawler depends mainly on water from the greater Zab, for instance in cases such as the Ifraz project which provides drinking water to the city. Meanwhile, there are some other tributaries that unite and flow into the greater Zab which can be mentioned as a reason for its larger quantity of water than the lesser Zab. The total water supply of the lesser Zab is greater than that of Sirwan River and the reason is due to the larger catchment area of the lesser Zab. The quantity of water in the rivers also depends on the geographic place that the river is located. Some rivers flow through rural areas and a certain amount of water will be utilized by the inhabitants of these areas.

The measurement of the amount of water in rivers is a difficult task. For instance, some rivers are used by rural areas before they flow into another river, such as the five boughs (tributaries) of the greater Zab. In turn the main rivers such as the greater Zab, lesser Zab,

Udhaym, Sirwan, and Khabur River flow into the Tigris. The quantity of water in these rivers is shown in table 5.2. This table contains information about the length, area, rate of water flow and water supply quantities. Unfortunately, no data on river discharge is available for the Duhok Rivers. For more information, see also table 4.7 in chapter four.

Table 5.2. Quantity of water from the rivers

Rivers	Length/km	Area/km^2	Rate of waste water (m^3/sec)	Rate of water to Tigris %	Total water supply (milliard m^3)
Upper Zab	473	26,470	421.4	32 6	14.32
Lower Zab	456	22,250	226.0	16 7	7.07
Uzaym	220	1,200	27.6	1 6	0.79
Sirwan	386	17,850	160.6	13 6	5.86
Chabour	160	6,268	-	-	-

Source: ministry of water resources, annual report, 2008.

The quantity of water in springs depends primarily on the rate of rain and snowfall. Water resulting from the rain and snowfall descends underground and then it flows back to the surface and forms springs. The quantity of water in the springs will increase if the rate of rain and snowfall increases and vice versa. Table 5.3 illustrates the predicted discharges of the springs. These rates will most probably vary from one year to another. For instance, in 2008, the discharges of the springs decreased extremely due to the low rate of rainfall. Drought has affected many springs in the Kurdistan Region. For more details about the discharge of the springs, see also table 4.7 in chapter four.

Table 5.3. Total Rainfall and Snowfall quantities in Kurdistan

	Hawler		Sulaimanyah		Duhok	
Year	Quantity of rain m^3/year	Quantity of snow, water equivalent, m^3	Quantity of rain m^3/year	Quantity of snow, water equivalent, m^3	Quantity of rain m^3/year	Quantity of snow, water equivalent, m^3
2000-2001	60,883,886	4,853,828	68,772,356	6,021,399	26,689,058	8,221,001
2001-2002	39,870,730	10,988,946	40,121,231	12,987,622	62,412,317	13,991,217
2002-2003	7,989,220	6,617,486	13,445,617	7,772,883	7,620,811	8,917,772
2003-2004	60,853,738	12,225,014	59,727,682	9,223,754	79,566,526	2,379,221
2004-2005	44,423,078	12,255,162	52,007,214	13,212,995	48,814,608	6,881,744
2005-2006	21,887,448	6,949,114	22,880,123	5,791,213	884,582	2,311,998
2006-2007	35,442,817	9,221,799	49,212,813	4,971,313	387,547	4,225,568
2007-2008	19,342,720	3,442,783	21,719,318	2,911,875	33,541	2,412,719

Source: Ministry of water resources, Federal Region of Kurdistan, Hawler. See also Table 5.8 in Chapter Four.

The annual forecasted discharge of the springs in cubic meters within the three governorates is as follows: Hawler 518,000-3,110,400m^3, Sulaimanyah 1,728,000-95,040,000m^3, and Duhok 518,400-3,110,400m^3. The numbers indicate differences in water availability as a basis for the development potential of the three governorates.

B. Rain- and Snowfall in the Kurdistan Region

Rain and snowfall in the Kurdistan Region varies from one location to another. In the mountainous areas, the rate of rain and snowfall is higher than on the plains. This process can be illustrated based on the quantity of rain and snowfall in the governorates. Rain and snowfall in the Hawler governorate varies from one year to another. According to the geographical location of Hawler, the rate of rain is more than the rate of snow particularly in the city and its vicinity. The amount of rain and snow are the main factors behind variability in the rivers and springs levels. This year, the rate of snow was very low and it only covered a few areas for a small number of days in the Kurdistan Region. In addition, the rate of rain also decreased in all parts of the region. The low rate of rain and snowfall are the factors causing insufficient water for irrigation and electricity generation in the region. Table 5.3 shows the total rain and snowfall in the Hawler governorate.

It can be inferred from table 5.3 that the quantity of rain in 2000-2001 was the highest in comparison to the other years. In addition, the quantity of snowfall in 2004-2005 was the highest in comparison to previous records. It should be noted that Hawler is a plains area, which results in the total amount of snow being smaller than in the mountainous areas. The Hawler region mostly depends on rain as a source of water for its rivers and springs. Unfortunately, no data is available from 2006 to 2008.

According to the table 5.3, the quantity of rainfall in the Duhok governorate increased in 2003-2004.[26] Afterwards, the quantity of rain decreased, and reached the minimum rate in 2007-2008. Nevertheless, a high quantity of rain does not mean that the governorate is not lacking water. This is because rainfall in this region is a seasonal factor. If the quantity of rain from the heavy rainfall seasons is not stored, the population cannot benefit from it. The low levels of rainfall result in the drying-up of many springs and a further reduction of the rate of water in rivers.

C. The Groundwater Sources and Quantities Available

In general, groundwater is important in the region but there is also a locality in the degree of dependence of the consumers and providers on this source. Both public and private interest groups attach high priority to the groundwater as a source. The Ministry of Water Resources has provided recent statistics regarding the groundwater reported in table 5.2. The table was prepared in March 2008, and it indicates the presence of a number of wells in the three major governorates. Wells are categorized in two ways: as legal and illegal. The majority of the region depends on wells as the sole source of drinking water. Wells are easy to use, they provide freshwater with high quality water considering the geographical structure of

---

[26] The rate of rainfall in 2002-2003 is low because the data covers only three areas within the Duhok governorate.

Kurdistan and its aquifer. The number of legal wells is 2,370, whereas the numbers of illegal wells is 300 in Hawler and 1,122 in Duhok. There are 12,022 legal and 17,230 illegal wells in Sulaimanyah. The illegality of wells is due to the lack of official permission for their establishment.

It is clear that Sulaimanyah has the highest number of wells, and this is because almost all of these wells are considered to be "shallow wells" and not properly constructed. They produce about 20 m^3 water per day. There is a high probability that many of the illegal wells are placed such that they are in contact with sewage waste resulting in the contamination of their water. This consequently leads to outbreaks of fatal diseases such as cholera. Research conducted by specialists at the Ministry concluded that the region does not suffer from a shortage of water availability. The inadequate amount of water arises for a number of reasons. The management of water resources is the main reason behind the complexity of the situation with water in the entire region. The number of wells in the three governorates and access by the using by sectors are reported in tables 4.2 and 4.3 of chapter four.

5.4. CURRENT ALLOCATION OF WATER BY SUB-SECTORS

Water resources in the Kurdistan Region are mainly used for households, industry, and agriculture. The largest consumption of water is the household sector. Industry follows as the second largest consumer group, whereas agriculture is not well-developed in Kurdistan, and this is why it is a significant consumer of water resources, but it does not crowd out other users. Undoubtedly, Kurdistan needs to develop its domestic production in order to increase its level of self-sufficiency instead of depending on the import of agricultural products from neighboring countries.

A. Agricultural Sector

Agriculture is one of the main water consumers in the region. As will be discussed in more detail in the next chapter, we have two types of agricultural crops: (i) cereals which are mostly dependent upon rainfall, and (ii) fruits, vegetables and legumes which mostly depend on irrigation. To determine the demand of water needed for future irrigation of cultivated land, we need to look at the current data available and analyze it, for example comparing current amounts of water used for irrigation, as well as the kinds of crops being grown in a given area. In a number of tables below we present information on the distribution of cultivated land areas in Hawler, Sulaimanyah and Duhok according to the type of the crops being grown on them during a 10 year period from 1997 to 2006. The information is obtained from the General Directorate of Planning and Follow up, Ministry of Agriculture (2007) covering Kurdistan region. The crops include: wheat, barley and rice.

Table 5.4 and figure 5.1 show that in 2006 the areas cultivated for wheat, barely and rice have declined comparing to the previous years. Meanwhile, we also note that agricultural areas have increased relatively in size since 1997 except for the year 2004, which was the year after the invasion of Iraq to remove the Baath regime from power. The reason behind the decline of cultivation is partly due to the prediction of little rain, and farmers risk averseness to losing seed and fertilizer. The amount of wheat produced in Kurdistan ranges from 300 to 375 thousand tons a year, while the need for wheat for the region is about 500 thousand tons. This clearly demonstrates that a quarter to one-third of the wheat consumed in the region is imported from abroad.

Table 5.4. Area cultivated for cereal crops in Hawler, Sulaimanyah and Duhok (in donum)

Year	Wheat			Barley			Rice		
	Hawler	Sulai-manyah	Duhok	Hawler	Sulai-manyah	Duhok	Hawler	Sulai-manyah	Duhok
1997	424,076	565,508	463,808	159,628	146,056	72,018	3,044	10,920	16,936
1998	442,374	531,727	335,574	222,234	247,545	82,929	1,957	8,545	11,299
1999	380,871	410,184	311,450	158,780	231,191	79,004	1,150	3,333	6,357
2000	319,029	522,447	319,029	274,948	330,197	73,260	885	1,844	5,298
2001	362,194	517,902	339,912	325,153	430,220	153,703	987	6,845	4,926
2002	531,371	653,300	486,077	438,989	489,109	128,177	496	4,523	5,923
2003	940,060	436,760	515,750	595,851	173,780	156,350	1,860	6,150	11,242
2004	395,850	280,447	393,240	344,643	208,636	109,618	1,800	8,410	19,240
2005	467,110	612,460	409,108	1,082,763	498,732	146,151	1,840	5,563	11,496
2006	507,552	481,638	363,258	970,175	432,822	162,976	1,365	6,742	7,007

Source: Ministry of agriculture, Statistics directorate.

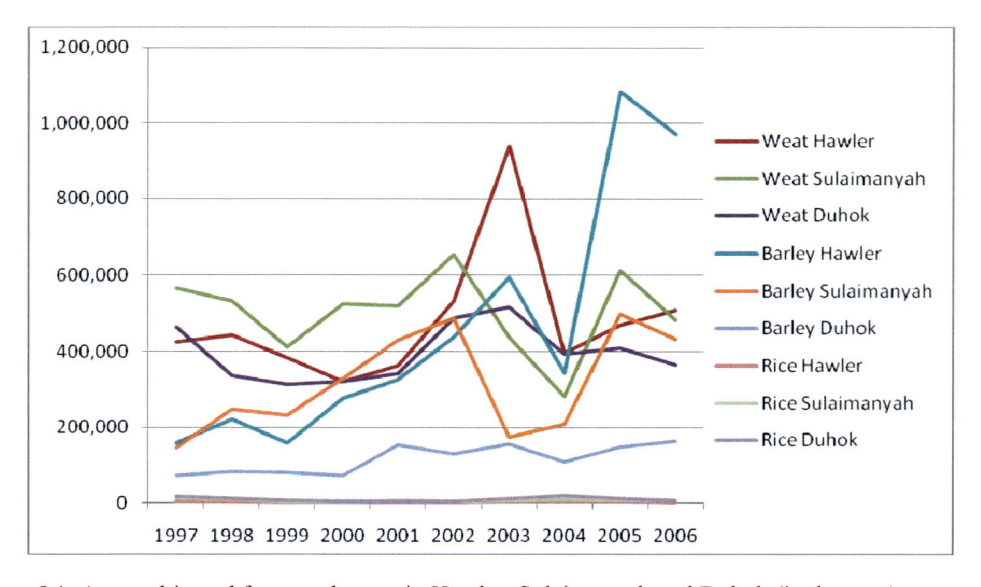

Figure 5.1. Area cultivated for cereal crops in Hawler, Sulaimanyah and Duhok (in donums).

The sum of the areas cultivated, measured in donum[27] for cereal crops in the three governorates are: Hawler 1,479,092, Sulaimanyah 921,202 and Duhok 533,241 in the year 2006. The land is fertile, but productivity of land measured in yield per hectare or donum is very low and, among others reasons, is due to low investment in agriculture, low skills, a lacking agricultural and trade policy and inadequate business and import practices. Tables 5.5 and 5.6 show the areas cultivated with the most common vegetables such as tomatoes, cucumbers, eggplants, squash, onions and water melons in the region during 1997-2006 and by governorate.

Table 5.5. Area cultivated for vegetables in Hawler, Sulaimanyah and Duhok (in donums)

Year	Tomato			Cucumber			Eggplant		
	Hawler	Sulai-manyah	Duhok	Hawler	Sulai-manyah	Duhok	Hawler	Sulai-manyah	Duhok
1997	6,692	9,778	16,680	1,744	887	723	1,496	1,104	1,257
1998	8,703	9,141	17,520	2,903	1,418	1,531	1,216	913	1,310
1999	8,586	11,093	9,303	3,356	1,729	1,198	1,523	765	1,278
2000	8,634	9,153	6,925	4,066	1,276	921	1,724	923	451
2001	13,742	8,817	5,768	7,775	2,996	2,197	2,859	969	890
2002	24,288	12,644	7,888	9,810	3,439	2,236	3,195	1,132	883
2003	25,340	24,330	25,850	15,375	10,795	4,497	3,416	2,198	1,065
2004	35,088	30,530	24,400	17,657	10,495	5,471	5,199	2,608	1,334
2005	32,485	25,685	21,740	13,515	10,952	3,635	2,732	2,397	625
2006	27,645	20,314	21,710	18,386	7,987	4,026	4,203	1,844	885

Source: Ministry of agriculture, Statistics directorate.

Table 5.6. Area cultivated for vegetables in Hawler, Sulaimanyah and Duhok (in donums)

Year	Squash			Onion			Water melon		
	Hawler	Sulai-manyah	Duhok	Hawler	Sulai-manyah	Duhok	Hawler	Sulai-manyah	Duhok
1997	834	503	1,585	6,288	2,949	1,611	468	3,440	983
1998	2,394	631	1,265	9,902	4,783	1,931	906	3,151	1,697
1999	1,997	399	1,498	6,224	4,403	1,579	2,221	4,338	894
2000	1,060	675	739	3,854	3,195	1,933	2,051	5,772	177
2001	1,635	1,058	533	6,797	5,075	2,225	4,989	3,077	3,249
2002	1,232	1,034	742	6,895	6,332	2,729	4,487	3,810	3,397
2003	3,663	3,960	2,290	2,008	4,850	3,000	9,193	6,770	4,524
2004	4,091	3,911	3,825	1,905	6,673	2,500	13,025	5,580	5,638
2005	2,673	2,428	3,635	7,415	5,750	1,100	9,760	5,480	2,975
2006	3,783	2,383	4,633	2,042	8,449	100	11,070	4,340	4,030

Source: Ministry of agriculture, Statistics directorate.

---

[27] Donum is a local measure of area. One donum is 2,500m^2 of land.

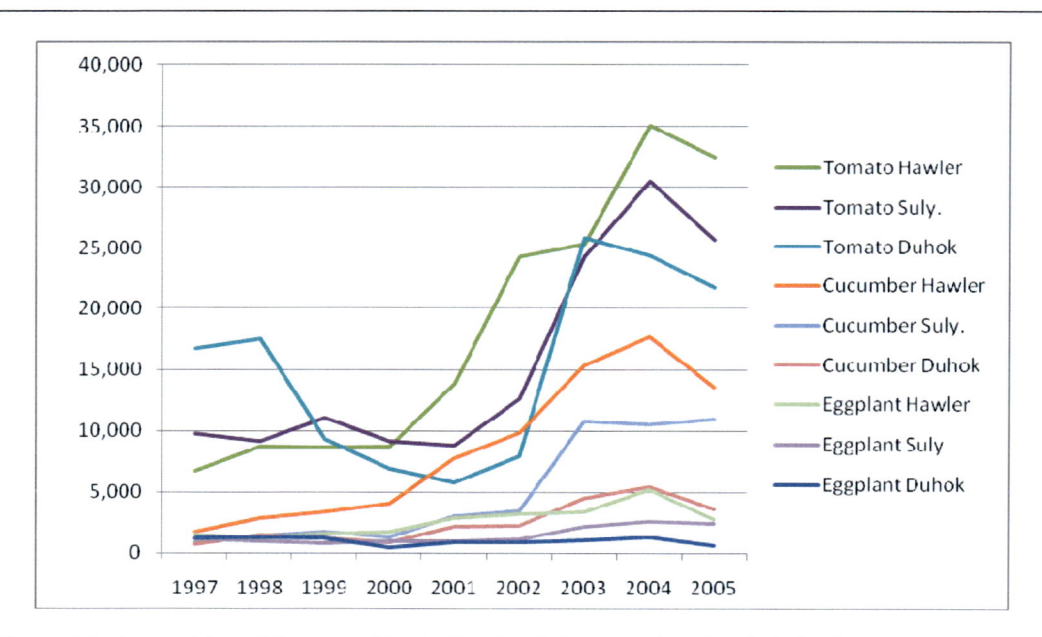

Figure 5.2. Area cultivated for vegetables in Hawler, Sulaimanyah and Duhok (in donums).

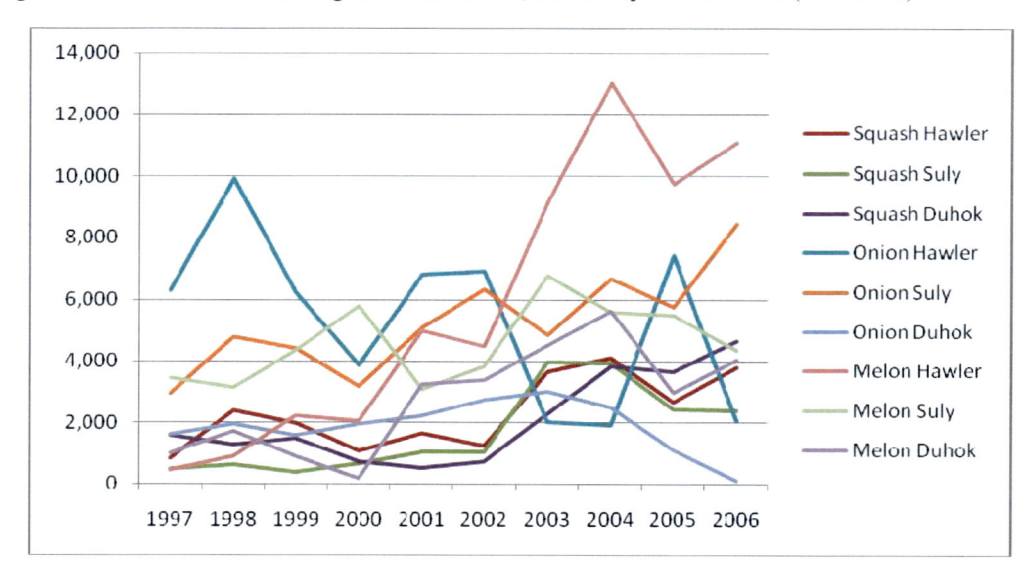

Figure 5.3. Area cultivated for vegetables in Hawler, Sulaimanyah and Duhok (in donums).

We separated tables 5.5 and 5.6 containing the 6 types of vegetables in order to show the charts in a way easily understandable to the reader. From the graphs we see that cultivation has increased in general since 1997. Although that is a good sign for the agricultural sector and for future food security, many vegetables are still imported due to increasing incomes and demand as a result of rapid population growth in the region and the oil revenue sharing program. The sum of the cultivated areas measured in donum for vegetable crops in the three governorates is: Hawler 67,129, Sulaimanyah 45,317 and Duhok 35,384 in the year 2006. The distribution and development of these areas are illustrated in table 5.7 and figure 5.4. For example, table 5.7 shows the areas cultivated for sunflower oil seed and is further divided into the three governorates observed for the 10 year period from 1997 to 2006.

Table 5.7. Area cultivated for Sunflower Oil Seed in the Kurdistan Region (in donums)

Year	Sunflower		
	Hawler	Sulaimanyah	Duhok
1997	3,064	9,391	1,400
1998	4,207	15,247	2,205
1999	3,129	12,829	3,513
2000	1,533	15,582	1,414
2001	5,648	20,427	2,995
2002	10,416	49,228	10,441
2003	3,762	51,115	4,530
2004	5,503	50,965	6,237
2005	3,909	45,485	2,740
2006	4,673	33,242	2,661

Source: Ministry of agriculture, Statistics directorate.

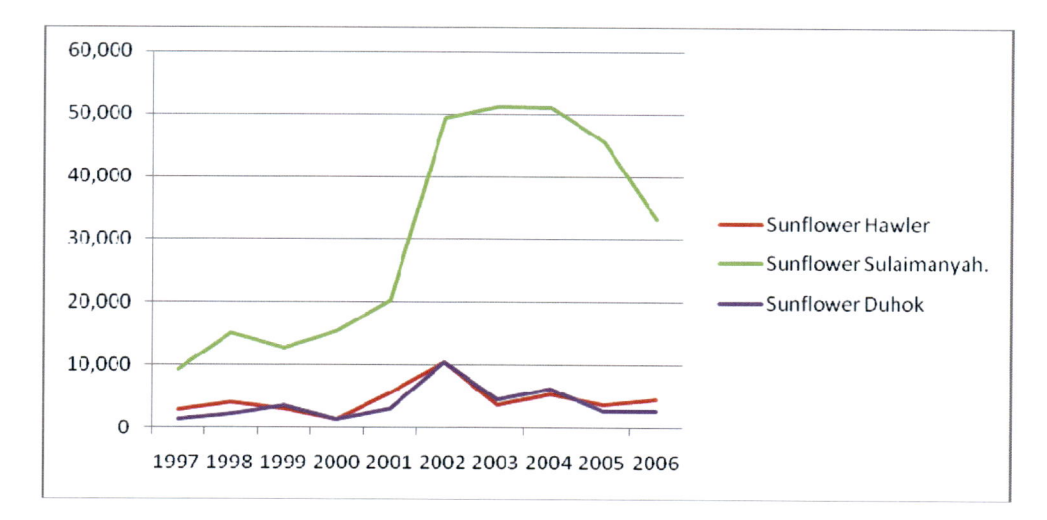

Figure 5.4. Area cultivated for Sunflower Oil Seed in the region (in donums).

Sunflower is the only crop representing oil seed crops in the Kurdistan Region because there is no other data available on other oil seed crops. From figure 7 we can see that from 1997 until 2004 land cultivated for planting sunflowers increased, but after 2004 a great decline occurred. The reason for this decline is related to production and sales-related costs and benefits of production, and is not linked to water scarcity problems. The sum of the areas cultivated in donum for oil seed crops in the three governorates are: Hawler 4,673, Sulaimanyah 33,242 and Duhok 2,661 in the year 2006. We see that the Sulaimanyah governorate takes the leading position in sunflower cultivation. Unfortunately the production is not used in the food processing industry, and as such it is not developed and all cooking oil is imported.

The last type of crop that we refer to is legumes. Table 5.8 and figure 5.5 show the areas cultivated for that purpose. Again, even in this case, the distribution of land across governorates and its development over time is used in the analysis.

Table 5.8. Area cultivated for legumes in Hawler, Sulaimanyah and Duhok (in donums)

| Year | Lentil | | | Chickpea | | |
	Hawler	Sulai-manyah	Duhok	Hawler	Sulai-manyah	Duhok
1997	6,710	17,343	11,316	18,682	198,719	159,071
1998	5,798	9,871	3,233	32,534	179,599	108,601
1999	2,868	9,210	2,535	21,010	162,789	84,810
2000	2,525	6,626	2,525	38,631	191,704	111,114
2001	2,215	6,708	1,178	87,413	260,518	250,121
2002	2,401	3,450	1,379	90,763	196,335	234,647
2003	3,369	3,250	4,756	16,334	176,323	77,560
2004	3,117	4,321	1,430	37,570	122,224	117,420
2005	1,613	5,899	2,267	51,373	83,637	120,455
2006	1,900	2,154	5,443	63,084	77,430	133,613

Source: Ministry of agriculture, Statistics directorate.

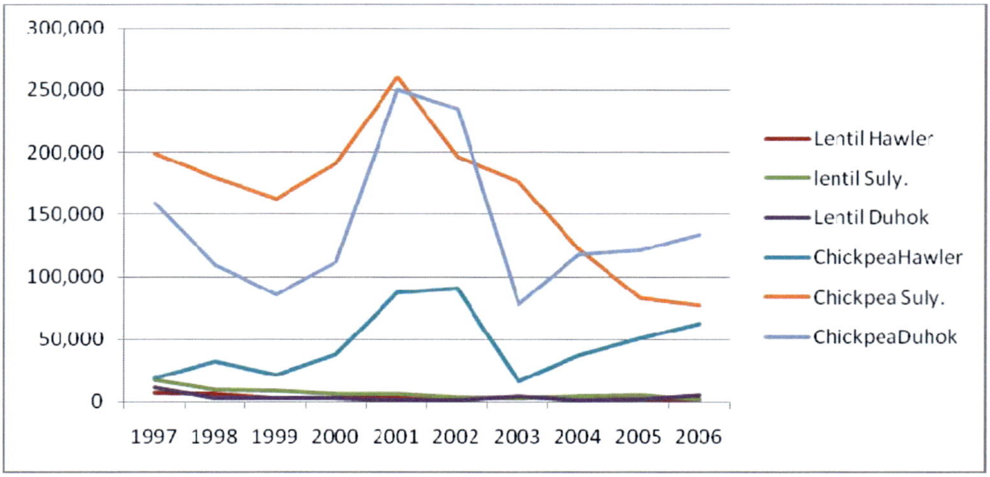

Figure 5.5. Area cultivated for legumes in Hawler, Sulaimanyah and Duhok (in donums).

Figure 5.5 indicates the areas cultivated for both lentils and chickpeas in the regional governorates of Hawler, Sulaimanyah and Duhok. Chickpea cultivation is more common than lentils in the region because a superior harvest of chickpeas is guaranteed by the land and water conditions in the region. Since 2001 the area of cultivation for both types of crops has been declining. This is despite the high local demand for these products. A significant amount of imported processed product has weakened local production and its expansion.

The total sum of the land areas cultivated in donum for legume crops in the three governorates are: Hawler 64,984, Sulaimanyah 79,584 and Duhok 139,056 in the year 2006. Here Duhok is more specialized in the production of legume crops. The total sum of all cultivated land area used in production of all these type of crops in the three governorates in 2006 is reported in table 5.9.

Table 5.9. Land area cultivated for all crops in 2006, (in donums)

	Hawler	Sulaimanyah	Duhok	Total
In Donum	1,615,878	1,079,345	710,342	3,405,565
In square km	4,039.7	2,698.4	1,775.9	8,513.9

It should be noted that tables 5.4-5.8 showed only the type of crops and their cultivation in areas for which data was available. The data is short of full regional coverage. Lack of import statistics does not allow an estimation of total need and local production to estimate the potential to expand the latter and irrigation needs. Table 5.6 demonstrates the total of areas cultivated in Hawler, Sulaimanyah and Duhok, as well as the region as a whole in both donum and square kilometers.

There are several factors that, in addition to the quantity of cultivated land, affect water demand for irrigation in agriculture. These include the type of crop, the age of the planted crop, the type of land, the season of planting the crop, moisture and temperature as well as the wind velocity. All of these factors affect the quantity of water necessary for the efficient cultivation of crops. The degree of effect varies from one location and crop type to another and each has its own coefficient to determine its effectiveness. Unfortunately, this information is not available for this region, and without these coefficients we cannot predict the water demanded for irrigation of cultivated land. It is also a negative factor to the prediction possibility of harvest and yield potentials.

The only factors we reliably know about the current status of agriculture in the three governorates of the region is the size of the area cultivated during the last few years and the type of crop planted in these areas. Table 5.6 includes data about areas cultivated in Hawler, Sulaimanyah and Duhok. There no doubt that the information available is incomplete, as it lacks complete coverage of cultivated land and type of crops produced. Without such information and in a detailed form and with high accuracy it is hard to plan and manage water resources. Despite the long tradition in data collection in agriculture (see Davis (1957) on land use in Iraq) and in the education sectors, this inability to produce basic statistics is a major handicap in the region.

B. Industry Sector

Groundwater is the water resource that is used by almost all of the industrial sectors for their production. Water used by each sector depends on the type of production of the given sector. For instance, the largest consumer of water is the sector producing prepared

Almas Heshmati

(prefabricated) concrete and iron products used in the construction and public infrastructure sectors. Due to the drought year, the rate of production has decreased. In addition, a low level of production leads to an increase in the price of the products. This has resulted in the increasing price of housing and implementation costs of public projects. Many buildings are not completed due to the high price of the materials used in construction. For example, many contracts that were undertaken by Turkish companies are left uncompleted.

Table 5.10 shows the situation of the industrial sub-sector in the Hawler governorate by depicting the number of factories, number of workers, water use in production and for drinking purposes. The corresponding information for the governorate of Duhok is reported in Table 5.11.

Table 5.10. Water use in industrial sectors in Hawler governorate, 2006

Type of production	number of factories	number of workers	Water use of industry (m^3)	drinking water
A. Mineral industry:				
Breaking stones	8	92	13,900	10,500
B. Food industry:				
Ice	29	96	41,000	8,120
Mineral water	2	25	4,600	280
Flour	9	169	1,035	16,520
Cookies	16	101	470	9,800
Soft drinks	1	5	1,100	560
Nuts	3	48	305	5,320
preparing skin	2	25	4,760	392
C. Plastic industry:				
Plastic	14	182	9,200	1,540
Doors and windows, PVC	15	107	730	7,560
D. Paper industry:				
Tissues	2	52	190	4,480
E. Faltered petroleum:				
Oil of car	4	51	2,200	5,750
F. Pipes and iron:				
White and black pipes	1	80	110	14,560
Iron	1	270	18,750	34,160
Ironsmith	325	1,574	9,185	98,750
G. Machines, electrical equipment & generators:				
Electrical equipments	1	18	95	112
Lighting equipment & generators	1	7	5	56
H. Metallic and construction industries:				
producing tiles and corner	1	30	2,800	336
Ceramic Tiles	2	22	2,400	184
Manual Brick	32	484	23,500	6,670
Gravel	27	331	16,700	4,480
Construction blocks	117	1,192	112,650	6,210
Shtiger	3	60	2,720	9,660
Mozaik Tiles	33	537	14,200	506

Type of production	number of factories	number of workers	Water use of industry (m^3)	drinking water
Prepared concrete	6	212	163,200	4,370
Asphalt	3	77	4,350	1,955
I. Furniture industry:				
furniture and carpentry	23	266	785	20,500
Furniture	18	241	7,200	2,016
J. Chemical industry				
chemical industries	10	215	12,690	2,016
K. producing car, trucks				
pipe of trucks	5	57	140	476
L. Producing equipments				
producing construction equipments	3	32	90	252
producing electric equipments	5	31	150	252
producing agricultural equipments	1	18	12	168
M. repairing cars				
washing cars	21	275	3,100	17,250

Source: Ministry of Industry, Federal Region of Kurdistan, Hawler.

Table 5.11. Water use in industrial sectors of Duhok, 2006

Type of production	number of factories	number of workers	water use of industry (m^3)	drinking water
A. Food industry:				
Mineral water	4	137	45,800	6,750
Flour	9	281	17,900	17,750
Cookies (snacks)	8	151	19,000	7,750
Soft drinks	9	227	1,750	17,000
cleaning skin	2	25	4,760	26,000
B. Paper industry:				
Tissues	3	35	680	25,250
C. Faltered petroleum:				
Oil (gas/engine oil)	2	30	840	25,500
D. construction industries:				
gypsum	1	10	12,000	84
Brick	36	368	21,500	32,250
mosaic tiles	21	266	2,810	23,250
concrete pipes	1	50	23,000	4,500
Prepared concrete	2	93	22,500	8,250
Asphalt	3	54	4,800	4,750
E. producing cars, trucks				
pipe of trucks (exhaust)	2	50	2,700	325
F. producing equipment				
equipment production	3	121	4,130	975

Source: Ministry of Industry, Federal Region of Kurdistan, Hawler.

It is evident from table 5.11 that in the city of Duhok few industrial sectors are established. This explains the low level of water consumption for industrial use. The construction industry is found to be the largest consumer of water. However, a majority of the sectors rely on wells for their production. There are few exceptions in which firms utilize a combination of surface and groundwater resources. The food industry comes in second place concerning its demand for water. The largest consumer of water in this industry is mineral water production. This industry depends primarily on surface water that flows from the mountains.

C. Household Sector

The General Directorate of Water Resources and the Ministry of Agriculture and Industry have conducted a study on water resources in the Hawler, Sulaimanyah and Duhok governorates.[28] The objective is to determine the current state of water resources in the Kurdistan Region. The report shows the most recent statistics that the General Directorate of Water Resource produced in August 2008 regarding drinking water for households. Aside from this, other studies were prepared concerning the agriculture and industrial sectors. The study shows that water resources in the center of the Hawler governorate consist of those originating from wells and those supplied by the Ifraz projects.

The number of wells is around 400 and the Ifraz project consists of three sub-projects, in general called Ifraz projects 1, 2 and 3.

The quantity of water supply from the three Ifraz projects for the center of Hawler is estimated. Project 1 supplies 1,450 m^3 per hour, project 2 1,950 m^3 per hour, while project 3 supplies 6,000 m^3 per hour. The total supply of the Ifraz projects is 9,400 m^3 per hour. Thus, the total water supply per day is 9400x24=225,600 m^3. The production capacity from the Ifraz projects can be compared to the quantity of water supplied from one well which is 25 m^3 per hour. The total production capacity, assuming 10 hours of operation per day, is estimated to be 25m^3x10hx400wells, which is approximately 100,000 m^3 per day. The total water supply obtained from both sources is 325,600 m^3 per day.

The total population in the center of Hawler is approximately 850,000 residents and growing rapidly over time. Every individual resident needs approximately 350 liters of water per day; which equals 297,500m^3 per day for the entire community. In addition to the base consumption amount a portion corresponding to 15 liters per day and per capita is used as a "security factor". Therefore the total required water quantity for Hawler area is 342,125m^3 per day. Given that the population and estimation of per capital and day consumption and security amount are correctly estimated, the water shortage is only 16,525m^3 per day. The actual rate of the water supply that reaches the consumers is estimated to be 100% of the supplied water. Thus the rate of the water shortage in normal cases is only 4.8% of the estimated need. The zero leakage rate in the system seems to be an exaggeration of the quality and capacity of the water supply infrastructure.

The primary sources of water to Sulaimanyah governorate are generated from the Dukan project, which equals 50,000m^3 of water per day. The secondary source is the Sarchinar project, which generates 30,000m^3 per day. The third source is the local well production, generating about 4,000m^3 per day. Therefore the total supply of water is estimated to equal

---

[28] See General Directorate of Irrigation & Surface Water (2008a, 2008b and 2008c) Ministry of Water Resources, Kurdistan Regional Government, No. 88, 373 and 951.

84,000m^3 per day. The Ministry of Municipality's estimation shows that about 20% of this quantity is wasted as a result of old networks which equal 16,800 m^3 per day. Therefore the actual supply of water to residents is 67,200 m^3 per day.

The population of Sulaimanyah is around 800,000 inhabiting the city center and suburban areas. According to Iraqi standards each individual requires 350 liters of water per day. Unfortunately, due to drought this recommended quantity was reduced to 200 liters per day, that being 280,000m^3 per day by Iraqi standards and it is only 160,000 m^3 in the period of drought. The actual water supply per capita is currently only about 85 liters. This implies that 115 more liters more water per capita are needed to cover every individual's basic and recommended needs. The available rate of 85 liters per day and capita is only 42.5% of the needed water provision. Water is distributed only three days per week from between 1-3 hours on each occasion. The rate of shortage of water based on Iraqi standards referring to 350 liters consumption per day is about 75%. The corresponding rate based on drought conditions is 57.5%.

There are three sources of water in the Duhok governorate. The first source is Duhok's primary project which generates 2,400 m^3 per hour (62% of the total water output) allocated to the "Chum Barakat" area. The second source is substitution water and the Gali Duhok projects that allocate water within Duhok city. These projects depend on the Duhok dam as the primary source of water. They both generate only 750 m^3 per hour. This is combined with the water that comes from "Chum Barakat" in order to improve its quality chemically, and it forms 19% of the total output. Groundwater is the third source. The number of wells that are functioning is around 120, but only 50 are used and generate 750 m^3 per hour.

The total supply of water from the above three sources is 3,900 m^3 per hour. The amount of wasted water is estimated to be 20% of the production. Therefore the actual quantity of water that reaches the residents is 3,120 m^3 per hour which is equivalent to 56,160 m^3 per day. The required rate of water based on standard measurements is 350 liters per individual and per day. Therefore, the shortage of water in Duhok is estimated to be around 50% of the recommended level. The differences in recommendation levels might have to do with the weather conditions.

D. The Major Factors Causing Water Shortages

After the Iraqi Gulf War, the central government withdrew its administration and security forces from the Kurdistan Region. Both the general and administrative body of the region was rather confused for some time because this action was rather unexpected. The Kurds had to find a way to manage the region even though they had little experience and almost all high rank public officials were in past non-Kurds. The initial attempt to govern the region was not satisfactory mainly due to a lack of resources, political disputes and a power-sharing struggle. The process has since then gradually improved due to exchanges of specialists, particularly with European countries and countries that have in recent decades been in a similar transition situation as the Kurdistan Region.

Kurds have been able to adjust to the variety and changing conditions from a sudden inexistence of governance, being subject to international and national sanctions, power sharing and globalization. In parallel the new governing body has been established and acquainted with the use of modern information, knowledge and has attained a certain level of proficiency in management in general. In fact the region has improved in various aspects. This does not mean that management of the region is smooth and free from problems and criticisms. There is a big gap in water management in the region as a whole, which the report above illustrated.

Another case of deficiency as a result of inability in governance is that in 15 years the region has been suffering from a shortage of electricity and it is obvious that the region relies on electricity to distribute water. Therefore, electricity generation and supply is a main target area for the regional government to induce radical changes. To control the water problem, that the regional government should first resolve the power supply problem. Despite serious efforts and significant investment programs, the regional government is still struggling to improve the power and water shortage problems facing the region.

E. Water Management in the Region

The region has its own policy for managing the water resources. The management of water is indirectly linked to or determined by the electricity distribution. The regional government is adopting a table system to distribute electricity to households. This method has been applied during the last 15 years of its governance. It applies to all sectors of the economy including households, agriculture, industry and commercial sectors. However, the tables are not uniform in their constructions across different water-using sectors and differ significantly from one sector to another. Variations also observed over time and across regional locations.

The system described above implies that each water using sector has a particular daily allocation of electricity and consequently of their water allocation as well. Drinking water for households is the most significant sector that has attracted official attention. In general the neighborhoods have access to clean water every second day. Households are expected to refill their private water tanks during the electricity and water supply hours. The same source is used for all household needs. The electricity shortage has had the positive effects of reducing the consumption of water and need for waste water treatment as well as the production costs. The system is a kind of distribution time rationing of the water supply.

5.5. OPTIMALITY IN ALLOCATION OF WATER BY USERS

A. Agriculture in a Governorate Perspective

The optimal allocation of water for irrigation purposes can be determined only when the determinants of water consumption have been provided according to a specific area of land, location of areas and types of crops as well as other characteristics of irrigated land. The Ministries of Water Resources and Agriculture should cooperate to enable data collection in such a way that researchers can easily access necessary information to conduct research related to irrigation.

Table 5.12 shows the arable and non-arable land areas in the Kurdistan Region's three main governorates. The information concerns total land area, rain-fed, irrigated and non-arable land all measured in hectares in 2006.

Table 5.12. The arable and non-arable areas in the regions governorates, 2006

Name of Governorate	Total area in ha	Arable Area			Non Arable
		Rain fed	Irrigated	Total	
Hawler	1,514,120	580,645	45,635	626,280	887,840
Duhok	931,398	254,892	46,650	301,542	629,856
Sulaimanyah	-	-	-	-	-

In a comparison between tables 5.9 and tables 5.12 we can conclude the following concerning the condition for the agricultural sector's use of water resources in the three main governorates of Kurdistan Region. Table 5.9 stated that 2,698.4 square kilometers have been used in 2006 for production, but table 5.12 does not provide any such information about arable areas in the Sulaimanyah governorate, thus we cannot comment on the irrigation issues in this governorate.

Table 5.12 shows that 6,262.8 square kilometers (626,280 hectares) of arable land is available in the Hawler governorate but only 4,039.7 square kilometers of it were cultivated in 2006. The difference, corresponding to 2,223.1 square kilometers, which is about one-third of the total arable land, is good for cultivation, but is not used for that purpose. The optimum goal is to use the entire arable area, because the region has an extremely low degree of self-sufficiency in the production of most crops. In the event that the cultivated areas exceed the level required to feed the domestic consumers, the surplus production can be exported to the rest of Iraq whose main part of the food supply in the past came from the Kurdistan Region.

Table 5.12 also reported that in the Duhok governorate, there are 301,542 ha of arable land while only 177,590 ha were cultivated in the year of 2006. This means that almost 45% of the total arable area was not used in 2006. It can be estimated that if the entire land capacity had been used, the quantity of water needed would have doubled in 2006. The regional government provides assistant to farmers and builds infrastructure for the development of the agricultural sector. However, the lack of interest in long term investment in agriculture and the sector inability to compete with the booming construction sector and high wages has limited the development potential in rural areas. The lacking trade and agricultural policy and business laws and regulations has further weakened the prospect of the development in agricultural sector.

By looking at table 5.12 we can see that in all three governorates great portions of the arable land is rain-fed. Rain-fed areas should be changed to irrigable areas in order to have a guaranteed level of harvest at the end of the cropping season. This will require an immense number of water divergence canals and it is the Ministry of Agriculture's plan and responsibility to create such a project in the Hawler and Shamamk plains.

B. Industry Sector

There is no optimal allocation of water estimated for the industry sectors. We lack basic data on the production and needs of the sector to estimate such. There is only a maximum rate and amount of water use designated for the industrial sectors. The optimal level of water consumption ideally should be calculated on the base of optimum consumption per production plant. In many locations there are wells that the sectors can utilize for their daily uses. However, the lack of a continuous electricity supply causes yet another problem for the industry sector as there is not enough electricity to operate the wells. We have already mentioned that the shortage of electricity is a major problem and development constraint in the region. The drought has limited further it generation.

The irony is that the industry cannot operate diesel-driven pumps to access water in sufficient quantities from wells located at their plants. The governance and public are expecting the industry sector to serve as a base or engine for their economic, social, security and technology development. If sufficient data had been available, the objective was to compute the actual rate of water use and by estimating the optimal use of water calculate the water gap or degree of non-optimality in water access for industrial production purposes. The information would be very useful in decision-making on resource allocation to reduce the gap and inequality in regional development. Mahzouni (2008) provides an excellent analysis of the participatory local governance for sustainable local periphery community-driven development in the Kurdistan Region. Minoia and Brusarosco (2006), in their integrated evaluation of impacts of dams on regional development, discuss the situation of the water infrastructure facing sustainable development challenges.

C. Household Sector

In section 5.4 under the sub-section for households we discussed the current situation for the water supply and mentioned the recommended quantities of water supply per capita and day. The optimal allocation of drinking water for a household can be computed according to Iraqi recommended standards where each individual requires 432 liters of water per day. However, according to the General Directorate of Water Resources, in 2008 the following estimations are applicable.

The overall quantity of water supply in Hawler governorate was estimated to reach 325,600m^3 per day. Given the population of approximately 850,000 persons, every resident's need for a lower level of recommendation of 350 liters of water per day and adding 15% security marginal the total required water quantity for Hawler area is 342,125m^3 per day. The water shortage is estimated to be 17,525m^3 per day. Given zero leakage in the supply system, the rate of water shortage in normal case is only 4.8% of the estimated need. Based on these calculations the optimal level of water supply is 383 liters per capita per day, which is equivalent to 325,600m^3.

The sources of water in Sulaimanyah governorate are fewer than those available to Hawler and the total supply of water is estimated to equal 84,000m^3 per day. After an estimation of 20% loss due to leakage as a result of old networks the actual supply of water to the 800,000 residents is 67,200m^3 per day. According to Iraqi standards each individual requires 350 liters of water per day in normal cases and 200 liters under drought conditions.

The actual water supply per capita is currently only about 79 liters which is only 39.5% of the 200 liters of water provision needed under drought conditions. Water is distributed only three days per week from between 1-3 hours at each occasion. The rate of shortage of water based on Iraqi standards is about 80%, while the corresponding rate based on drought conditions is 77.4%. These indicate the extent of non-optimality in the supply of water in Sulaimanyah.

The current total quantity of water available at the Duhok governorate reaches 3,900m^3 per hour. The amount of wasted water is estimated to be 20% of the production quantity. Therefore the actual quantity of water that reaches the residents is 3,120m^3 per hour which is equivalent to 56,160m^3 per day. The required rate of water recommended is 350 liters per individual and per day. Therefore, the shortage of water in Duhok is estimated to be around 50% of the recommended level.

The calculated degree of non-optimality or disequilibrium between demand and supply in the three governorates of Hawler, Sulaimanyah and Duhok is estimated to be 3.5%, 57.5% and 50% respectively. It should be noted that the calculations are based on different standards or recommended levels. The differences in recommended levels might have to do with the different weather conditions.

Here disequilibrium refers to shortages of supply. In the Kurdistan Region many factors affect the disequilibrium. Unbalanced water resources affect differently different sectors. The factors affecting disequilibrium in water resources are: ineffective management, power shortages for operating the system, water availability, snowfall, rainfall and our ability to store water that is not in use at a given time in order to prevent wastage. Each of these factors has a direct impact on the instability in supply of water resources. Factors that lead to the loss of water are: evaporation, pollution and the use of old and inefficient networks.

5.6. SUMMARY OF SOURCES AND QUANTITIES OF WATER

This chapter is an analysis of the current state of the allocation of water resources in the Kurdistan Region. The chapter is divided into several parts based on the situation of water resources in different governorates and sectors of users. The chapter illustrates the sources and the quantity available, the current allocation, the optimal or desired allocation, and estimation of in-optimal or disequilibrium by each of the sectors.

In the first part of the chapter, the sources and quantity available are illustrated. The sources of water are divided into three main parts: surface water, groundwater, and dams. The first source is illustrated through dams. Although there are few dams in the region, they are considered to be one of the main sources of water. The primary function of dams is to store water that can then be used for different purposes. Surface water includes the rivers and the springs. The quantity of water in each is illustrated through the discharge of the water. Surface water also includes the quantity of rain and snowfall, measured in each governorate over a 10-year period: 1997-2006. Lastly, groundwater is illustrated in the form of wells. The quantity of water in the wells also depends on the rate of rain and snowfall in each governorate.

The current allocations of water by users are divided into three parts. Water resources in the Kurdistan Region are mainly used by households, industry, and agriculture. The largest consumer of water is the household sector. Both types of water, surface and groundwater are used by households. Industry represents the second main category of consumer. It generally uses groundwater for its production. Agriculture is not well developed in Kurdistan and this is why agriculture is not a major consumer of water resources. In addition, the Kurdistan Region needs to develop its domestic production capacity as an alternative to its high dependency on neighboring countries for the import of agricultural products.

The optimal allocation of water to the sub-sectors differs from one sector to another. It is difficult to measure the exact optimal water use allocation of agriculture and industry sectors. In agriculture, we can only compare the land used for agriculture and irrigation and that not for either and in the industry sector case no optimal allocation can be estimated. The optimal allocation for households depends on the population in each governorate and the availability of water and applicable usage recommendations.

The in-optimal allocation of the sub-sectors depends on the gap between their optimal allocation based on certain recommendations and their actual allocation. The differences between the current and the optimal distribution to the sectors equal the degree of in-optimality in the distribution of water at the sub-sector level. In another words, it indicates either a shortage or excess supplies of water resources. Here in-optimality suggests a shortage of water. In the Kurdistan Region many factors affect the disequilibrium of water resources. These imbalances in water resources affect the various sectors in the region such as household, agricultural, and industrial sectors differently.

Several of these causal factors can be accounted for in the distribution analysis, while others need planning and investment. Here disequilibrium refers to shortages of supply. The factors affecting disequilibrium are: ineffective management, power shortages for operating the system, water availability, snowfall, rainfall, our ability to store water, evaporation, pollution and the use of old and inefficient supply networks.

Chapter 6

CHARACTERISTICS OF THE MAIN USERS OF WATER RESOURCES[*]

ABSTRACT

There are several user groups of water resources and they differ greatly in their numbers and shares of the total consumption. Most users are the households who use water for drinking, cooking, construction, gardening and hygiene. The second largest group, again in terms of number, is the agricultural sector. The sector including farming, horticulture, forestry, fishery and aquaculture use water for drinking, for feeding animals and for irrigation, mainly of farmland. The industrial sector is the third group which uses water for the production of bottled water and for different simple process industries. The last category of consumers is the state/municipalities for the preservation of nature, for water security, recreation and tourism as well as for production of electricity. Each of the four categories is characterized here by the capacity of its users and their demand for water. In addition to a quantification of their demand and its justification, different externalities and impacts associated with their usage of water are discussed. Different measures, as part of public water policy to prevent or to reduce the magnitude of such negative externalities, are also discussed.

6.1. INTRODUCTION

The main users or consumers of water resources in a typical society differ by their type, number, needs and consumption behavior. There are four main categories of consumers of water resources. These are household, agriculture, industry and municipality/services. The user groups differ greatly in their share of total consumption and in respect to the outcome of their uses of water. Here outcome refers to both the direct and indirect effects of water consumption. The direct effects are in the form of the difference in quality of water before and after its consumption while the indirect effects are in the form of pollutants resulting from different ways of using it and the results of possible crowding out effects.

---

[*] Contributions by Binar Jawhar, Aumed Muhammed, Nabaz T. Abdullah and Zozan Othman to earlier versions of Sections 6.2-6.5 and by Fatima Osman to section 6.6 are acknowledged.

The largest group of consumers is households who use water for drinking, cooking, hygiene and other household activities. Households differ by location and are grouped into urban and rural areas. The rural inhabitants are closer to the source of water and unlikely to have access to water processing, treatment and distribution systems. Despite closeness to the water source and access to greater quantity at no cost, difficulties in preventing the contamination of drinking water by sewage water mean that the quality of water in rural non-agricultural areas is much lower than in urban areas. Due to economies of scale and inequality in opportunities, treatment of drinking water in these areas is rare.

The second group, again in terms of number, is the agricultural sector. The sector including farming, horticulture, forestry, fishery and aquaculture uses water for drinking, for animal husbandry and for irrigation of mainly farmland. Kurdistan Region was until recent decades mainly an agricultural society. The central government policy in the 70s and 80s led to the systematic destruction of rural life and rapid urbanization. Thus there have been rapid changes taking place in respect to the agricultural sector. The sector is relatively small but still consumes large amounts of water for irrigation due to use of old and ineffective irrigation and production technologies. The sector from business and profitability perspectives is unattractive compared with the construction and service sector.

The industrial sector is the third group which uses water in various production processes. The Kurdistan Region is not an industrialized society and has no such developed industries. The main users of water resources related to industrial processes are those of the cement industry, in the production of drinking water, the construction industry, the restaurant industry, and the food processing industry. The latter is however insignificant and most of the food and soft drink supplies are imported from the neighboring countries. It is just in the last two years that bottled water has been produced domestically. There is hardly any manufacturing industry worth mentioning. Thus, this small and negligible industry is not to be considered as a major user and pollutant.

The last category of consumers is the municipalities. The water in this category is used for the preservation of nature, for water security reasons, for recreation and tourism as well as for the production of electricity. The first two types of uses are an investment to protect the environment and to enhance national security. Recreation and tourism in a geographic location such as the Kurdistan Region, where the majority of population is concentrated in plains and warm areas, requires intensive use of water for the irrigation of parks, recreational centers and city plantations. The production of hydropower-based electricity is a major user of water.

Each of the four categories mentioned above is characterized in this chapter by the capacity of major users and their demand for water in the water market. In addition to the quantification of their demand and its justification, different externalities and impacts associated with their usage of water are discussed. In addition different measures as part of public water policy to prevent or to reduce the magnitude of such negative externalities are also briefly discussed.

The rest of the chapter is organized as follows. In the first section the development of agriculture as a user of water is discussed. The focus is on types of crops and their demand for irrigation, water saving techniques and consumption of water, dams, pollution, regulations and water saving policies, statistics and water consumption awareness. The second section covers the development of the industrial sector and major industries and their demand for water in the region of Kurdistan, as well as issues of safety and stability in the supply of drinking water. The third section is about recreational, tourism and other public services including the impacts of tourism and recreation on the demand for water and positive and negative environmental impacts. The fourth section is a discussion about the development of the population in urban and rural areas and their increasing demand for water resources. The focus is in particular on the water conditions in the cities of Sulaimanyah and Hawler. The summary and conclusion follows in the last section.

6.2. DEVELOPMENT OF THE AGRICULTURAL SECTOR

A. An Introduction to Agriculture and Irrigation

Water is considered as the main source of life. It is directly and indirectly related to human well-being. Agriculture is one sector of the economy which depends to a very high extent on water, and it is the main source of water consumption in the agricultural areas. Kurdistan is an agricultural-based area or society. The population used to depend on agriculture in the Kurdistan Region because of its fertile land which was suitable for farming. The region is relatively wealthy in water resource availability, and the population depended on agriculture to make a living.

Since many years ago, this area has been well known for its richness in both groundwater and surface water sources, but now the region is facing a scarcity of water for irrigation in the agricultural areas because of insufficient rainfall in the past few years. The lack of rain and prospects for planning has frightened the farmers and most of them are not ready to take risks in farming, especially because of changed climate conditions and the warming phenomenon. The farmers predict low and no rainfall and they are unwilling to risk losing the initial investment plugging, seed and fertilizer without getting any payoff for their efforts. Moreover the plain southern part of the region is facing this problem more severely than in the northern part. The northern mountainous area is in a better position concerning rain and snowfall and spring water conditions.

B. Agricultural Types of Crops and Their Demand for Water

The agricultural land can broadly be divided into two types of irrigable lands, which are irrigated and rain-fed land. The irrigation system may differ from one location to another and differ according to the farms' financial situation and technology capability. In general the irrigation system is old, ineffective and not optimal compared with those with more water saving technologies used by developed nations.

The Kurdistan Region's population in rural areas was highly dependent in the past and still is mostly dependent on rain-fed farming for production of wheat and barely crops. These are two main crops in the region which most farms in plain areas are specialized in. However, the specialization does not imply high productivity and yield. There are new techniques in irrigating wheat and barley fields in which it was not often used previously. One way is through sprinklers, which can be used more broadly in the future for solving the problem of irrigation in areas lacking sufficient rainfall and water storage. This will of course be conditional on public irrigation support programs.

Regarding fruit and vegetable farming, they usually do not depend on the rain directly, but indirectly through ground and surface waters to a larger extent. In the northern part of the region which is the mountainous areas, farmers mainly use surface water in their farming. On the other hand, in the southern part of the region which is the plain areas, the farmers use groundwater for irrigation to a larger extent. In addition, they use other techniques such as those using wells, and a small share of surface water which are rivers and streams in the areas around them.

Consumption of the groundwater has increased in recent years because digging wells has become very cheap and most people are able to have a well or, if necessary, more than one well. The use of wells is more common because of the availability of technology and private and public financial resources to invest in wells. The farmers use the wells and water pump machines regardless of how small their piece of land is. Also the surface water, in most places, is not stored through large or small dams. Thus, the farmers are encouraged as the only alternative available to use groundwater for irrigation in agriculture, even in the dry seasons.

C. Water Saving Techniques and Water Consumption

There are no well-established rules and regulations existing for water management and water usage in the farming sector and even if there is any such, farmers may pay little attention to these rules and there is no effective mechanism to monitor applications and to impose penalties on those who violate such rules. The condition results from the lack of good management of water, low education and environmental awareness. Therefore the land owners consume free unregulated water without many productive farming activities on their lands.

In order to control the irrigation and to provide incentives to farmers in their use of groundwater as a source of irrigation water, the irrigation times should be controlled by setting gauge systems to measure the quantity of water consumed. It should be possible that the areas that use groundwater can be monitored in their consumption of water by setting counters on the wells and by limiting consumption adjusted to the season of the year and rainfall. There should be strict rules to prohibit the excessive use of water for other purposes than legitimate cultivation of land. Fines should be applied in cases where violations are made to save the groundwater from systematic misuse. The Government should protect groundwater and give priority to using surface water as a main water supply by better management of wastewater, in particular water used for hydro-based power production.

D. Dams

The most important source of water utilized for irrigation in most places is dams, which cover 30-40% of the irrigation needs worldwide (see table 6.1). There are more than 45,000 dams worldwide, while only three of them are in the Kurdistan Region. These are the Dukan, Darbandikhan, and Duhok dams. There is plan to build several new dams, construction of some of which is already in progress. The planned and existing dams were discussed in a more detailed form in chapter 4.

Table 6.1. Summary of the Dams in the Kurdistan Region

Dam	Completion date	Catchment area (km^2)	Length (m)	Height (m)	Storage (BCM)	Power (MW/h)
Dukan	1959	50.00	325	108.00	6.800	120
Darbandikhan	1961	120.00	535	128.00	3.000	37
Duhok	1988	2.56	..	60.50	0.052	..
Bekhme	Not completed	140.00	840	265.00	17.100	2,500

Source: UNICEF Report 2001.

Note: In the table above the supply of the Dukan dam is 120 MW/h, but according to information available on the Ministry of Water Resources website the power supply by the Dukan dam is around 400 MW/h.

There was another major project for establishing a dam in the Bekhme village. The project started early in 1984, but it was suspended because of the first the Iraqi-Iranian and First Gulf Wars. The project was later further postponed due to the Second Gulf War. The most expensive and advanced equipments at the site were looted in the period of the central power vacuums in the aftermath of the coalition's invasion of Iraq. It will cost the region billions of dollars to purchase the equipment again and this delays the project further with negative consequences for the agricultural sector and reconstruction and development programs.

Dukan dam is the biggest one which together with Darbandikhan dam is used as a hydropower source for the region. In addition to being a power supply, Dukan dam supply water for irrigating Taqtaq plain area. Thus, most irrigation of the Taqtaq plain is by this dam and it is useful for groundwater recharge. It is obvious that in the winter season water increases and the level of the rivers and streams rise. In this season floods may happen and the water flows away without taking any advantages from it. It is necessary for the government to construct more dams in different areas for water storage which can be used later in irrigating agricultural land, groundwater recharge, generating hydropower and preventing flood disasters.

E. Water Pollution

Water pollutants come from point and non-point as two main sources. Their effects on aquatic systems largely depend on whether polluted waters are non-flowing (lakes and ponds) or flowing (rivers). The former systems are generally more susceptible because of the slow turnover in water quantity. The major water pollutants are organic nutrients, inorganic nutrients, infectious agents, toxic organics, toxic inorganic, sediment and heat. Each of these sources is described below. This section does not aim at a systematic review of water pollution, but only a brief description of the issue.

Organic nutrients come from feedlots, municipal sewage treatment plants, and industry. They promote the growth of natural populations of aquatic bacteria. Bacterial decomposition of organic materials results in a decline in dissolved oxygen, with dire effects on other oxygen-requiring organisms. Two inorganic plant nutrients of major concern are nitrogen and phosphorus. These come primarily from septic tanks, barnyards, heavily fertilized crops, and sewage treatment plants. These cause excessive plant growth that clogs navigable waterways. The bacterial decay of plants in the fall results in a drop in dissolved oxygen, which may suffocate fish and other organisms. Luckily, fertilizer usage per unit of land and the total quantity used is quite low in Kurdistan and a less serious problem as a source of pollution.

Water may contain pathogenic bacteria, viruses, protozoans, and parasites (infectious agents). Untreated or improperly treated sewage, animal waste, waste from food-processing like meat-packing, and some wild species are the major sources of infectious agents. Waterborne infectious diseases present a special problem in developing nations with poorly developed sewage systems and sewage treatment facilities. Inadequate sewage systems and treatment plants are thus a serious danger to health in the Kurdistan Region.

Toxic organic pollutants include a large number of chemicals, such as pesticides and PCBs, many of which are non-biodegradable or slowly degraded, biologically magnified and carcinogenic. Toxic inorganic pollutants include a wide range of chemicals, such as metals and salts, from a wide array of sources. Mercury is a particularly troublesome pollutant because it is converted into methyl and diethyl mercury in aquatic ecosystems by aerobic bacteria. These forms of pollutants are more toxic than inorganic mercury.

In the Kurdistan Region there are no chemical factories which pollute water, also water sources in the region mainly flow out of the region, but little of it originates in other neighboring countries through rivers and rivulets. The way which mostly pollutes water in this region is through leakages from sewage systems and rainfall when the air is polluted. The urban traffic is high, but the car density is still relatively low and probably not a major source of air pollution, although the number of vehicles is increasing rapidly and in the absence of a good traffic and environmental policy it might become a problem for health and safety. In summary water can be considered to be clean in the Kurdistan Region for agricultural purposes.

Crops are affected with polluted water used in irrigation. Polluted water in irrigation has many negative externalities and effects. It might reduce the harvest or make the crop contaminated and unusable for human consumption. Furthermore, seeds might not be used again for farming as the soil will be polluted and its effects will remain for many years to come. In August 1990 Iraq was forced out of Kuwait and in the middle of February 1991the Iraqi government set on fire its oil wells. The smoke reached and covered the southern Kurdistan area. The rain, which was polluted with carbon, affected grain crops, but this was a special case and it does not happen often.

F. Regulations and Policies for Water Savings and Consumption

Regulations and policies for water management are necessary in the region because the region is predicted to have a deteriorating situation concerning the problem of aggravated water scarcity and its lower quality in the near future. These issues will be discussed in more detail in the chapter 7.

Pricing water is one of the successful and self-financing policies worldwide which have been adopted for controlling the usage of water and getting the biggest benefits from it. Pricing water should be applied to the water consumption in the urban and rural areas.

However, it is not very practical or applicable to apply it to the agriculture sector in the region, at least not for the next few years. Pricing of water as a lump sum per unit of land area can easily be implemented and monitored. However, the farmers are currently facing difficulties in farming for various reasons. An increase in the production costs in the form of pricing water might become a burden to them. Some form of public compensation to encourage farming would be required.

It should be noted that pricing in itself does not necessarily solve all the problems of water misuse, pollution, and scarcity in society. Public intervention in the form of regulations and their implementation is necessary. Regulations which are enforced and sizable penalties which are borne by the perpetrators are probably the most efficient elements in this equation. Such measures are expected to bear fruit both in the long and short terms. There is limited experience in trafficking regulations and processing penalties associated with their violations. This could serve as an example for regulation in the water area.

Data resources are one of the most important issues to be dealt with to help in setting policies for the best management of the water resources available in the region. For instance, a time series data can show actual water resource conditions, its allocation and the rate of water quality and quantity including decline in specific periods of time. Using data can help to predict water supply, demand, consumption and shortages in future and it is possible to set policies for optimizing usage of it based on this. Unfortunately there is no such systematic data collection available to help researchers in their work and to use these data for decision-making.

Land owners and those employed in agriculture in the rural areas must be aware of the importance of water savings and management. This can be done by training the rural working population through regular meetings and consumer representatives' participation in workshops on awareness organized by the Ministry of Agriculture. Alongside awareness campaigns, rules and regulations should be introduced and guidelines, incentives and instruments should be introduced so that consumers are forced to commit to those in order to reduce the waste of scarce water resources.

6.3. DEVELOPMENT OF INDUSTRIAL SECTOR

A. Industrial Sector and Water Demand

The industrial sector is one of the users of water resources for different industrial processes. In developed countries the industrial sector is a main user, but in the Middle East region water use in the industry is characterized as negligible and yet it puts extra pressure on water resources. The pressure stems from the demand for water and also industries pollute the local environment. The intensity in the need for water resources differs from one industry to another according to the industrial production structure, material handling operations, and industrial processes.

Demand for water is increasing according to the industrial sector and characteristics of their production and in many industrialized and semi-industrialized societies they consume more water than households. The daily per capita water use for each person is approximately 50 liters in order to meet present and future needs. We can see that Asian regions are mostly concerned with the use of groundwater. This has put a lot pressure on the water resources and it will lead to shortages of water in the future.

Fresh water is the fundamental resource of many economic, agricultural, and social activities in a society. The activities include food and energy production, transportation, waste disposal, industrial development, and health. Yet, in the recent years there have been some shortages in water resources in many countries including the Middle East. There are several reasons for shortages in the supply of water, such as population growth which leads to an increase in demand for water, and global climate changes which makes both demand and supply for water problematic.

According to the geographical locations, people depend on rivers, lakes, and groundwater sources. Water-related conflicts are not uncommon in some regions due to a shortage in the water supply. International laws for resolving water related conflicts should have a significant role in managing internationally shared water resources. There are some characteristics of water that makes it a source of strategic competition such as a low rate of water, the inequality in the extent to which the water is shared by several regions, the ability of basins, and access to alternative fresh water sources (Gleick, 2008).

B. Major Industries in the Kurdistan Region

There are several industries in the Kurdistan Region that are potential consumers of water. These are not yet well developed, but several are already major users of water. Their water demands may vary by season and also change over time as a result of expansion of the industry and also as a result of the regional government's water policy and availability of water. The different industries using water include: Agriculture, Aquaculture[29], Horticulture, Forestry, Fishery, Mining, Manufacturing, Electricity generation, Construction, Hotels and Restaurants, Tourism and Recreation, Health, Petroleum, etc.

A shortage of water is one of the problems that the Kurdistan Region has been facing in recent years. A lack of water started in 1999 and is a result of low or no rainfall and the diversion of water upstream. Then the regional government was able to manage the situation for a short term but recently the problem of a shortage in the water supply became aggravated for several reasons. A lack of water has caused other problems such as lowered production in agriculture, supply of food, generation of hydro power, inflow of tourism, and start ups of manufacturing companies in the region. Altogether it affects growth in the economy, hampers the establishment of new firms and the creation of employment opportunities.

Currently the Kurdistan Region's agriculture is extremely low in productivity and production. Local production is small and insufficient to satisfy the domestic demand. The region mostly depends on the neighbors' support in providing food for the region for instance, from Iran, Syria, and Turkey. Most of the products coming from these countries are of low quality which has negative effects and a long term influence on the welfare and health of the population. There is insufficient production of domestic products for several reasons. The rural population does not work as it did in the past because most of them receive transfers

---

[29] The fishery industry and aquaculture in Kurdistan is not yet well-developed. The regional government supports the establishment of fish farms by providing equipment, loans and education. Seung and Waters (2006) provide a review of regional economic models for fishery management in the U.S.

from regional government that make them avoid working in their fields. Another reason is the shortage of production equipment, such as vehicles and also water, and raw materials. Otherwise Kurdistan has good access to fertile land for agriculture, forest and fishery production.

Water is the basic source of power generation in many countries with good access to hydropower sources. The majority of households in Iraq are connected to the national electricity network. It is important to identify the source of the electricity, namely whether the household depends on private generators or a public electricity supply. Furthermore, there is another issue that we have to take into consideration, which is the stability of the electricity supply. If the household has less than 12 hours electricity per day or it has low voltage then it is considered as having instability in the electricity supply.

One of the major sources of electricity in the Kurdistan Region is hydropower. There are several criteria to indicate the safety and stability of water sources. The UN definition for improved water supply is 'household connection, public standpipe, borehole, protected dug well, protected spring, and rain water collection'. Another criterion includes the measurement of hours that the household reports the shortages in the water supply on a weekly basis (Tabulation report, 2004). Many industrial sectors lack electricity due to the shortage of water which makes them use private generators for their daily activities.

Kurdistan depends mainly on the Dukan and Darbandikhan dams for its water supply and power generation. Dukan dam is constructed on the leaser of Zap River and Darbandikhan dam on the Sirwan River. Besides these lakes, it also depends on generators that are provided for each province. These generators are diesel driven and cannot alone provide electricity demanded by the population. For this reason, the regional government has provided supplementary public electricity for the rural and urban areas. Northeast of Iraq embraces high fold mountains such as Pirmam which have important water basins. The range culminates in fine peaks over 10,000 feet above sea level. It is indicated that the basins of Sulaimanyah are the largest and most important basins for cultivation (Davies, 2008).

Recently, Kurdistan has faced problems with its water supply as a result of the low level of rainfall and insufficient dams and their capacity. In 2008, the rainfall in Hawler was very low and only about 194 mm. The average rainfall is expected to be higher exceeding 400 mm. There are several strategies according to which the government is trying to build dams all over the region.

C. The Industrial Sector Data

The data used in this section are obtained from the Ministry of Industry, Kurdistan Regional Government. The data covers the entire year of 2007 and is further extended to include March 2008 (see table 6.2). These data are changing due to the drought. For instance, the sub-sector producing construction material called 'blocks', does not produce enough blocks due to the lack of water in the drought season. The data covers only the governorate of Hawler as a case study, while those of other governorates, including Sulaimanyah, Duhok, Kirkuk and Mosel, are missing due to unavailability at the time of data collection.

Table 6.2 provides information about the type of industrial production, number of factories and workers, and quantity of water used for production and human consumption in each sector. The industrial sectors are divided into mineral, food, plastic, paper, faltered petroleum, pipe and iron, machineries, and metallic and construction. Each of these especially those in food, machinery and metallic and construction are further divided into a number of sub-sectors.

Table 6.2. Water use by type of industrial production in Hawler, 2007

Type of production	number of factories	number of workers	water use of industry	drinking water
A. Mineral industry:				
Breaking stones	8	92	13,900	10,500
B. Food industry:				
Ice	29	96	41,000	8,120
Mineral water	2	25	4,600	280
Flour	9	169	1,035	16,520
Cookies	16	101	470	9,800
Soft drinks	1	5	1,100	560
Nuts	3	48	305	5,320
C. Plastic industry:				
Doors and windows, PVC	15	107	730	7,560
D. Paper industry:				
Tissues	2	52	190	4,480
E. Faltered petroleum:				
Oil of car	4	51	2,200	5,750
F. Pipes and iron:				
White and black pipes	1	80	110	14,560
Iron	1	270	18,750	34,160
G. Machines, electrical equipment & generators:				
Electrical equipments	1	18	95	112
Lighting equipment & generators	1	7	5	56
H. Metallic and construction industries:				
Ceramic Tiles	2	22	2,400	184
Manual Brick	32	484	23,500	6,670
Gravel	27	331	16,700	4,480
Construction blocks	117	1,192	112,650	6,210
Shtiger	3	60	2,720	9,660
Mosaics Tiles	33	537	14,200	506
Prepared concrete	6	212	163,200	4,370
Asphalt	3	77	4,350	1,955

Source: Ministry of Industry, Federal Region of Kurdistan, Hawler.

Several industrial sectors are developing in and around the city of Hawler. The existing sectors are few but are rapidly growing in number and their production capacity. In the following section, the report briefly introduces the readers to the existing structure of the industry. The classification is not scientific or based on existing international ISIC codes, rather reported just in an ad hoc way by following the way the data is presented to us.

Furthermore, economically it is not any more meaningful to separate production and drinking water usages. However, since the data is available to us in a disaggregate form we try to analyze the two sources.

The *mineral industry* consists of mainly breaking stones. There are 8 stone-breaking factories with 92 workers. Water is used for two purposes in the industry: for processing in production and for human consumption. The water specified for the process is more than the water that is used by the factories for the process of breaking stones. The water that is used by the factories is 13,900m^3 annually, while the rate of drinking water in each firm is 10,500m^3.

The *food industry* is another industrial sector that includes several sub-sectors like producers of ice cubes, mineral water, flour, cookies, soft drinks and nuts. Ice cube production includes 29 factories with 96 employees. The water that is used by each factory is 41,000m^3. In addition firms use water for drinking, equivalent to 8,120m^3 each. Mineral water is another sub-sector that includes 2 factories with 25 workers. The rate of production water used for the industry is 4,600m^3 and the rate of drinking water is 280m^3. Flour sub-sector includes 9 factories with 169 employees. The rate of water used for production and drinking is 1,035 and the 16,520m^3, respectively.

The industry producing cookies consists of 16 factories with 101 employees. The rate of water used by the industry is quite small, 470m^3, and the quantity for drinking is 9,800 m^3. The soft drinks sub-sector includes only one factory with 5 workers. The rates of water used for production and drinking are 1,100m^3 and 560m^3 respectively. The last sub sector in the food industry is that producing nuts. It has 3 factories and 48 workers. The water consumption rates are 305 and 5,320m^3. The total rate of water consumption by the food industry is 72,590m^3. This high rate is mostly due to the high rate of water used in the production of ice, mineral water, and soft drinks.

The *plastic industry* only consists of the PVC door and window sub-sector which includes 15 factories with 107 workers. The sector uses 730m^3 water for production and 7,560m^3 for human consumption.

The *paper production industry* includes only the tissues sub-sector with 2 factories. The number of employees working in this industry is 52 workers and the rate of water used by the industry is 190m^3 for production and the drinking water rate is 4,480m^3.

Faltered petroleum production includes the sub-sector dealing with automobile oil . It has 4 factories with 51 workers. The rates of water used by the industry for production and human consumption are estimated to be 2,200m^3 and 5,750m^3. It can be noted that this industry, with only 4 factories has a high rate of water consumption.

The production of *pipes and iron* include two sub-sectors producing white and black pipes, and iron. Producing white and black pipes includes one factory with 80 workers, while there is one iron-producing firm with 270 employees. In the two sectors water consumption for production is 110 and 18,750m^3, while their water use for human consumption is 14,560 and 34,160m^3. The iron sub-sector uses much more water than the production of white and black pipes.

The sector involved in the production of *machines, electrical equipment and generators* includes electrical equipment, the production of lighting equipment, and the generator sub sectors. The two sub-sectors each consist of one factory with 18 and 7 workers. Their consumption of water for production is 95 and 5m^3, while water used for drinking is 112 and 56m^3.

The *metallic and construction material* industries include several sub-sectors such as: ceramic tiles (2, 22), manual bricks (32, 484), gravel (27, 331), blocks (117, 1192), Shtiger (3, 60), mosaics (33, 537), prepared concrete (6, 212) and the asphalt sub-sectors (3, 77). The number in parentheses indicates the number of firms and employees. The sub-sectors linked to construction blocks, bricks and tiles are among the largest groups in both number of firms and employment size. They and the sub-sector producing prepared concrete are the main users of water, both in production and for drinking. The largest users of water in production are those involved in the production of blocks ($112,650m^3$) and prepared concrete ($163,200m^3$), while the main users of drinking water are Shtiger ($9,660m^3$) and bricks ($6,670m^3$).

D. The Safety and Stability of Drinking Water

In Duhok 11% of the water is classified as unsafe for drinking, 67% is stable and safe for drinking, while 22% is unstable but safe. In Hawler, 1% of the water is unsafe for drinking, 67% is stable and safe for drinking, and 32% is unstable but safe. In Sulaimanyah, the corresponding number are that 10% of the water is unsafe for drinking, 55% is stable and safe for drinking, and 35% is unstable but safe. (Tabulation report, 2004).

In Kurdistan statistics, if any, are produced for the main cities of Hawler, Sulaimanyah and Duhok. The statistics are then represented as if they cover the entire governorates. There is a large difference between the three main cities, but an even larger gap between those and the smaller cities which are often neglected in many ways, such as in statistics, in budget allocations and in development. It is unclear whether the numbers above represent the cities or governorates.

Industrial sectors also have negative effects on supplying fresh water. One of the disadvantages of the industrial sectors is pollution, which adds toxicity to fresh water. A lack of regulations resulting in the uncontrolled disposal of the waste collections of farmers and dumps from many manufacturing factories pollute lakes and rivers. For this reason, water in the lakes and rivers is mostly not suitable for agriculture. These pollutions have other negative side effects, such as spreading several types of diseases such as cancer (Wu et al., 2008). The small scale of industries and their low concentration and the non-toxic nature of production suggest that the Kurdistan Region, despite its lack of regulations, is currently not subject to such negative effects.

Iraq has recently negotiated with the UAE to get support for developing Iraqi industries which include the development of industrial sectors such as cement, iron and steel, engineering, fertilizer, glass and ceramics, mechanical industries, automotive industries, electrical industries and information systems. The aim of these investments is to raise the production and productivity of various firms and plants to match their capacity and needs. Iraq's Ministry of Industry and Minerals is responsible for the operation of 60 publicly owned companies and 240 publicly owned factories and plants located throughout the country. It is estimated that these units need around $2 billion to transform these facilities with up-to-date technologies and standards.

Iraq in general is facing a crucial situation which influences the future of the country. The country has suffered three decades of continued instability, but now there are opportunities to use new techniques (Ali S. Omar, 2008). The need for investment is not only attributed to an improvement in the capacity of existing plants, but also to upgrade the technology level in the industries. The exit of many plants is due to their obsolete technology and the age of the firms. This process of constructive destruction of capacity is seen as a natural and healthy measure to upgrade the technology with more environmentally-friendly technology and to enhance the productivity and management of firms.

Another issue concerns the textiles industries in which the majority of the production is distributed in the domestic market. However, this domestic production can meet the needs of only 10-20% of the population. In addition, there is also another problem with the quality of the production (Abdulghani F. Al-Jafer, 2008). The level of self-sufficiency in the domestic-based textile production is extremely low. The negative trend is due to unregulated trade with textile products and the domination of East and South Asia in the market, as well lagging in upgrading the domestic textile industry.

6.4. DEVELOPMENT OF RECREATIONAL, TOURISM AND OTHER SERVICES

A. Introduction to Tourism

Tourism and recreation attracts many visitors from elsewhere to the region. It is a service that could improve the community's well-being. For example, new residents or tourists demand more goods and services, resulting in a more diversified economy with higher wages. Income levels could rise, along with levels of publicly provided services such as education, transportation, improved health, electricity, sanitation, clean water and other measures of community welfare. Investment in tourism and other infrastructure services generates new employment opportunities and together with it, poverty rates could be expected to decline. Development of the sector, in addition to economic advantage, will affect the well-being of the local population under the existing conditions of restricted travel and great security concerns. For a study of the potential for tourism development in non-metropolitan areas see Gibson (1993). Practice and policies of outdoor recreation and rural development is discussed in Marcouiller and Green (2000).

The share of the service sector increases, outweighing the decline in the share of agriculture and industry sectors of the economy. As a result of higher labor productivity, higher incomes and leisure time, tourism expands. The outflow negatively affects the trade balance and is considered as imports, while the inflow improves the trade balance and is considered as export revenue. In general tourism and recreation, by using natural resources, result in improving socioeconomic well being. The sector leads to a higher employment growth rate in the service sector with spillover effecting the other sectors. Income level is also positively affected by tourism. Although the cost of living is increased by higher housing costs, the increase offsets only part of the income advantage. Tourism and recreation result in lower local poverty rates and improvements in other social conditions, such as local educational attainment and health.

Recreation and tourism have potential advantages for communities. They can add to the promotion of business startups, growth and profitability. Landowners can benefit from rising land values. Growth can provide jobs for unemployed people, and this can help some of them to escape from poverty. Recreation and tourism, although seasonal in character, can help diversify an economy, making the economy less cyclical and less dependent on the ups and downs of a few industries and income sources. It also gives underemployed manufacturing workers and farmers a way to supplement their incomes and remain in the community. Benefiting from growing tax revenues and growth-induced economies of scale, local governments may be able to improve public goods and services. In addition, local residents may gain access to a broader array of private sector goods and services, such as medical care, shopping and entertainment. While other types of growth can have similar benefits, recreation and tourism may also provide greater diversification.

Kurdistan's beautiful scenery, archeological sites and history of religious tolerance are major factors which could help to transform the region into a popular tourist destination. Once the tourist industry is established in the Federal Region of Kurdistan, the companies will then be able to add to their business interests in the region. The new Austrian Airlines office in Hawler marks an important step in encouraging other European countries to promote direct investment and travel to the region. The air fare is extremely high, more suited for business, and less for tourism.

Tourism in Kurdistan is mainly of a local character and limited to the short spring season. Another smaller source is refugees living abroad who during Christmas and summer holidays visit their relatives at home. As such they are not consumers of hotel or other services. Furthermore, no activities around tourism have been developed to attract tourism and keep them busy. The quality of service is low, the airfare is extremely high, there are not many handicrafts produced or found in the market and the Ministry of Tourism has not been able to provide education in services, to promote the production of handicrafts and to market industries. The Bazars are more like Chinese suburban markets rather than Kurdish Bazars. The hotel capacity is often used by business people or conference participants who are financed by the public sector. Lack of a taxation system and registration of business revenues make tourism uninteresting to municipalities from a tax revenue perspective.

B. Economic Impacts of Tourism

Recreation and tourism both have positive and negative economic impacts on recreation areas. On the positive side, recreational development helps to diversify the local economy and it generates economic growth (Gibson, 1993). It achieves this partly by acting as a kind of export industry, attracting money from foreigners to spend on goods and services produced locally (Gibson, 1993). It also stimulates the local economy through other means. Infrastructure, such as airports, highways and water systems, often must be upgraded to meet the needs of tourists, and such improvements can help to foster the growth of non-recreation industries in the area by attracting entrepreneurs and labor and by providing direct inputs to these industries (Gibson, 1993).

Recreation can involve significant economic spillover effects, however, many of the goods and services it requires are imported to the community. For example, temporary foreign workers are often attracted to the area to fill vacant jobs in hotels, restaurants, municipalities, etc. Many of the recreation-related establishments (restaurants, hotels, and tour and travel companies) are owned by national or regional companies that repatriate their profits. Thus, part of the revenue from tourists ends up leaving the locality. Another economic drawback involves the seasonality of recreational activities, which can create problems for workers and businesses during off seasons (Galston and Baehler, 1995), though this may actually be a plus for places where seasonal recreation jobs are timely, coming when farmers and other workers normally have an off season.

The greatest economic concern is that recreational development may be less desirable than traditional forms of rural development because it increases the incidence of service employment with relatively low wages. According to Deller et al. (2001), "There is a perception that substituting traditional jobs in resource-extractive industries and manufacturing with more service oriented jobs yields inferior earning power, benefits, and advancement potential" and that this may lead to "higher levels of local underemployment, lower income levels, and generally lower overall economic wellbeing".

In addition, many researchers are concerned that recreation may result in a less equitable distribution of income (Marcouiller and Green, 2000). These problems may be compounded by the higher housing costs in some recreation areas (Galston and Baehler, 1995). These concerns reflect findings from some individual case studies. Deller et al. (2001) found that rural tourism and amenity-based development contributed to the growth in per capita income and employment, and they concluded that as a result of the positive impact from tourism on income "the concern expressed about the quality of jobs created appears to be misplaced".

C. Impact of Tourism on Water Consumption and Environment

The growth of tourism is often associated with the search for complementary water sources to satisfy the great demands on water for this growing economic sector. The combination of water needs for agriculture and tourism has lead to the construction of a significant number of dams. At present in the Kurdistan Region there are 15 dams, with a combined storage capacity of 8 million m^3. Dams are certainly necessary for a water supply, energy production and flood control. However, they have negative effects on the environment and on the population along the sites.

The indiscriminate construction of dams with extreme impacts on the environment is to be avoided. A recent study of the World Resources Institute highlights the fact that dams alter the dynamics of rivers in terms of water flow regimes and transportation of sediment. Dams reduce the speed of the rivers' flow and provoke water stagnation, which decreases the capacity of the river to break down organic pollutants and therefore to combat water pollution. This leads to changes in the chemical and physical characteristics of rivers that adversely affect fish species, which also suffer from the alteration of their migratory patterns.

Another adverse effect of dams is related to altered water regimes in rivers and their impact on the environment and living conditions of many fish species. The artificial time and volume of water released by dams has an impact on waterfalls, rapids and riverbanks and wetlands, which are essential feeding and breeding areas for many aquatic and terrestrial species. Multi-disciplinary evaluation studies of all measureable and un-measurable effects should be a precondition for construction of dams at any size, location or purpose. The local capacity for such evaluation in the region is weak or non-existing.

D. The Tourism Industry and Increased Water Demand and Urban Development

Tourist areas suffer from significant fluctuations in the number of local dwellers that have to be supplied with freshwater. Water consumption peaks normally occur in the dry season, when tourist demand overlaps with high water demand by the agriculture sector. The increased demand requires significant public investment in new water sources. Such investment in an excessive and unbalanced form alters nature with negative environmental externalities with crowding out investment effects.

Tourism leads to urban development because it needs facilities not only to host, feed and entertain tourists, but also to transport them and care for them. Moreover, economic growth is normally associated with the growth of the local population which provides services to tourists. All these facilities occupy land and transform the landscape and the natural dynamics of lands located near tourist resorts. Furthermore, accommodation and its rapid expansion has a major impact on water resources, land use and the ecosystems in cities and their neighboring land areas.

The tourism industry should be directly concerned with the negative impact of its activities on freshwater because decreasing overall water use can lead to cost savings and restrict the quantity of water use especially during periods of drought. Also reducing water use can conserve and protect the local water resources upon which hotels, restaurants and the local community businesses depend. This is even more relevant if overexploitation of water or water pollution is causing deterioration to the freshwater ecosystems that symbolize a tourist destination. Moreover, preserving the quality of local water resources can reduce the need for costly drinking water treatment processes and water conservation can enhance reputation among guests and others who are concerned about reducing water consumption and protecting local nature related resources.

6.5. DEVELOPMENT OF POPULATION AND ITS CONCENTRATION

A. Introduction to Population and Water Demand in Kurdistan Region

One of the most important temporal issues is the shortage or limitation of water availability and low quality of water. This has a negative impact on the environment, demography, formation and well-being of society, the economy and even the psychology of the population. This problem does not exist only in Kurdistan but everywhere in the world, especially in Asia, the Middle East and Africa and it is predicted to deteriorate continuously until 2050.

In the case of Kurdistan and as a result of a series of dictatorship regimes, water wealth has witnessed many disastrous policies in the past decades. Saddam's regime demolished more than 4500 villages, whose sole work was in the agriculture sector. By this inhuman action the agriculture sector was systematically destroyed. Besides, the policy forced the civil population to leave their places of origin in the villages heading toward cities. The policy aimed at isolating the Kurdish people from political parties. This has led to an increase in the population in the cities through urbanization of life. See map 6.1.

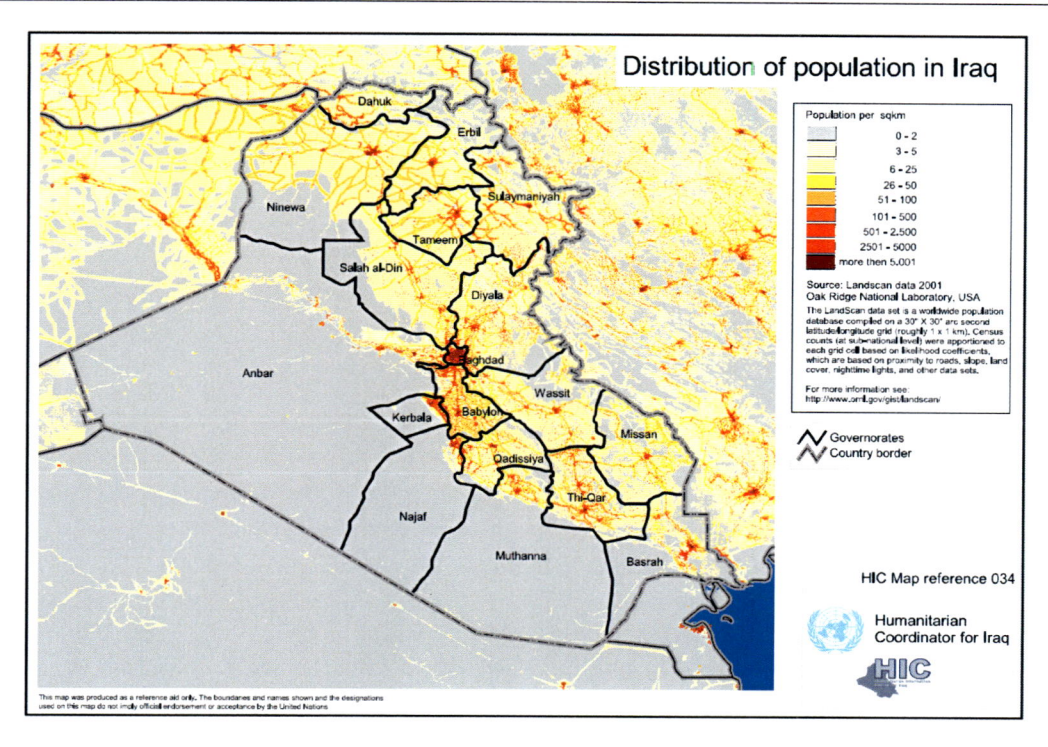

Map 6.1. Concentration and distribution of population in Iraq.

In addition, the unconscious use of water in the cities has had negative impacts on the water conditions. Another reason is that people do not realize the importance of water wealth in their daily planning and usage. They are simply not aware of proper ways for using water and avoiding wasting it. There is a significant reason behind water problems, which is drought and the diminution of rate of rain that the region has faced in recent years. All these reasons have led to an intensified water problem in the region.

Kurdistan has excellent sources of fresh water, mainly spring-based water flows. The region has never faced a lack of water as a major problem in the past 30 years. The region has used the available natural sources of water, such as they are, without any need for treatment before using them. The problem of a shortage of water has emerged particularly after 1991 and is a new phenomenon. Several factors have caused this problem. One of the most important reasons is the rapid increase in the number of the urban population without building up the necessary infrastructure to face the water demand of the growing population. Thus the lack of demographic planning and public investment in water infrastructure is the main factor causing the current and alarming state of water, its access, quality and management.

Kurdistan Region has witnessed a huge increase in its population especially after 1991. Based on some limited statistics available, the average annual growth of the population in Iraq was 3.0% from years 1981-2005. The average improved water source in Iraq was 82.0% from 1981 to 2005. There are several reasons for the increased population, changing demography and population movements. Firstly, thousands of Kurdish families who had been forcibly displaced returned from different places of deportation to Kurdistan. The high but normally increasing rate in the number of people already inhabiting the region is a second factor. In addition, thousands of Arab families have been relocated to Kurdistan for political and safety reasons since 2003. More than two million residents populate Hawler governorate, while approximately two, and around one million populate the Sulaimanyah and Duhok governorates, respectively. The total population in the region is about five million.

In addition, a large number of foreigners have arrived in Kurdistan for different purposes, such as establishing businesses, work or being displaced from other parts of greater Kurdistan. The plain area of the region has been facing drought and limited water availability almost every four or five years. This has led to losing some of the regions' natural sources of water. Many villagers have been displaced by moving toward the urban areas because of water scarcity. All the mentioned reasons have led to the high increase mainly in urban and but also in rural water consumption. For more details about the urban and rural population structure and its development in major cities see table 6.3 (UNDP, 2005a, 2005b, 2005c).

The demand for water has increased due to the rapid development of the region. The major cities in Kurdistan have expanded in their scope. Both public and private sectors are working on constructing new institutions, public infrastructure, houses, and typical villages for this purpose. These projects are associated with constructing service institutions such as hospitals, schools, parks and kindergartens. In addition, large quantities of water are needed in the short-term in order to complete these projects, while in long-term, huge networks of water should be connected to these new places to supply them with water for multiple purposes. The Kurdistan Region is mostly dependent on groundwater, dams, and springs. Hundreds of legal and illegal wells have been dug in recent years.

Water has played a significant role in Iraq's history. Most Iraqi households obtain their drinking water through pipes. A total of 78% of all households in the country have drinking water piped directly into their dwelling, but there are large differences between regions, rural and urban areas. In general 88% of Iraqi households have piped water as their main source of drinking water. This portion varies between regions from 98% of urban households of Baghdad and in the center, respectively, to 77% and 75% in the south and north respectively. The other main source of drinking water is through tanker-trucks in the south where it is 19%, and water piped to the yard or compound in the north which is 19%.

Rural households have different drinking water sources from their urban counterparts. Based on the "Iraqi living conditions survey, 2004", only 43% of rural households have their drinking water piped into their dwelling. About 13% depend on tanker-trucks and only one fourth of rural households get their drinking water from unsafe natural sources such as rivers, lakes and streams. For distribution of drinking water supply by regional location and by type of water supply see table 6.4.

Table 4 shows the drinking water supply as a percentage of all households for urban-rural, main regions and the cities of the Kurdistan Region and Iraq. The information provided covers: sources such as pipe to dwelling, other pipe water, public tap, open well, covered well, tanker-truck, unsafe natural source, other and the total number of the population. The differences in access and safety across comparison groups are large. The rural areas are the most disadvantaged group among the consumer groups.

No more than 9% of all Iraqi households purify their drinking water, 5% of which are in rural areas. The analysis shows that purified drinking water is more common in the northern parts of Iraq, where 15% of all households purify their drinking water. It is most remarkable in Sulaimanyah where 22% of the drinking water is purified. The differences are attributed to the sources of water and also, to a higher extent, to the water policy of municipalities or lack of effective water safety measures.

Table 6.3. Distribution of population in 2004

		0-14 years	15-64 years	64+ years	Total	Mean age	Median age	Un-weighted n	Total number (in 1000)
Urban-rural	Rural	45.0	53.0	3.0	100	21.8	17.3	49,863	7,141
	Urban	37.0	59.0	3.0	100	24.5	20.6	93,601	19,991
Main regions	South	41.0	56.0	3.0	100	23.1	19.0	67,167	9,729
	Baghdad	36.0	61.0	3.0	100	25.4	21.6	18,686	6,55
	Center	42.0	55.0	3.0	100	22.8	18.6	38,515	7,275
	North	36.0	60.0	4.0	100	24.5	20.5	19,096	3,577
	Duhok	42.0	55.0	3.0	100	21.9	18.2	7,349	472
	Nineveh	43.0	54.0	3.0	100	22.3	17.7	8,005	2,554
	Sulaimanyah	34.0	62.0	4.0	100	25.4	21.5	6,230	1,716
	Al-Tameem	37.0	60.0	4.0	100	25.2	20.9	6,408	854
	Hawler	37.0	59.0	3.0	100	24.1	20.0	5,517	1,389
Average of north		38.6	58.0	3.4	100	23.8	19.7	66,324	37,838
Average of Iraq		39.0	57.0	3.0	100	23.8	19.8	143,464	27,132
Average of total		38.8	57.5	3.2	100	23.4	19.7	750,482	154,579

Source: Iraqi household survey, 2004.

Table 6.4. Drinking water supply, in percent of all households

		Pipe to dwelling	Other piped water	Public tab	Open well	Covered well/ borehole	Tank truck	Unsafe natural source	other	Total	Un-weighted n	Total number (in 1000)
Urban-Rural	Rural	43	3	4	2	2	13	26	6	100	6798	966
	Urban	88	4	0	0	0	6	0	1	100	14839	3287
Main regions	South	64	2	1	0	0	19	13	1	100	9839	1485
	Baghdad	97	1	1		0	0	1	0	100	3264	1145
	Center	81	1	1	1	1	5	5	5	100	5392	1016
	North	70	18	2	3	3	1	2	2	100	3142	606
	Duhok	74	4	1	2	9	1	7	2	100	1074	70
	Nineveh	83	1	1	2	0	2	1	10	100	1088	350
	Sulaimanyah	72	10	3	4	4	1	2	3	100	1089	302
	Al-Tameem	94	1	1	0	0	0	4	1	100	1075	144
	Hawler	65	33	1	1	0	0	0	0	100	979	234
Average l of north		77.6	9.8	1.4	1.8	2.6	0.8	2.8	3.2	100	1061	220
Average of Iraq		78.0	4.0	1.0	1.0	1.0	8.0	6.0	2.0	100	21637	4253
Average of total		77.8	6.9	1.2	1.4	1.8	4.4	4.4	2.6	100	11349	2236

Source: Iraqi household survey, 2004.

The mean annual outflow of Dukan's dam since 1958 has been 2,352.0 MCM. Of this amount 28.3 MCM is used for Sulaimanyah's domestic water purposes. This does not include the amount used for irrigation in agriculture. Darbandikhan dam is the second largest dam in this city, its annual discharge within the last 39 years is 2,169.0 MCM and it includes a proportion for irrigation which is not known. The Lower Zab discharges mostly around 1,000.0 to 4,000.0 MCM and the amount fluctuates based on the rate of rainfall, while the mean annual discharge of the Upper Zab is 4,190.0 MCM measured at Bekhme. The storage capacity of Duhok dam is about 52.0 MCM. This dam was mainly used for irrigation in dry seasons, but it is currently used for local purposes as well.

B. The Demand of Water

In general, the average quantity of water consumption per capita differs from one country to another. Based on climate and other factors, the water consumption rate can be determined. Water consumption depends mainly on the seasons. The summer season always witnesses the highest rate of demand for water. The temperature is high in the summer season and it sometimes reaches $45°$ centigrade or more. That is why people in Iraq including the Kurdistan Region consume a high quantity of water per capita in this season.

As mentioned previously, the population is growing significantly. UNICEF statistics in 1997 show that the population in the Kurdistan governorates capital cities was the following: Hawler 1,054,567 residents, Sulaimanyah 1,076,412 residents, and Duhok 703,503. Thus, the majority of the Iraqi Kurdistan's total population of around 5 million lives in these three cities. The annual population growth of the entire country is 3.5%. The local water consumption was estimated to be about 107 MCM in year 2000, and 249 MCM for agriculture and industry. Therefore the entire water consumption in Hawler, based on the same statistics, was 356 MCM in year 2,000. The required rainfall in Hawler is around 600 to 700 mm per year, while it is 400 to 500 mm in Sulaimanyah. In fact the total rainfall in these cities and in the region is much lower than that required to meet the water demands or recommended levels in the region.

C. Water Conditions in Sulaimanyah City

The KRG has faced severe difficulties in supplying water to its population. Many political and economic problems have come into existence which they have affected the water situation. Firstly, the UN imposed economic sanctions in 1991 on Iraq as a result of the Iraqi occupation of Kuwait. The Iraqi government at that time imposed another parallel economic sanction on the Kurdistan Region. Thus the Kurdistan Region was subject to two sanctions: one was imposed indirectly by the UN and the other by the regime directly. In this way the KRG, without sufficient financial and technical resources, was unable to solve this problem. That is why it allowed people to dig wells in their houses in Sulaimanyah city, with the purpose of getting water to their households. Indeed, people started to dig permitted wells in their own houses. Many necessary instruments were imported from neighboring countries.

During several months hundreds of wells were completed especially in the new neighborhoods and places that suffered from a shortage of water. See Map 6.2.

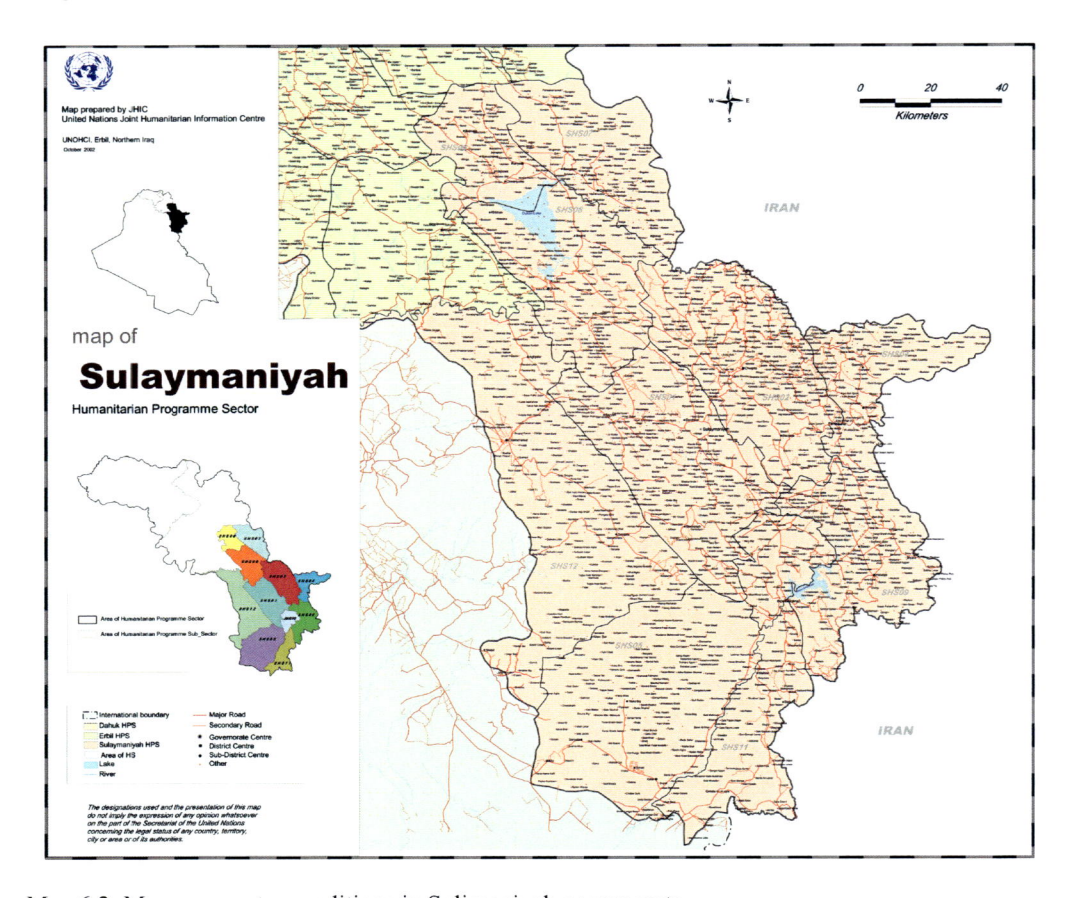

Map 6.2. Map over water conditions in Sulimaniyah governorate.

As a result of testing the quality of well water, and based on chemical and physical properties, laboratory results point to the magnitude of the problem and its danger to the health of the citizens. Among more than 1,440 legal wells that have been tested, of which 779 were appropriate for human use, while the remaining 664 were not suitable for drinking or cooking. Many of those samples were taken for checking in September, which is a very hot season. The high temperatures led to the salt dissolving and the water becoming more contaminated.

Thus, tests taken during this season are not representative of the degree of contamination, yet they suggest presence of severe problems with water quality in Sulaimanyah.[30]

---

[30] For assessment of the water resources of Hawler, Sulaimanyah and Duhok governorates see UNICEF (2001a, 2001b and 2001c).

D. Water Conditions in Hawler City

Hawler is the capital city of the Kurdistan Region. Its major problem is the distance from sources of water and the scarcity of water. Many attempts have been exerted to find a real solution for this problem in the last15 years. All were found to be either temporary solutions or not to be very useful in practice. People in this city depend heavily on two major resources of water. First, the Ifraz projects, which are three projects numbered as 1, 2 and 3. Second, there are about 350 wells for domestic use in Hawler, each one supplies 500 to 800 cubic meters of water per day. The mechanism of the Ifraz operation is firstly, drawing the water and secondly, sanitizing it, and then distributing the water to households. The procedure of filtering water operates in five stages. This process becomes more complex as the population of the city increases constantly. See Map 6.3.

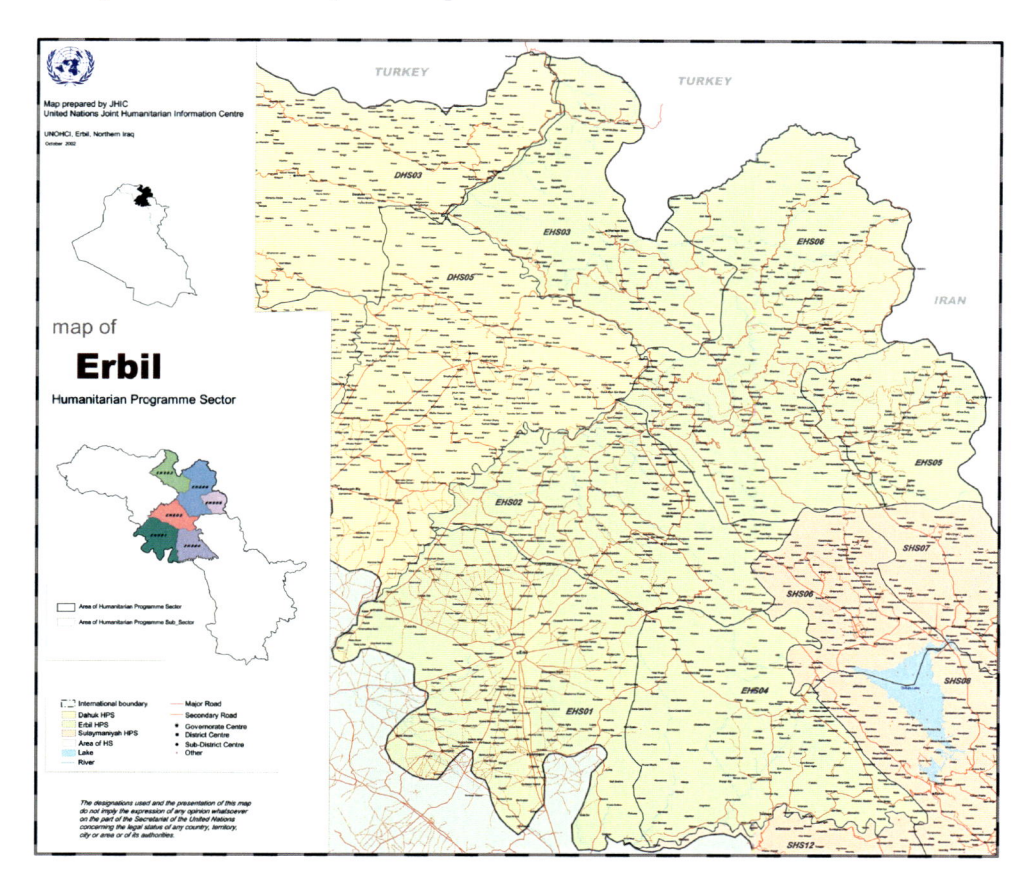

Map 6.3. Map over water conditions in Hawler (Erbil) governorate.

The total number of wells in Hawler plain is 802 including its urban areas. An interesting result is found after testing samples of well water. The results show that all water samples are considered to be fresh water. This mean that the quality of well water is excellent, based on UNICEF research conducted in the year 2001. However, since 2001 the population has increased significantly and major economic development has taken place in the city in the areas of private housing and the construction of public infrastructure. These might have led to a deterioration of the quality of the well water.

Using water is free in Kurdistan, but it is also very disorganized and mismanaged. There are no strict rules in the region that prohibit people from violations of those regulations. Clean water is used for drinking, but the same water is used for all other uses as well. In agriculture, people use clean water to irrigate their plantations. The same case is adopted in industry, trading and many other areas. Thus, a lack of regulations and proper management of clean water mean that resources are wasted. The situation is not likely to be sustainable in the long term, given the population development and urbanization rate. Mitlin (2002) discusses the issues of urban water center competition and regulation.

All the estimates of population growth in Iraq show a lower growth rate during the period of the Iran-Iraq war (1980-1988). After the end of the war, the population growth rates have been stable, forecasted by various population estimates. The estimation of the population is based on age cohorts showing that 39% of the population in the entire country is aged less than 15 years, while 57% of them are aged from 15 to 64. The rate of population in the northern governorates of Hawler, Duhok, Sulaimanyah, Nineveh and Kirkuk shows that 38.8% are aged below 14 years while 58% are in the age interval of 14 to 64.

On average, 33% of Iraqi households have an unstable supply of water. Baghdad seems to have more problems with its water supply than any other places, where 36% of the city's households have an unstable supply of water. The most unreliable source of drinking water is water piped into public taps and yards. Close to half of the households depend on this unstable water supply. It should be noted that there are no guarantees that piped water to household connections is safe for drinking. Water pollution from this source may occur, making the water unsafe.

There are only 54% of households who have access to a safe and stable supply of drinking water; 29% have drinking water from safe sources but with an unstable supply; and another 17% of all households have neither safe nor stable drinking water. This gives an estimated number of more than 722,000 Iraqi households with unsafe and unstable drinking water. The average household size is five members. There are relatively large differences between the geographical regions in Iraq when it comes to the safety of drinking water.

6.6. GENDER AND WATER RESOURCES

A. Female Responsibilities

The issue of gender and water resources is important and is an integral part of water management. Women play a central role in the provision, management and safeguarding of water. Thus woman as collectors, providers, users of water in household and in agriculture and guardians of the living environment have considerable knowledge about water. Their tasks cover quality and reliability, restrictions and storage methods. These key factors should better be reflected in an institutional arrangement for development, policies and programs and management of water resources (UNICEF, 2008; FAO, 2008).

Gender for a long time has been integral to Australian aid activities. Project quality and sustainability are improved by strategies to include both men and women. To enhance the role of gender AusAid (2000) provides a list of references and resources on gender guidelines on water supply and sanitation – a supplement to the guide to gender and development. The list contains manuals, books, articles and relevant internet sites on gender and water supply and sanitation issues. In addition references are also given which are related to the lessons learned in water supply and sanitation, gender issues and gender planning and participatory methods.[31]

Despite international recognition and active efforts to promote gender issues and water management, women's involvement in the decision-making process on water management in the MENA region seem to be a complex and under-represented issue. Minoia (2007) attempted to identify links between theoretical approaches and empirical data. Empirical study of gender issue and water management in the Mediterranean basin, the Middle East and North Africa shows that gender topics in water management are scarcely addressed in institutional politics, needs and expectations. The role of women in improving education and increasing awareness about water problems within the community of users is also neglected. Women's participation in the water management process could represent a challenge to the power hierarchy and old and inflexible culture structures in the MENA region where the role of NGOs and civil society organizations are limited to a large extent by the ruling powers.

Water plays an important role in human life. Males and females have different perspective and uses of water resources. Men use water for irrigation in agriculture, in industry and in construction, while women use it mostly in households for drinking, cooking, cleaning and washing. The quantity and quality requirements are thus different by gender and often complement each other. This motivates the idea that there is a greater role to be played by women in water management. Evans et al.'s (2002) study of awareness of environmental risks and protective actions among minority women in Northern Manhattan shows that a 'healthy home - healthy child' campaign and other interventions are effective. A high percentage of women were aware of such risks and took action to reduce them, but there was room for an educational campaign to reach women in different ways to protect their families.

Lipchin (2006) argues that projects for sustainability require the use of an integrated approach that takes into account the overall cultural context in which and by which water is used by the population. He suggests that community measures like income, health, education and resources, and available measures like quality, quantity and consumption coupled with the participation and empowerment of local communities should be a preferred methodological approach in water management. Such an approach is used to study how the differences and communalities in water culture influence attitudes and perceptions toward the Dead Sea Basin water use. The basin is shared by Israeli, Palestinian and Jordanian consumers.

B. Females in Rural Areas

The women differ by rural and urban living conditions and water usage. One main task for women in the rural areas is finding suitable water sources. This becomes more important

---

[31] For other mostly internet references on gender and water issue see: Dublin Principle 3 (1992) on women and water management, Rathegeber (2000) on women and water resource management in Africa, UN (2008) on gender, water and sanitations, Rural women securing household in Jordan (2006), FAO 0n women and water resources, and National Commission for Water on water and women (2007).

as the spring season approaches its end and with the start of the summer season the water availability is significantly reduced. The women's search for water sources is intensified and time-consuming. In order to manage the household and take care of younger children they get assistance from older children, mainly the females. This leads to the loss of valuable time with younger family members with negative effects on their education, health and social well-being. Evidence of the positive relationship between the improved health of children and better hygiene and easy accessibility of water in Tanzania is reported in McCauley, West and Lynch (1992).

In many villages with limited water sources, the water resource is stored in open spaces for different usages. These storages are used in parallel for household water consumption, as well as for animal husbandry. The common and shared water source by human and animals will create optimal conditions for transfer of diseases between and among the two groups of users. Significant quantities of water need to be transported to the home for human consumption, cleaning and washing, as well as for feeding animals, cleaning their places and processing milk and other outputs. Often females shoulder such a heavy responsibility.

In order to improve water accessibility, many families dig wells in the housing area. To bring up the water from the well requires technical solutions and investment which is probably beyond the budget of the families. The lack of electricity or its shortage leads to the use of manual solutions which demand human power. Thus, such limitations have implications in the form of added hardship for women. Their participation in agriculture with less technical education and tools makes women spend more time and face greater difficulties in the irrigation of farms and plant management.

C. Females in Urban Areas

Concerning families in the urban areas, the water access and their uses differ from that of the rural areas. Here electricity, pumps and technical storage determine the availability of water in the local household area and the optimality in its quantity. The quality of water and its accessibility is however determined by the water services provided by the municipality, its frequency in access and quantitative transfer. In Iraq, including the Kurdistan Region, access to clean water which is publicly provided has in many places in recent years been limited to a few hours per day. This is due to the limited water supply, inadequate infrastructure and ineffective use of water resources. This together with a limited electricity supply reduces the water supply to the household and as well the household ability to utilize supplied water resources in a desirable way.

Increased storage of water alleviates part of the problem but it deteriorates the quality of stored water in the housing area. The monitoring of all steps of water storage and the separation of drinking and non-drinking water storage takes up a significant part of women's time. The lack of pricing and billing mechanisms has led to the misuse and ineffective use of water resources and the municipalities' inability to invest in necessary infrastructure. Many families heat the drinking water in an attempt to avoid the risks of catching different illnesses. The process of heating, in addition to the advantage of killing different bacteria, has a number of disadvantages as well. These include: the fact that gas and electricity are required to heat the water. These are scarce energy sources, and the cost is also a limiting factor to the quantity heated. In addition certain viruses are not eliminated by heating the water, and heating has negative effects on the quality content of the water.

D. Female, Pollutions and Health

Ethelston (1999) reported that the population of the MENA region has doubled since the mid-1960s, reaching 370 million in 1995. Assuming the same growth rate, the United Nations predicts that the MENA population will increase to 600 million by 2025. At a fertility rate corresponding to 2.0, the world's population is estimated to reach 8 billion by 2050. The development and forecast for the population in Iraq and neighboring countries is reported in table 6.5.

Table 6.5. Development of population in Iraq and neighboring countries

Country	Population size in million				Rate of increase	Total fertility rate	
	1965	1995	2004	2025	1990-95	1960-65	Recent
Iran	24.663	62.324		84.463	2.36	7.3	2.8
Iraq	7.976	20.095		41.014	2.80	7.2	5.7
Jordan	1.962	5.734		12.063	3.11	8.0	4.4
Kuwait	0.471	1.690		2.974	2.27	7.3	3.2
Saudi Arabia	4.793	18.253		39.965	3.04	7.3	5.7
Syria	5.325	14.200		26.292	2.78	7.5	4.2
Turkey	31.151	61.276		87.889	1.62	6.1	2.8

Source: Ethelston (1999), Water and Women, The Middle East in Demographic Transition, Middle East Report 213, Millennial Middle East: Changing Orders, Shifting Border, Winter, pp. 8-12 and 44, Table 1, page 9.

Table 6.6. Population characteristics of Kurdistan Region, its main cities and Iraq, 2007

Governorate	Hawler	Sulaimanyah	Duhok	Total Kurdistan Region	Iraq	Kurdistan Region %
Population	2019688	1917936	973118	4910742	27583009	17.80
City center ratio (%)	60.35	43.35	28.70	-	--	--
Area (km^2)	15074	17023	6553	38650	434320	19.82
Density	95.43	109.68	148.5	127.06	63.51	

Source: Ministry of Plan, Kurdistan Regional Government.

Table 6.5 reports the development of the population in Iraq and compares it with the development in its six neighboring countries: Iran, Jordan, Kuwait, Saudi Arabia, Syria and Turkey. The information includes the population size in millions, the rate of increase of the population, and the total fertility rate for three years 1965, 1995, 2004, and the projected value for 2025. The rate of growth is based on 1990-1995, while the fertility rate is based on 1960-1965 and recent numbers. The growth rate in population differs among the countries and the fertility rate has declined over time. Iraq, despite its high mortality rate the last two decades, has both a high fertility rate and high population growth.

The population characteristics of the Kurdistan Region and its main cities in 2007 are reported in table 6.6 and compared with those of Iraq. The bases for comparison are: population, city center ratio, area in km^2, and population density. The table shows that more than two million residents populate the Hawler governorate. While approximately two, and around one million citizens populate both the Sulaimanyah and Duhok governorates, respectively. The total population in the region is close to five million.

The consumption of water for human use in the form of drinking, cooking, washing and hygiene is often proportional to the size of the families. The rapidly increasing population will increase the demand for water supplied from existing and new sources of water. Human consumption is the main source of the pollutants in water. Household wastewater contains significant chemical elements in the form of the remains of shampoo and various cosmetics and hair colors. Thus the gender aspect of household pollutants can easily be established.

The discharge of chemical elements from households and their mixtures cause severe contamination of water and are a significant negative externality to the environment. Their separation is costly and the failure in their cleaning results in severe illnesses, reduced production potential and a burden for families, in particular to the women in the families.

In order to clean water and to provide safe water to households, the level of certain contents is altered in the supplied water. Magnesium and calcium added to drinking water are two such elements. There are established relationships between these and deaths from acute myocardinal infarction among women. The protective effects of these elements based on a study of women 50-69 years old who died in 1982-1993 in 16 municipalities in Southern Sweden and a control group are shown in Rubenowitz, Axelsson and Rylander (1999).

The literature on the relationship between water pollution and human health is vast. China's double digit annual economic growth rate, rapid industrialization and urbanization since the late 70s, coupled with inadequate public investment in the basic water supply and water treatment infrastructure has resulted in widespread water pollution. Over half of the population consumes water whose contamination level exceeds the permissible level. The situation is worse for the rural population. Wu et al. (1999) analyze the recent links between water resources and pollution and trends in the increased risk of exposure to infectious and parasitic diseases and show that the problems have become more acute.

6.7. SUMMARY AND CONCLUSIONS

In similarity with all other societies, the main consumers of water resources in the Kurdistan Region differ by type, number and their consumption purpose and behavior. There are four main categories of consumers of water resources which differ greatly by their share of the total consumption. The groups differ also by the outcome of their uses of water in the form of negative direct and indirect externalities. The direct effects are in the form of the difference in the quality of water before and after its consumption, while the indirect effects are in the form of pollutants resulting from different ways of using it and crowding out other potential users.

The largest user in terms of numbers is households who use water for drinking, cooking, hygiene and several other household activities. Households differ by location and are grouped into urban and rural areas. The rural inhabitants are closer to the source of water and unlikely to have access to modern water treatment and distribution systems. This has to do with the degree of contamination in water, low political influence on budget allocation and the minimum economically efficient scale of operation of the processes. Despite the closeness to the water source and access to greater quantity at no cost, due to difficulties in preventing contamination of drinking water from sewage water and access to clean water in rural non-agricultural areas and other factors mentioned above, the quality of water is often much lower than that in the urban areas.

The agricultural sector is the second largest group in terms of number, but the sole largest in terms of water quantity used. This sector, including different sub-sectors like farming, horticulture, forestry, fishery and aquaculture, uses water for drinking, animal husbandry and irrigation of farmland. The Kurdistan Region was, up to 2 decades ago, mainly an agricultural society. The central government policy in the 70s and 80s led to systematic destruction of rural life and speeded up the rapid urbanization process. Thus there has been a rapid change in the agricultural sector and in the demography of the region. The sector is relatively small but still consumes large amounts of water for irrigation due to the continuous use of old irrigation systems and production technology. High wages, the large investment requirement with long-term perspectives, low short-term profitability, and speculative investment behavior in the market make it impossible for agriculture to be competitive to attract productive investors to the rural areas. The task is much more difficult at a time of non-productive investment in the booming construction sector.

The industrial sector in the Kurdistan Region is still almost non-existent, but it is to be considered as the third group which uses water in various production processes. The development of such an industry has been one of the priorities of the Kurdistan Regional Government and activity through its investment law and various incentive policies promotes its expansion.[32] The main users of water resources related to the industrial process are those of the cement industry, the production of drinking water, the construction industry, the restaurant industry, and in the food processing industry. The construction industry might be the largest group. The food processing industry should play a major role, but unfortunately most of the food and soft drink supplies are imported from the neighboring countries. It is just in the last two years that most supplies of bottled water are locally produced. Local production and the recycling of bottles should be promoted. There is hardly any manufacturing industry in the region. Local production of materials used in construction and agriculture should be produced locally.

The last category of consumers classified as the state/municipalities is also a major consumer of water. The water by this category is used for the preservation of nature, for water security reasons, for recreation and tourism as well as for production of electricity. The first two types of uses are environmental and nature-related public investment. Recreation and tourism in a geographic location such as Kurdistan, where the majority of population is concentrated in plains and warm areas, require intensive use of water for the irrigation of parks, recreational centers and city plantations. There have been comprehensive public and private investment programs to build up the necessary infrastructure for the development of the tourism industry. The capacity exists but the services are not utilized in an effective and economically profitable way. The reason might be lack of experience, ineffective

---

[32] See also report by Iraq Ministry of Industry and Minerals Commercial Investment Summit (2008) on investing in Iraq's public and mixed industrial sectors.

advertisements and organization, excessive investment in an unknown area, and the issue of security, expensive services and transportation costs. The production of hydropower-based electricity is also a major user of water. There are plans to increase the capacity in this respect to ease the shortage of electricity.

Each of the four categories mentioned above is characterized in this chapter in its capacity as major users and their demand for water in the expanding water market. Given limited time and space, in addition to quantification of their demand and its justification, different externalities and impacts associated with their usage of water were discussed. Different measures as part of public water policy to prevent or to reduce the magnitude of such negative externalities are also briefly discussed and will be further discussed later.

In addition to the four user categories of water resources we reviewed the literature on the role played by women and the relationship between gender and water management. Gender plays a major role in relation to water supply, sanitation and activities that promote awareness of environment risks and protective action taken to enhance the health of the family, in particular the welfare of children. Women's involvement in the decision-making process on water management in the Middle East is underrepresented due to its cultural complexity and limited influence by NGOs and civil society organizations.

Chapter 7

A NEW WATER RESOURCES PLAN AND POLICIES FOR THE KURDISTAN REGION[*]

ABSTRACT

This chapter proposes a new water plan and policies for the Kurdistan Region. The plan and policies in its design have benefits from the experience in other developed countries with environmentally effective policies. The proposal is region-specific by accounting for the characteristics of the Kurdistan Region. First the public infrastructure is analyzed to see how this affects positively or negatively the water resources. Second, the evolution of water resource laws and regulations is reviewed to provide a picture of the current legal and regulatory conditions. Implementation of the existing laws and regulations and their use in practice and outcomes in the form of statistics and quality monitoring is also investigated. Third, in moving towards a new plan and policies, we propose periodical and serial publications and research as crucial measures for water management. These are used in the forecast of demand and supply in the emerging water market. In doing so, we account for the realities of economic development in the Kurdistan Region and discuss the issues of self-sufficiency and vulnerability. Fourth, we arrive at the proposed new water plan and policies for the region. As components of the plan and policies we emphasize the importance of: data, research and publications; water laws and common pool relations; project evaluations and ranking; water policies and incentives; the role of water in sustainable development; and capability and skill upgrading. Finally, we elaborate with how to estimate the resources that are needed and the costs of implementing selected water policies.

7.1. INTRODUCTION TO WATER PLAN AND POLICIES

The Middle East is a region like many other regions of the world characterized by scarce water resources and a population that is growing fast and increasingly concentrated in a few urban areas. Water scarcity is both increasing in magnitude and expanding in the region. Under such conditions, water is a constraint on the sustainable future economic and social development in the region. Improved efficiency in water use, combined with reuse of water can minimize the shortage of water. The main water sources in the region are of a common

---

[*] Binar Jawhar and Zozan Othman have contributed to earlier versions of Sections 7.2 and 7.3.

pool character and are consequently considered both as a source of conflict as well as interstate cooperation. Thus, regional water-sharing agreements are instruments for conflict avoidance among the region's countries.

Based on the conditions described above, it is desirable that governance and sustainable development of common water resources should be given more attention. Part of such a strategy is necessary for regional co-operation in development, in joint regional planning and in management of water resources, increased interregional trade and in building up regional institutional arrangements. The logic and importance of collective action has already in several cases made it possible to develop sound co-operation in water issues, although in practice the principle of equality of access to water is not achieved.

The Kurdistan Region in northern Iraq is not an exception from the rest of the Middle East. Similar commonality and collective action conditions apply to this region as well. Water scarcity is less compared with that downstream but is still increasing and is a binding constraint on the region's economic and social development. It should be noted that the scarcity or sizable reduction of water is often a result of neighboring and upstream countries' active policy of divergence of water. Among other causal factors are changes in population structure and concentration within the region, climate changes as well as increasing hydropower electricity production. Therefore it is important to investigate the current economic, social and water resource conditions in the Kurdistan Region and to evaluate alternative sources of water. It will be helpful to identify them and to propose measures to enhance the effectiveness in the use of water resources which reduces the shortages in the water supply and negative environmental effects.

This study aimed to assist the Kurdistan Region institutions to access the necessary information about the state of water resources in the Middle East region in general and those in the Kurdistan Region and its neighboring countries in particular. The information contained in this report will help to enable the Ministry of Water Resources to play a proactive role in the management of water resources within the region and in interstate cooperation in relation to common pool water resources. In recent years the region has suffered from the diversion of water and construction of dams upstream, negatively affecting the water flows which is a violation of international laws. The law does not account for minorities' views but only states. However, Kurds through the central government Ministry of Water Resources will be able, by utilizing information, to have a direct effect on future interstate relations. Water resources are an integrated part of the developed trade relationship between the Kurdistan Regional Government and its neighboring countries with mutual significant benefits that cannot be risked as a result of disagreement over common pool water resource issues.

The report aims to examine the current practices of water management in the region and suggests ways to encourage the region's decision-makers to pursue sustainable resource development through interstate co-operation. The project will focus on: a comparative study of water resources among Iraq and its neighboring countries, conducting an analysis of water resources and the water user sector to quantify the availability and sub-optimality in their supply, designing water policies and suggesting measures that improve regional water planning and management, developing models and methods to project demand, supply and water gap, suggesting alternatives for provision of water on the basis of sustainable long-term and minimum cost solutions, suggesting necessary mechanisms on how to approach interstate cooperation, proposing optimal practices of within region and interstate cooperation in water resource management, and suggesting investment opportunities for increased public investment in the water market.

The rest of this key chapter is organized as follows. First the development of public infrastructure and investment in water resources are discussed. Second, water resource laws and regulation with emphasis on irrigation is discussed. Third, water resource statistics and quality monitoring are investigated. Fourth, periodical publications, data collection and management and research collaborations are elaborated on. Fifth, a forecast of demand and supply and cost-benefit evaluation of public projects are described. Sixth, the realities of economic development in the Kurdistan Region and how it affects the resources and implementation potential is evaluated. Seventh, the issue of increased self-sufficiency and vulnerability is raised. Eighth, the above issues are discussed in the context of a new water plan and policies for the region with an emphasis on data, research, incentives, water laws and regulations, and education and capacity training in the implementation and evaluation of investment projects in water areas. A summary of the chapter is presented.

7.2. Public Infrastructure and Investments in Water Resources

In this section we provide a review of the public infrastructure in general and investment in water resources in particular in the Kurdistan Region. The focus is on the development in the last two decades as a result of increased local self-governance and globalization of knowledge, technologies and economies, in particular the development in a number of important areas including an increased flow of foreign direct investment (FDI) and its heterogeneous regional and sectoral distributions, the increased public investment in recreation and tourism, information and telecommunication technologies (ICT), institutions like the Ministry of Water Resources, international airports in Hawler and Sulaimanyah, dams planned and those under construction, irrigation and water supply projects and education as infrastructures for development.

A country's economic performance is to a great extent determined by its political, institutional and legal environment. The regional government has made comprehensive investment programs to build up and to adapt its institutions and governance to a higher and international standard. In order to encourage inward FDI the regional government has undertaken a number of proactive policy measures to strengthen the infrastructure and to affect investment behavior through its new investment law (see Heshmati and Davis, 2007). Inflow of investment to the region has been significant, but it has mainly been directed at the construction and services sectors. Investment in services has a direct effect on water resources. Comprehensive programs have also been in water areas like the construction of dams and in building up infrastructure for supplying water. These were partially discussed in previous chapters. We have no access to the public budget to illustrate the amount of budget or its share of the total for the region.

A number of infrastructures are a prerequisite to the inflow of FDI and the effective use of capital investments. The Financial Market, its functions and incentive instruments are crucial to the success of the investment policy. Another important infrastructure for inward investment is support institutions, public guidelines and the size and potential of small and medium enterprises and start-ups policies. The labor market policy options and measures to promote the development of the region are the third category of infrastructure measures. The fourth infrastructure factor is the formulation of a model for industrial development in the region. These issues will be discussed later in the section on the realities of economic development in the region. The establishment of Science Parks as a fifth factor is a necessary condition for the region's industrial development. Science Parks are found to have a positive effect on productivity growth, technology, management and skill transfer.

The Kurdistan Region was cut off from communication with the outside world in 1988 and gained its self-governance in 1991. Intensive use of satellite services, broadcasting and telecommunications, the presence of many NGOs, comprehensive regional development programs together with technology advancement led to the profitable transfer of new communication technologies to the region. The connectivity in the form of computers and cell phones is relatively high, but the absence of effective regulations, a lack of cooperation among service providers and ineffective public institutions has led to the underutilization of communication resources. The Kurdistan Region sees this new sector as a major contributor and significant infrastructure and an enabler to its economic development.

In regard to ICT as investment in infrastructure for development, it will impact performance and the productivity growth of sectors like water resources, in particular in quality control and in data collection and analysis. The economic benefits of ICT will be observed in sectors with high levels of ICT diffusion. In order to derive the full economic benefits of ICT, other factors such as the regulatory environment, skills, the ability to change organizational set-ups as well as innovations in ICT applications affect the ability of firms to seize the benefits of ICT technology. The contribution of ICT to economic growth is positively related to the level of development and adoption of complementary policies. These polices include basic infrastructure, competitive market, market opening, effective laws, regulations, law enforcement and the educational system.

Many aspects of globalization have been positive to development in the Kurdistan Region, but several have been negative. Among the negative aspects worth mentioning are foreign cultural dominance, the unbalanced development in the urban and rural areas, a high dependency on imported labor, difficulties facing competition in agriculture, undermined local production, and the lowered self-sufficiency and security in the region. Rapid development has not resulted in a sufficient level of technology, skill and management transfer, but a high dependency on imported labor to build up and maintain the existing infrastructure. In-sourcing of labor to the construction and service areas, and outsourcing of most production previously produced domestically is negative evidence. Rapid development not combined with taxation and redistribution has also generated inequality and raised poverty and its concentration among certain groups. The region is dependent on foreign labor and contractors for building dams, but local labor manages the operation of constructed dams.

The establishment of the Ministry of Water Resources and its introduction in the new Regional Government in 2006 is to be considered an important investment in development infrastructure (see Chapter 9 of this report). It reflects the desire of the Regional Government to address the problems of water resources, which is one of the most complex problems facing the region. The most important challenge is the problem of water scarcity and the challenge of providing clean drinking water to different communities, the creation of an integrated sewage system network in urban areas, sewage treatment and overall management of water resources. Another challenge is to combat the environmental degradation of the depletion of water resources and polluting soil, air and water. The Ministry strives to balance the competing water demands of households, irrigation, municipal and industrial, hydropower generation, and environmental requirements. The goal is to transform the Ministry into a dynamic and efficient organization that meets current requirements and is able to optimize the future utilization of diminishing water resources.

The education sector plays an important role in the development of the Kurdistan Region. Alongside the previous public institutions several new institutions have been established in the region. The Ministry of Education and Ministry of Higher Education and Scientific Research plan and implement the region's educational policy. The region has five universities located in the main cities of Hawler, Sulaimanyah, Duhok, Koya and Kirkuk. The quality of education has remained low, the system is highly bureaucratic, ineffective and not able to produce graduates with the ability to be creative and productive. They are unable to produce education of a high quality that corresponds to the needs of the society. The difficulties in reforming the highly politicized higher education system have led to establishment of new universities that are more autonomous in their operation. The American University of Iraq-Sulaimanyah, and the University of Kurdistan-Hawler, Jihan University and Eshiq University in Hawler are four such examples. Currently these universities are weak in their research and innovation cooperation but the Ministry of Water Resources will certainly gain from cooperation with them.

7.3. WATER RESOURCE LAWS AND REGULATIONS

Water covers more than 2/3 of the earth's surface and it is vital for all life on the earth. Managing water resources and the way of using them is very important for every region as as well as to the Kurdistan Region. It is important to promote high quality in water and to prevent shortages of water in the future, and especially to deal with the factors that relate to global warming and non-cooperative behavior among neighboring countries with common pool water resources. Moreover, neighboring countries are building huge dams and irrigation projects that reduce the surface water which flows to downstream countries like the Kurdistan Region. This is why using water resources appropriately is important for making a better life for existing and future generations. Based on the Ministry of Water Resources, there are water laws, but these laws were introduced a long time ago and despite being out-of-date are still used at the present time.

A. Water Laws

Most countries have different types of laws, one of which is environment and water laws. In Kurdistan these two institutions are separate and operate as two separate ministries. Water laws are there to regulate all issues related to the supply of and demand for water, the relationship between consumer and utilities, the obligations of the regulators, etc. A few of these are listed below:

- Providing good quality drinking water for all the population in the region. The water should cover the population's needs for the present and future life.
- Providing water for all the sectors, such as households, industry and agriculture. The water should also be provided for the present and future needs of these sectors.
- Testing the quality of water resources and allocating supervisors to deal with this. This process is for providing good quality water for future needs.
- Searching for new sources of water and techniques of water management.
- Protecting water resources.
- Providing human resources for all the water sectors and raising the quality of production.
- A good and proper management of the water resources.

B. Goals and Strategies of Water Resources

There are several general goals and strategies of water resources which are to enhance the efficiency in the use and management of water. These include: increasing the rate of water, improving the quality of water, assuring availability and continuity in the flow of water resources, improving quality and conditions in irrigation and techniques, and finally flooding prevention and management. Each of these is described below:

I. Increasing the rate of water in traditional and non-traditional ways:

- Providing and preparing private projects in water resources such as dams, irrigation networks, springs, and rivers.
- Designing and carrying out projects of a preventive, reformative and water saving nature to reduce the use of water resources.
- Using new resources of water such as the reuse of treated wastewater.
- Nutrition of groundwater.
- Imposing the issuing of licenses to those who want to use groundwater.
- Using modern and alternative technologies and practices for reducing wastewater.
- Providing alternative ways to store water for different purposes.
- Following up on the implementation of issues that are agreed on and protocols of water in the region.

II. Improving the quality of water:

- Protecting surface and groundwater from pollution and contamination.
- In resource allocation, one should give priority to nature.

III. Assuring the availability and continuation of water resources for the sectors that consume water:

- Designing, promoting and building private projects to relieve pressure on public the provision of water and shortage.

IV. Improving the operation of the systems and quality of the groundwater through inter-connected irrigation systems and assuring the continuation in the flow of water:

- Assuring the protection of the quality of water in the system of transportation and distribution of water resources.
- Measuring the quantity of water in the system of transportation and distribution of water resources.
- Guidance on how to use water to enhance a better use of scarce water resources.

V. Removing the danger of flooding and controlling floods:

- Building both small and large dams.
- Building appropriate channels to transform flooding.

C. Irrigation Laws

Irrigation is one of the most important topics in research on water and is heavily regulated. One of the Iraqi laws on irrigation states that all the rules should be followed properly and any irrigation project should be decided under the supervision of the Minister of Agriculture. People have the right to work on their own projects but their irrigation activities should all be monitored and regulated by the government. The government has the right to allocate water to different locations and the areas should be under their supervision which includes having engineers for irrigation. The engineers have the right to give comments and recommendations about the work and ask to be guided by the authorities. Farmers have no right to get water for their agricultural land without being permitted to by the government and only if it does not harm others' businesses. Anybody who does not follow these rules will be penalized by the government through sentences and fines.

Another irrigation law has been introduced which is about buying and owning water pumps. This law includes eleven parts. It states the necessity of providing water pumps for agriculture and other purposes. The old water pumps should also be replaced with new ones. According to the type of water resources, different types of the water pumps should be used. Different types of water pump should be provided for different branches of irrigation. Those who buy water pumps should have a license and a handwritten certificate to buy them and the license should be modified.

In summary, no law has been modified or updated but there are some new projects that are suggested and they are now under discussion. One of the projects includes getting the use of the rivers and springs in the region. Unfortunately, there is no systematic management of water resources. For instance, the same water pump is used for different types of wells regardless of the type of the soil where the wells are dug.

There are some important recommendations that are important to follow. All the households should have one main pipe that is connected to a gutter. All the households need to have floats in their tanks so that it prevents wasting water. All the households have the right to be provided with water from an official distributional channel. Meanwhile, the radius of the pipes should not be more than half an inch.

7.4. WATER RESOURCE STATISTICS AND QUALITY MONITORING

A. Databases and Monitoring the Quality of Water

Every region and country in the world needs to have its own statistics. Data is fundamental to the establishment, development, and operation of institutions, their regulation and the monitoring of activities of any country. Databases exist to identify and analyze problems then set up solutions. A database is important for specialists. It fills the gaps when any studies come into existence. In addition, it may possibly help to avoid repeating any problems that may occur in the future. The availability of databases is necessary in each ministry. Most of the ministries in Kurdistan are suffering from a shortage in statistics and a lack of databases. Recently they have started to establish data collection and analysis units. Water Resources is one of the ministries that has made serious efforts to establish such a unit and collect and process the data to analyze and monitor the factors and events that affect water resources in the region.

It is necessary for a database to have good management and operation. Updating statistics is another step towards careful regulation with successful outcomes. The world is a mass of changes where everything surrounding us is continuously changing. This change has a language which is statistics. Research cannot be done without statistics. The aim of statistics is to determine the weaknesses and strengths in each state. This will lead to movement towards stability and development. The Kurdistan Region after 1991 does not have systematic data collection and thereby lacks precise information on many issues such as population, production, consumption, employment, trade, etc. As a result of political disagreements and separation the data produced, if any, are inaccurate or incomplete due to low coverage. Nowadays the region is attempting to have its own bureau of statistics to manage its affairs.

New data can be used to generate statistics which has advantages in many respects. Firstly, the data is used to classify and compare the past and present states of water in the region. Secondly, it is used to predict and affect future development. It should be noted that emphasis is incorrectly put on statistics. The focus should be on data collection, not the statistics. When data is collected different statistics can be drawn from them. Poor data produces poor statistics. However, good data, if used well, can produce good statistics.

Quantity monitoring of regional plans and programs is significant in the region. Basic water quantity monitoring activities in the Kurdistan Region are performed for the groundwater and drinking water distribution systems. Progress in water quality monitoring has been made in developed and many developing countries for conducting water quality monitoring to eliminate the risks associated with waste of water. Water quality sampling collection must be conducted using proper methods. Advanced and developed laboratories for testing the samples of water need to be established.

The Kurdistan Region should bring new and developed equipment for geological purposes which will be used to get accurate results for testing water or layers. Thus, the objective is to reach a higher level of satisfaction and safety. It is possible during a short time to have the best water resources if and only if the Kurdistan Regional Government come up with a new and superior plan and apply a typical effective water policy. These are what the region needs as strategies for water monitoring activities. The Regional Government should handle a development plan, the operation, continuation and upgrading of monitoring networks and sampling programs. Besides standard sampling and data management, it should evaluate the monitoring and sampling technology developments.

Water quality networks should be established in the Kurdistan Region for different types of water monitoring activities. There networks must be developed for surface water groundwater and basins. After the specific monitoring plan is organized, water quality data should be reviewed in detail at least annually. Then an evaluation of the plan should be held. If the plan and data has changed then the monitoring plan and program may require a certain level of modification. Standard water quality sampling, quality assurance, quality control, and field data management procedures and protocol should be continuously developed and adopted to the local conditions.

B. The Efficient Way for Using Water

The cost for equipment, chemicals and energy used to improve water supply and its availability is constantly increasing. The region supplies water especially for residents through hundreds of powerful generators which need millions of gallons of gasoline. Utilities are developing new water-saving equipment which has some potential benefits. Emergency conservation measures and water supply exchange agreements can reduce the demand or increase supply in drought years. Similar measures can extend short supplies during other emergency conditions (Maddaus, 1987, pp 33). In the Kurdistan Region all material and technologies is imported as turnkey packages. There is little capability for maintaining such equipment with local labor and no skills to modify or adopt them. Energy is also imported from refineries in Turkey which make the cost very high. Thus, under such conditions it is hard to be efficient in water supply from technology and energy use perspectives.

C. Potential Benefits

There are several potential benefits of water and cost-saving equipment and a few of them are described below:

- Energy saving: Reduction in water use can result in significant energy savings. This is because water heaters are largely used particularly in the winter season through heating and air-conditioning.
- Wastewater reduction: Conserving water inside the home and reducing its use by businesses and industries will decrease wastewater.
- Reduction of cost: in most communities increasing water use efficiency results in cost reduction. The costs are lower because of reduced energy and chemical use in water supply and wastewater treatment.
- Protection of the environment: efficient wastewater use can reduce degradation of the environment by increasing stream flows and the water level in existing reservoirs and by reducing the lowering of groundwater levels and mining of groundwater basins.

Unfortunately the general level of education and capability in the Kurdistan Region is quite low in order to be able to take advantage of benefits of imported cost-saving technologies and their adaptation to local conditions.

D. Identifying Demand and Supply Problems

In order to promote the smooth provision of water services at the lowest cost, the nature and extent of supply and demand problems should be identified. To define the problems, the following questions need to be asked:

- Is the problem system-wide or limited to one part of the service area?
- Is its major cause short term (like drought, supply and contamination or other emergency) or long term?
- If long term, is the problem caused by leakage, inadequate storage, pipeline delivery capacity, pressure, inadequate source of supply?
- Does the supply shortfall occur seasonally (during high demand season), at specific peak demand periods each day, or in other ways?
- Is a low or high reduction needed to match supply with demand?
- Is the need to meet regional or state grant conditions or regulatory requirements a major factor in the reduction of demand?

It is quite common that providers and consumers in the Kurdistan Region face many problems on a daily basis. To the set of questions above more question of local specific character can be added such as those linked to quality, reliability and overuse of water. The demand and how much of it can be supplied with the current system was outlined in chapter 5. The magnitude of the shortage outlines the size of the problem and indirectly lays out the directions where solutions can be sought.

E. Water Conservation Methods

The water conservation methods are applicable to a variety of urban, residential, industrial, commercial, and government users. The different categories of water users and reduction in their water use are defined as the following:

- Residential users include those in both single family and multi-family buildings.
- Commercial users include office buildings, hotel restaurants, car washes, retail businesses and shopping centers.
- Industrial users are the industries requiring water for cooling, manufacturing, and processing.
- Government users include schools, prisons, military installations, public hospitals, public buildings, parks, and high-way landscaping.
- Agriculture users are supplied by the water utility.

Reduction of household water use: It is necessary to reduce water use inside homes. Water uses vary according to the climate, and landscape. Summer always witnesses a huge demand and use of water. That is because of the high temperatures in summer and the water is used in different ways, for example there are increases in the frequency of showering per day, washing houses to have a cooler housing environment, washing clothes, water uses for local air conditioning, and other daily uses. The weather conditions together with a lack of education in proper use of water have made the households in the region highly prone to overusing water increasing the wasted proportion. The degree of consciousness in the preservation of water and its rational use is low. This is mainly due to the fact that water is free and there are no laws and tie regulations on how to use water. In addition, it is vital to underline that the infrastructure of the society may lead to some of the excess water usage.

Reduction of commercial and industrial water use: Commercial establishments and public institutions use water mainly for sanitation and for landscape irrigation. A significant reduction also may be achieved if the majority of water public and private users modify their current operation procedures and gradually introduce, for instance, water recycling practices. Commercial establishments, public agencies and institutions, by being relatively large water users, should have significant economic incentives and obligations to save water.

Reduction of agriculture water use: Despite the weakness of this sector, agriculture is considered to be one of the most significant sectors. Irrigation in this sector should be efficient in the region; farmers use clean drinking water for irrigation. The irrigation technologies in open fields are old and ineffectively operated. Investment resources and education are important factors for possible changes in irrigation.

A common measure to bridge the three user sectors of water use is to develop wastewater management systems and their treatment in reusing it in agriculture. The economic and environmental benefits of the recommended system above can be estimated in order to be considered as a solid and feasible measure that suits the region.

F. Suggestions for Regulating Water Use

In order to regulate the use of water the General Directorate of the Ministry of Water Resources in 2008 has suggested the following measures:

- Setting up gutters and water regulators in order to control the water flow and use. The charge level can be progressive in relation to the quantity and differ by user. The revenue should be used exclusively for maintaining the water infrastructure.
- Introducing and implementing the approved rules and laws applicable to all residents.
- Applying these rules and punishing the violators.
- Controlling the distribution of water, the application of regulations and recycling measures to minimize abuses.
- Applying water pricing system and using water resource monitoring programs.
- Dividing the major cities into several zones for best water monitoring and distribution.
- Repairing the old and damaged water networks with respect to the hydraulic model.
- Providing incentives to consumers to follow regulations and increasing their consciousness in environmentally efficient water consumption.

In the remaining parts of this chapter we elaborate on these issues and suggest the introduction of laws and regulations and guidelines for their implementation consistent with modern technology and knowledge.

7.5. PERIODICAL AND SERIAL PUBLICATIONS ON WATER RESOURCES

The great importance of water resources and their increasing scarcity in many parts of the world and increasing environmental concerns has led to the development of mechanisms to monitor our supply and consumption of water. Not many countries have a Ministry of Water Resources like the Kurdistan Region, which is solely responsible for water issues. In general water and environment are a part of the Ministry of Agriculture's activities. The presence of such institutions in the Kurdistan Region is an indication of the great emphasis on water and the vital role of water in the region.

One of the main tasks of the Ministry of Water Resources should be the production of research, reports and statistics for multiple purposes. One main purpose would be to inform investors, the public and private sectors and the general population about the state of water resources in the region. The Ministry of Water Resources, in cooperation with the Ministry of Agriculture and Ministry of Environment, should produce an annual report on the water resource conditions and changes in them over time. Ideally the annual report should be complemented with the publication of special research and technical reports, and monthly and quarterly reports on a regular basis. This section proposes the publication of special research reports, monthly bulletins, quarterly reports, annual reports, and the establishment of an informative Ministry website, research and statistics directorates, a library, and research funds. Several of these, like the website and the statistics directorate currently exist but do not function properly and they need improvement.

A. Periodical Publications

The *Special Reports* should be designed to deal with specific issues with a impact on water resources. They should be in the form of research reports such as an investigation into a specific problem like the construction of a dam, irrigation projects, hydropower generation or issues related to the demand and supply of water by different users. Such reports usually require the collection and analysis of facts and data to be used in the preparation of documents to be used as a basis for making policy decision. The report should account for important aspects of water such as the financial, economical, political, security, social, technological and environmental impacts of water-related decisions. These reports could be a part of a research report series as an official publication from the Research Department of the Ministry. The reports should be distributed to ministries, university libraries and relevant colleges and departments. The reports could be written in either English or Kurdish and in each case with Arabic, Kurdish and English summaries.

A *Monthly Bulletin* should serve as an ideal media channel to inform and communicate with the general public and the private and public institutions and non-governmental organizations about the water resource conditions in the Kurdistan Region. The monthly reports will serve as a discussion forum for discussion of various water laws, water projects and water survey results, such as those on water dams, irrigation, drinking water, industrial use and recreational projects, their benefits and costs and their associated environmental externalities. A summary of research reports could be published here to improve their dissemination. The contributor should be the public, the MOWR employees and internal and external experts. It should be published and distributed to different universities, colleges, schools and public institutions as part of a democratic system and basic educational program. The articles published in the Bulletin could be written either in English or the Kurdish language. The contributors should be the Ministry's employees or general public contributors with opinions and suggestions for improvement of the service.

The *Quarterly Reports* should serve as an outlet for the publication of statistics collected on water resources and their utilization. It should also provide a discussion of methods and outcomes to improve upon the methods for a better analysis of data. In addition to the presentation of serial preliminary data it should inform the public and investors about investment opportunities, decisions made regarding water resources, the planned and budgeted projects to be implemented, progress in the implementation of ongoing projects, and the expected outcome of completed projects. It should cover changes in the organization and policies of the Ministry, the activities of each directorate and forecasts about the demand for water by different users and the supply of water in the form of different water sources. Quantification of the water available, water needed and estimation of the gap as well as a forecast for the coming quarters are among the types of information required and are suitable to be published in the Quarterly Reports series on a quarterly basis.

The *Annual Report* is the last in the series of publications recommended to be established and to be produced at the Ministry of Water Resources or alternatively as part of and in collaboration with the activities of the Ministries of Agriculture and the Environment. The annual report should have a number of objectives. First, it should contain an annual final statistical series covering all activities of the Ministry and general statistics on water resources, water supply and demand as well as the different projects implemented and their outcomes. Second, detailed statistics on the population, water demand, water consumption, water supply by main sources and their quality and accessibility as well as by main users and their location like cities and governorates should be given in detail with explanations of calculation methods and variable definitions and data sources. Third, a special series, supported by tables and graphs should report on the annual activities of each main water source, such as rivers, dams, springs, on wastewater and water treatment. Finally, examples of important indicators of water are found in various periodical and yearly water-related international and country case publications. Prior to a systematic publication of yearly reports such a list must be made available and continuously updated. Attention should be paid to the multipurpose of the data to be collected and the way it is processed and reported in the Ministry's and national statistics yearbooks.

B. Statistics, Research and Their Dissemination

In our view each ministry in the Kurdistan Region should have two sections, units or directorates working with them, i.e. Statistics and Research. These two directorates and their function will be determinants for the achievement of the established goals of their ministries.

They will have a great impact on the organization, activities and performance of all other directorates and also on the creation of networks and collaborative activities with external organizations like universities, research institutes, NGOs, individuals and research teams.

The *Directorate for Statistics* should plan and implement the collection of data and to process and disseminate it on a systematic basis. The outcome is published in the ministry's periodical publications. In addition it should on a regular basis organize in-house training of statisticians and conduct research covering its range of activities. In particular the research, training and seminars should deal with the methods of data collection and processing of the data to create suitable indicators. The area of data collection should cover all aspects of both users and sources of water resources as well as their characteristics. The information on the different market parties' characteristics is useful in the evaluation of public policy effects. In general a professional unit like a bureau of statistics can serve all the ministries and their affiliated sub-units. The establishment of such a unit in each ministry is both costly and time-consuming. However, in the absence of such a national unit, the establishment of the ministry level unit is the only available alternative.

The *Directorate of Research,* in addition to general research program and collaboration with external researcher, should as a main objective play an important role in the publication of various forecast indicators on different aspects of water such as demand, supply, investment and quality. The organization of seminars and conferences on water resources should be another major task of the Directorate. The organization of seminars and collaborative research activities leads to the identification of future potential employees and information about their abilities and potential. This unit is essential and it should closely cooperate with universities and research institutes outside the Ministry.

These series of publications should be made available online and free of charge on the *Ministry's website*. The Ministry currently has a website[33] which contains basic statistics and information about its activities. The publications will enhance public awareness of the importance of water resources, ease the monitoring of different public water-related projects and resources, as well as bring external researchers' attention to research conducted at different national and international universities. An online publication is an important link between the Ministry and decision-makers, producers, consumers and national and international audiences. The web-site informs about and presents the activities and policies of the Ministry and changes in laws, rules and regulations that affect the water market for social planners, households and industries. It can also serve as part of the E-government program that the KRG is promoting.

A full list of publications and additional unpublished statistics and brief reports should be kept in the *Ministry's Library* of resources. The library, in addition to the acquisition and collection of published material and important documents and agreements linked to water, agriculture and environment, should acquire important international literature on water resources elsewhere and make it available to both in-house and external researchers and decision-makers. The data collected and library resources will encourage students and researchers to write about water resources serving the Ministry and society's objectives and welfare.

---

[33] http://www.krg-mwr.org

C. Research Funds and External Collaboration

It is important to establish *Research Funds* to encourage research in water areas. This enhances the internal research capacity and close collaboration with universities and external research institutes and non-governmental organizations and donors. The research funds should cover both earmarked and general funds financing specific research and non-specific research areas. The specific areas should be related to both long-term and short-term development and evaluation of their cost and outcomes. The non-specific are required not to exclude potential research of a capacity-building character and those enhancing our knowledge about water resources.

The source of funds could be the national budget or acquisition of funds and resources from external sources such as NGOs and international aid agencies. Application forms and instructions with and without specific deadlines should be provided online and committees should be established to process applications and to follow up research and their dissemination. Research funds should in particular be allocated to design and conduct various surveys, data collection and the acquisition of secondary data sources, conference participation, organization of conferences and workshops, acquisition of research material, publication of research, and research external collaborations. All these activities are to be considered as investments in human capital who is the Ministry's future potential employees and research collaborators.

7.6. ANNUAL FORECASTS FOR SUPPLY AND DEMAND OF WATER

A. Economics of Water Resources Market

The water market in Kurdistan is still traditional and with little regulation. Here, as in the case of the goods market, the emergence of a market for water services is the process by which often (public) providers and buyers determine price and quantity and terms for its distribution. The public sector water agencies play a major role in the market and its function. They are those who, from the social point of view, discover good financial and environmental opportunities. In the context of public policy application, two general observations are that water resources used in production and consumption are limited and consumers may want more but face water scarcity and cannot have everything they want. In such a case society faces a number of questions related to water sources: their availability, the supplier and receivers of the service, transactions, and who and how the above questions shall be answered.

This study is an economic-oriented study of the water market and its management. Thus economics in this context is the study of how to cope with water scarcity and how to allocate limited water resources among competing requirements in Kurdish society. Here the scope of economics involves the issues of water resources as a public wealth, its associated costs and revenues, and the consideration of water as a resource for industrial production and the full spectrum of human life such as poverty and inequality dimensions. We use the existing economic theory to explain behaviors in the market and to design models and use available information to provide a basis for predictions of demand and supply for water.

The discipline of economics is divided into macro-economics and micro-economics.[34] Micro-economics is about how to measure, explain and predict demand for products and services. Questions of interest are what determine prices, outputs, effects of government policies and incentives, and the welfare of consumers. Here we use micro-economics to promote general interests and for a better understanding of water resource management. Macro-economics, on the other hand, is the study the national economy or resources as a whole or the major components such as total production and investment. The typical question here is what determines the general price of water, revenue, demand and supply levels, and the effects of government monetary and budgetary policies on the national water market.

Water from the perspective of property rights is a public resource for which we need to define the permissibility or specify its utilization by users. Communal property rights concern resources like water, parks and streets, which everyone has the right to use. Public goods perspective is employed if there is no cost to use more of the resources and users account for the effects of their use on the others' use. In some cases, private owner individuals are given the right to exclude others from the use of the resource. Monopolies can also result in the under-use of resources by a single user. An example of the limitations of communal property rights is pollution, which is a consequence of such rights of access to land and rivers. It is a product of the anti-social behavior of the users. Another limitation is where some users use water beyond their needs as the water is free. Good water management depends on incentives that are needed for people to do what they are expected to do. We aim if possible to apply the economic principles developed to assess access and use of water and to evaluate the effects of policies and to search for improvements.

B. Demand and Supply for Water Resources

A market can be competitive or non-competitive. A competitive market is characterized by a large number of producers and consumers, each of which has a small share of the market and is unable to affect the prices. The producers are price takers. Here we deal with public goods, namely water resources with no price, but are aware of its shortage and scarcity and desire to be priced. There is competition in its alternative uses. Thus competition can be based on the price or non-price aspects of water and the value of production to society should determine the exit and entry of firms at least but not limited to the market for household consumption.

Demand is what consumers want and it is applicable to all human behavior including water. In economics it is defined as the inverse relationship between the price and quantity that consumers are willing to buy, everything else given. The slope of the demand curve is negative, meaning that as the price decreases, the purchasing power of the consumer increases, and the consumer buys more. The quantity sold at a particular price is called the quantity demanded. Factors that affect market demand are called the determinants of demand, including taste and preferences, own goods (water) price, the price of alternative goods (soft drinks), the income and number of consumers, expectations about price and incomes,

---

[34] For a comprehensive reference on micro-economics with emphasis on the economic way of thinking of managers and public goods and services provision and regulations discussed in this section (7.6) see McKenzie and Lee (2006).

regulations, or factors like the weather. Each factor may lead to an increase or decrease in demand. Goods can be inferior, luxury or normal and a necessity like water. Demand for water is stable and less volatile to changes in price, income and other determinant factors.

Supply is the relationship between price and the quantity of goods supplied by a producer. It is the schedule of the quantity that producers will offer at various prices during a given period, everything else given. Unlike in the case of demand, the slope of the supply curve is positive. The quantity supplied depends on the production cost and different incentive factors. Determinants of supply are productivity change due to technology change, changes in profitability of producing other goods, changes in scarcity of productive resources, and weather conditions. Changes in these increase or decrease the supply. However, the supply of water may be restricted to a maximum level turning the supply curve to vertical.

The interaction between supply and demand is called market equilibrium, where demand is equal to supply (Figure 7.1). It is common that a market can be in disequilibrium in the form of both surplus and shortage. Market surplus is the amount of quantity supplied that exceeds the quantity demanded at any given price. Market shortage is the amount of quantity demanded that exceeds the quantity supplied at any given price. In the market there are tendencies for price and quantities to move towards equilibrium. In the case of water, the disequilibrium is seasonal and dependent on weather conditions, public investment policies and environmental concerns, regulations and income conditions. Regardless of income and demand conditions, supply can be restricted due to the availability of water. In a case with shortage of water the line with maximum supply will be located to the left side of equilibrium quantity.

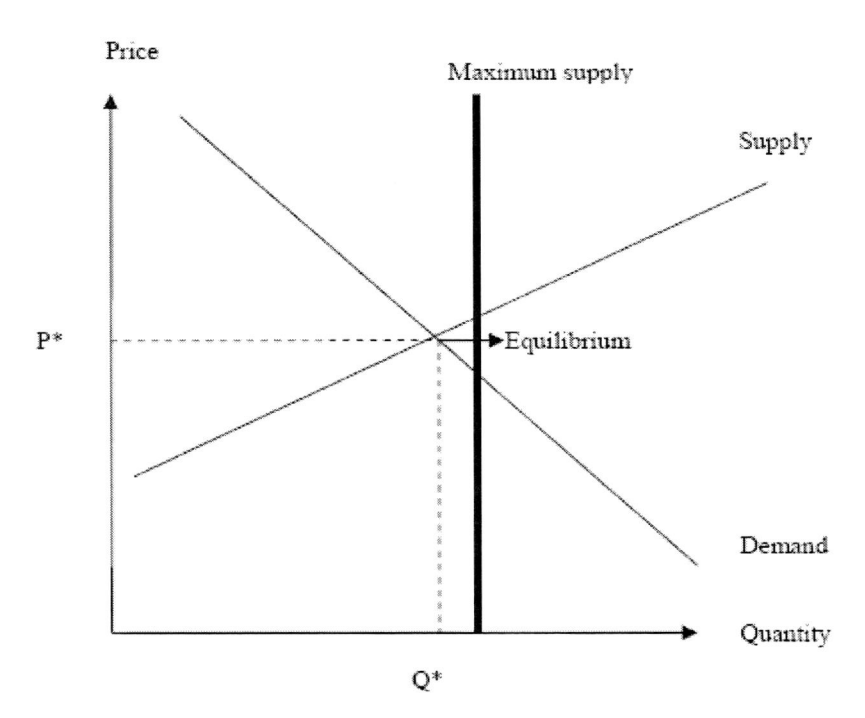

Figure 7.1. Demand and supply of water resources.

C. The Role of Price in the Market

If the actual level of price is higher than the equilibrium price, it results in market surplus and competitive pressure that will push the price down to the equilibrium price. A price that is below the intersection of the supply and demand curves will create a shortage, a greater quantity demanded and competitive pressure will push the price up to the equilibrium price An increase in demand raises both the equilibrium price and the equilibrium quantity. A decrease in demand has the opposite effect, namely a decrease in the equilibrium price and quantity. An increase in supply causes the equilibrium quantity to rise but the equilibrium price to fall. Finally, a decrease in supply has the opposite effect, namely a rise in the equilibrium price and a fall in the equilibrium quantity.

In order to protect consumers or the environment, price ceilings and price floors are introduced as a mechanism to regulate demand and supply. Price ceilings and price floors are government-determined prices above or below which goods cannot be sold. The policy is often used to regulate the consumption of goods and services like milk, oil, electricity, bread, rice, public transportation, health, etc. The use of the competitive market system has the advantage that it coordinates the decisions of producers and consumers. Thus the competitive market is more efficient as it allocates resources with efficiency. It is a situation where the welfare of the parties is reduced by changes in the production level. In such an efficient market the determined price-quantity combination is acceptable to both consumers and producers.

The optimal level of output and prices and issues of competition and decisions have each both long and short run aspects. Each of these may be fixed in the short run, but be flexible in the long run. In addition the competitive market has a number of shortcomings such as income distribution effects on consumption of luxury goods, production costs like pollution from cars which are imposed on people who do not drive a car, competition can promote socially undesirable products and services like cigarettes and alcohol, causing social problems, the un-measurability of product quality, and product proliferation where too many of the same product like aspirin is supplied and unethical methods are used in marketing.

In summary, the water market is a system that provides producers like the state, municipalities, hydro-power companies or suppliers of drinking water with incentives to deliver services that meet the needs of society. In such a market the producers compete and produce in a cost effective manner. A market implies that consumers and producers can freely respond to incentives and without constraints, but the water market with public goods nature requires tie regulations. Prices and quantity for bottled water tend to move towards point of equilibrium with maximum efficiency. Market shortages and surpluses, imposed price ceilings and floors, and insufficient information lead to imperfect markets and a tendency to acquire monopoly power affecting both supplies and prices.

D. Cost-Benefit Analysis and Government Interventions

Cost is the value of most preferred alternatives not taken at the time the choice is made. Benefit is the monetary measure when a choice is made. Cost-benefit analysis (CBA) is a calculation and comparison of all costs and benefits associated with a given course of action like a water project. In general, in relation to public or private projects, such analyses are made and are used as a basis for decision-making. If benefits are greater than the costs, choices are made. Time and risks affect the costs and benefits of a choice, implying the calculation of present values which is the value of future costs and benefits in terms of the current value. CBA is a useful method in public project selection and decision-making. CBA is a rational behavior that maximizes an individual's satisfaction. However, people do not necessarily maximize their satisfaction in practice. Thus, there may be conflicts between the economics of individuals and common interests. Here common interest means a collection of private benefits received by the consumers. Water is a public good where the benefit is received by all members of the society.

One objective of the use of government interventions or controls in the market is to soften the impact of price changes. Examples of government controls include excise taxes, gasoline price controls, a minimum wage, and pollution controls. Both producers and consumers pay tax, and taxes are not always passed on to consumers. An imposed tax affects the price, demand and consumers seek to substitute it. The tax burden can differ among producers and consumers. The producers' opposition to taxes depends on how responsive consumers are to price changes. Fraud and a black market, the rising price of uncontrolled goods and problem of law enforcement are other negative consequences of interventions in the market. To assure a fair and equitable distribution of services like water sometimes rationing is needed. A minimum wage has labor market effects in the form of increased supply of labor. In the context of water a minimum price level is some form of water ransom. It also has social effects in the form of increased negative health effects. As a positive effect, many families gain from the ransom and stabilize their consumption and economy, reducing the household wastewater discharge.

In a competitive market, producers minimize production costs and improve the quality of services provided. If maximum efficiency is not achieved, market failure occurs, i.e. part of the excess benefit is not realized. External costs and benefits are part of the total cost and benefits of production to society. Government imposes penalties to reduce the external costs. Social welfare benefits justify government actions to subsidize and supplement private efforts. Government action has pros and cons. Small distortions can be internalized, not requiring government actions. Government actions and their violations are costly and have their own external costs. They can take different forms like persuasion, public production and its regulation, production standards, price controls, taxes, fines, and subsidies. It is difficult to choose the most efficient remedy for externalities. Moral hazards and adverse selection can be problems. Government controls have important implications for the type and efficiency of policies. In order to be justified and undertaken, the benefit of government actions must exceed their costs.

Some adjustments to changes in economic conditions are predictable, such as the relationship between changes in prices and demand for goods and services. The behaviors are governed by the law of demand. The law of demand allows the prediction of rational behavior when the expected benefits exceed expected costs. It helps to make general predictions of consumer behavior and tendencies. Adding up the wants of individuals makes up the market demand. Price elasticity of demand measures changes in demand in response to changes in prices. Demand can be elastic or inelastic. Elastic demand is when demand is sensitive and responds more than the price change. Inelastic demand is insensitive to price change. Elasticity of demand together with the cost of production determine the prices that firms charge, which in turn affects consumers' total expenditure and firms' revenue and profit conditions, and competition among firms.

Goods can be substitutes or complements. Two products are substitutes if the demand for ones goes up (down) when the price of the other rises (decreases). Lagged-demand for goods is when the greater the quantity purchased today, the greater the demand tomorrow. Today's consumption affect tomorrow's. Network goods feature is when the greater the number of consumer (e.g. computers), the greater the benefit buyers receive. The value depends on how many others buy the same goods. Rational addiction is when tie-in (e.g. cigarettes) between current and future consumption of goods or activities is present. Demand for addictive goods is not inelastic in the long run. A price increase in current time may not reduce current demand but it may reduce future demand. In the context of water substitution between private well or public supply of water and size of house are substitution, lagged demand and network factors.

E. Determinants of Public Policy

Here we shift our focus to the functioning of government and examine the process of the determination of public water policy, decision-making and its implementation. Policies can be different and one policy can be preferred to another. Government production makes up a large proportion of the production of services provided and the economics of politics has various implications for how businesses are operated in the region. The cost of externalities in the private sector should be weighted against the cost of inefficiency and bureaucracy in the public sector. No system is perfectly efficient and we have to choose carefully between them and their combinations. The benefits of public programs are not evenly distributed among the population and the resulting inequality in benefits can be significant. Special and privileged groups like farmers, union and public servants are active in acquiring knowledge about legislative proposals. Thus, government programs are often designed primarily to serve special group interests rather than general public interests. However in the case of water resources the weight attached to private and public interest groups might be equally important.

Almost all economic activities have at some time been subject to some type of government regulation. Examples of regulatory agencies are the various utility commissions, consumer protection and the environment. Examples of regulated industries are gas, electricity, water, sewage and fisheries. In the literature there is little research on why and how regulations happen, but the two strands of theory are public interest and the economic theory of regulations. Here government is seen as a supplier of regulatory services, such as restrictions on entry to a market and the import of goods and services or payment of subsidies. Theory cannot predict regulation or deregulation and they are a result of measures for obtaining a desired outcome. The public interest theory of regulations suggests that regulations improve the efficiency of the market. However, in practice, often the benefits of regulations are over-estimated and their costs under-estimated. Regardless of pre-introduction evaluation results, it might be necessary to conduct a post-implementation evaluation of effects and outcomes.

The economics of government bureaucracy are important especially in the region of Kurdistan. In industrialized countries, some corporations are much bigger in their organization than government departments. Private bureaucratic organizations are more effective than their public counterparts because their objective is profit maximization and it is monetarily measurable. Governments have a multiplicity of complex and non-measurable objectives and, due to monopoly not being imposed, to competition to reinforce their objectives. Often governments produce goods and services that are not subject to any competition. The interest of corporate bodies and consumers may coincide from a social point of view but government bureaucracy and their voters do not. Bureaucracy is constrained by political, but not market forces. Instead of profit it maximizes the size of their operation, power, influence and benefits, increasing the waste of consumer surplus. Improved managerial efficiency, increased competition, downsizing and the cost benefit analysis of public programs are some suggested measures to make government bureaucracy and its operation more efficient.

A natural monopoly is a market structure where the average cost of production declines with the size of its operation and the market will be served most cost effectively by only one producer. The electric utility, urban water services and waste management, where market entry is restricted, are among (public) services with such characteristics. The existence of a natural monopoly is not a good justification for regulation of the market and barriers to entry and inelastic demand also allow monopolistic behavior and for charging monopoly prices. The public electric or water utilities and railroads are the kind of services that require high investment in infrastructure and large scale production which serves as a barrier to entry. Since output produced is below efficient output, a subsidy is required to offset the loss, leading to tax increases. It leads to inefficiency in resource use, price discrimination, and weakened firm incentives to control costs, although from political, security and self-sufficiency perspectives a limited degree of inefficiency might be justified. Regulation of monopolies has been justified by being in the public interest and to achieve national goals. In public choice theory, a firm wants a monopoly to suppress competition and regulations are supplied by politicians for rent-seeking.

F. Forecasts of Supply of and Demand for Water

A forecast of supply and demand is important to investment, employment and production decisions. Banerjee et al. (2004) and Banerjee and Martin (2008) discuss alternative methods of forecasting agricultural water demand and the econometric and engineering prediction of demand and value for irrigation. In order to forecast supply and demand for water resources we need access to key information about the current state and future development of the main sources and users of water resources. There are different ways that supply and demand can be predicted. These can be classified into parametric and non-parametric approaches. Each of the two methods is described below in more detail.

Non-Parametric Approach

A simple non-parametric approach may be of the form that the supply of water resources is computed by adding up the water sources (rivers, springs, dams and treated wastewater) by the quantity of water, while the demand is a simple aggregation of the water users (farmers, households, municipalities and industries). The aggregation should be based on the latest information and adjusted for a number of factors like changes in the structure of the population, land size, industry structure and uncertainties and risks, as well as possible effects of water policies and regulations. The formula for prediction of supply is written as:

$$SU\hat{P}PLY_{t+k} = \sum_{j=1}^{J} SOURCE_{jt} \times \sum_{m=1}^{M} CERTAINTY_{m,t+k} \tag{1}$$

where $SUPPLY_{t+k}$ is the supply of water in the next k years, $SOURCE$ refers to the current or latest quantity of main water sources and CERTAINTY refers to the certainty in the realization of the current level in the next k years. The supply can be estimated for each source separately but also as a total supply in an aggregate form. The sources might be weighted or just use the same weight, as they are all measured in quantity of water. It is a predicted or estimated factor. Concerning the certainty factor, one can use mean value (1.0), estimated lower (<1.0) or upper (>1.0) levels of the certainty factor m. The factors can be given different weights.

The certainty variable, for instance in the case of a dam, might by itself be a composite factor and multidimensional consisting of a large number of factors. Each of the factors must be taken into account in the prediction of the supply of water by each source. The calculated supply of water will generate a mean, upper and lower predicted values for decision-makers. A higher level may reflect optimism in relation to rain and snowfall, an improvement of the conditions for the management of water, an increased number of wells and dams, treatment of wastewater, and a lower diversion of a river at upstream locations. A lower level may be attributed to a negative expectation of the factors above.

In a similar way, demand for water resources by different users can be computed by adding the water users, such as farmers', households', municipalities' and industries' consumption of water. Again the aggregation should be based on the latest information and adjusted for a number of factors like changes in the structure of the population, land size, industry structure, risks, and the effects of economic, environmental, political, social and other policies on demand for water. The formula for the prediction of demand can be written as:

$$DE\hat{M}AND_{t+k} = \sum_{j=1}^{J} USER_{jt} \times \sum_{m=1}^{M} CERTAINTY_{m,t+k} \tag{2}$$

where $DEMAND_{t+k}$ is demand for water in the next k years, $USER$ refer to the type of users or latest quantity of water source consumption and $CERTAINTY$ refers to the certainty in realization of the current level of demand in the next k years. The demand can be estimated for each type of user separately or as an aggregate national demand. The consumer groups can be weighted differently based on their number, needs or share of GDP or just use the same weight as they are all measured in quantity of water. Certainty is an estimated factor and it can take values 1.0, lower or higher than 1.0. The factors making up the certainty index can be given different weights. It is a composite factor and is multidimensional consisting of a large number of factors which must be taken into account in the prediction of demand for water by each type of user. Again the calculated demand for water will generate a distribution including mean, upper and lower predicted values of demand for decision-makers. It accounts for risks and uncertainty by producing a confidence interval for demand. A higher level may reflect shortage and the need for more investment in water resources or a more effective utilization of existing water resources.

Parametric Approach

We have already described what the market for water resources is and defined the characteristics of supply and demand showing the relationship between prices and quantities for water resources. Factors that affect market demand are called determinants of demand and include taste and preferences (+/-), water price (-) and quality available (+), the price of alternative goods like soft drinks (-), income of households (+), number of consumers (+), their expectation about price (-) and incomes (+), regulations/implied taxes (-/+), or factors like weather (+/-). Each factor's expected effects are reported in parentheses. The determinants of supply are productivity change due to technology change in water management (+), changes in profitability of producing other sources of water (-), changes in scarcity of productive resources (-), and weather conditions (+/-). The supply of water may be restricted to a maximum level. The interaction between the supply and demand is called market equilibrium, where demand is equal to supply. In the market equilibrium price and quantity of water are cleared.

If there are no quantitative restrictions in terms of access to water, the demand for water could be modeled as:

$$
\begin{aligned}
DEMAND_{it} = {} & \beta_0 + \beta_{inc}INCOME_{it} + \beta_{pwat}PWATER_{it} + \beta_{poth}POTHER_{it} \\
& + \beta_{msize}MSize_t + \beta_{reg}\text{REGULATION}_{it} + \beta_{oth}OTHER_{it} \\
& + \beta_t TIME_t + \varepsilon_{it}
\end{aligned}
\tag{3}
$$

where *DEMAND* is demand for water for household, farm, firm or municipality in period t, *INCOME* is the household income, *PWATER* is the cost of use of water to the household, *POTHER* is the price (index) of alternative goods and water services, *MSIZE* is an indication of market size or network effect, *REGULATION* is restrictions in the use of water, *OTHER* is factors beyond our control like the weather and other external effects, and *TIME* represents technology and trend in water consumption over time. Several of these variables might be vectors of characteristics. The model can be aggregated across household or farms and written for the national market for water as:

$$
\begin{aligned}
DEMAND_t = {} & \beta_0 + \beta_{inc}INCOME_t + \beta_{pwat}PWATER_t + \beta_{poth}POTHER_t \\
& + \beta_{msize}MSIZE_t + \beta_{reg}\text{REGULATION}_t + \beta_{oth}OTHER_t \\
& + \beta_t TIME_t + \varepsilon_t
\end{aligned}
\tag{4}
$$

where *INCOME* is the national income, the prices *PWATER* and *POTHER* are price indices, *MSIZE* is the aggregate size of the market and *REGULATION* are dummy variables or quantitative water restrictions or implied taxes on water, while *OTHER* incorporates a number of variables that are source, user or region specific. The variable *TIME* captures the effects of technology, weather and demographic changes. The term ε_t captures pure random error terms and it measures error in water demand and information that has been left out due to our ignorance.

The parametric models in (3) and (4) can be used to predict aggregate water demand for a source across different users, or aggregate water demand for a group of users across different sources as follows:

$$\hat{DEMAND}_{t+k} = \hat{\beta}_0 + \hat{\beta}_{inc}INCOME_{t+k} + \hat{\beta}_{pwat}PWATER_{t+k} + \hat{\beta}_{poth}POTHER_{t+k}$$
$$+ \hat{\beta}_{msize}MSIZE_{t+k} + \hat{\beta}_{reg}REGULATION_{t+k} + \hat{\beta}_{oth}OTHER_{t+k}$$
$$+ \hat{\beta}_t TIME_{t+k} \tag{5}$$

where $DEMAND_{t+k}$ is predicted demand in the next k years. The time horizon for prediction, k, can be 1 to several years. The longer the time, the less reliable the prediction will be. In order to predict the left hand variable, future demand, in addition to the estimates of the vector of coefficients, $\{\beta_{inc}, \beta_{pwat}, \beta_{poth}, \beta_{msize}, \beta_{reg}, \beta_{oth}, \beta_t\}$, we need an estimation of future values of the right hand or explanatory variables associated with these coefficients.

The coefficients sign, size and significance are important in an analysis of the result and their use in prediction. If the model is properly specified and estimated and tested, it can be used to predict future demand. To each coefficient a probability and standard error are attached. These together with variations in the estimation of future values of the explanatory variables are used to construct a confidence interval for the predicted water demand. Confidence intervals are routinely estimated. The interval is useful in making expectations about the effect of public policies, optimization of public investment and in optimal provision of services.

The intercept coefficient, β_0, is an estimation of the minimum demand for water to exist and is independent of the characteristics of user or water policies. The remaining coefficients measure changes in demand in response to changes in the explanatory variables. If the left and right hand variables are expressed in a logarithmic form, the estimated coefficients are interpreted as a percentage change in demand in response to a one percent change in respective explanatory variable, ceteris paribus. The regulation or implied taxes coefficient is interpreted as a percentage change in demand in response to changes in the regulation of taxes. Finally the coefficient of time measures the percentage change in demand as time elapses over one year. It captures a shift in demand in response to technological change used in water supply and management.

A Comparison of the Two Approaches

The two methods each have their benefits and disadvantages. The non-parametric is simple and requires less data to compute and predict supply and demand for water. It requires only quantity of water by users and sources and an accounting for expected changes as a result of policy and in the structure of users and sources of water.

The parametric approach on the other hand has a number of benefits. The main one is that it allows the estimation of the effects of polices like imposed taxes and regulations on the demand and supply of water conditional on other observable factors and their effects. A quantification of specific effects is a significant help in decision-making. Another advantage is the accounting for interactive effects and their causation and the direction of effects. The identification of factors and their positive or negative effects and by how much is a third advantage of the parametric methods. A fourth advantage is the use of statistics to construct confidence intervals for estimated effects and predictions of supply and demand. The disadvantage of the parametric approach is the assumptions of the functional form of the relationships, data requirements and complexities in modeling behavior, the estimation and interpretation of the results.

7.7. REALITIES OF ECONOMIC DEVELOPMENT IN THE REGION[35]

In this section we investigate the current state of a number of factors that are vital to the development of the Kurdistan Region. These include in particular the labor market, the mismatch of education and labor market demand, the health and technology resources and several other factors like economic development plans and policy, reconstruction capacity building, inflow of FDI, industrial development model and macro-economic policy of the region. These factors as development infrastructure directly or indirectly affect the water supply, water policy of the regional government and its financing, implementation and effectiveness.

Currently there are no national accounts and no national statistics covering public or private sectors activities in the region in a published form available to researchers. A lack of basic statistics does not allow quantification of the magnitude of any macro-economic or micro-economic indicators to analyze the socio-economic effects of public policies in general and those of water resources in particular. A lack of qualified statisticians and resources to plan, collect and process statistics has been a limitation. Despite significant resources allocated, no reliable data are available for research and policy planning, analysis and evaluation. During completion of this project we have received support from the Ministry of Water Resources to access data. Most of the data made available to us are raw data and there are no clear objectives for their collection and no user of such data clearly identified. The data is of a multipurpose nature, but it is not classified nor checked for consistency.

A. Job Market and Training

Analysis of the labor market conditions in Heshmati (2007a) led to the identification of a number of factors that are determinants of the negative labor market outcomes. The focus was on: the inability of local labor to take new jobs created mainly in construction areas; the high wage rate that is determined by the booming construction sector; low local labor productivity and competitiveness compared to foreign and non-local labor; high profitability of imports and distribution of goods compared with locally produced ones; and the absence of well-

---

[35] For a comprehensive analysis of the economic realities of the Kurdistan Region see Heshmati (2008a) and for recent trends in development economics research with experience from the Kurdistan Region see Heshmati (2008b).

functioning institutions and active public policies to promote local production. Low quality of labor has resulted in high dependency on foreign and non-local labor. It is a result of ineffective public organizations, rapid expansion and mismanagement of higher education in the region. The generous public employment policy has also resulted in a low pay-off for education, encouraged laziness, raised expectations, a high wage and inflation rate, and lowered the work morale.

Thus, low labor productivity and a high wage rate are two main factors negatively affecting both national and foreign investment decisions in the region. The most urgent step to be taken is to formulate a general labor market policy program. Necessary labor market institutions are to be established to enhance the function of the labor market. Several incentive programs targeting primarily the private sector to promote positive development such as youth training, placement programs, wage subsidies, tax rebates, credit guarantees and business startup support programs should be introduced. There should be guidelines to promote discipline and to boost high morale at work. The costly system of multiple employments should be discouraged and eliminated. Such steps have already been taken but are not practiced effectively.

The job market in modern economies is constantly facing a transformation process. Old jobs are destroyed and new ones created. Many of the new jobs created are innovation-driven, where new or modified products are introduced to search for new demand and markets. The rise of the knowledge-based economy has also generated a new global infrastructure with ICT playing an increasingly important role in services and production (Heshmati, 2008b). Despite massive public investment in education and expanded capacity, the Kurdistan Region has never been more dependent on the import of human resources and imported goods previously produced locally (Heshmati and Chawsheen, 2008).

Modernization of the education system and its competitiveness is a prerequisite for a balanced and sustainable economic development in the Kurdistan Region. The issue of reform and modernization of the education system needs to be initiated, discussed, proposed, implemented and evaluated. It should be done by reviewing the educational reform process of the transition economies in East Europe and Central Asia. The massive import of goods and labor is an indication of a significant mismatch of the education produced and labor market requirements which suggest that improved matching of education and skills is necessary for the economy to function effectively. A study of development will guide planners in the allocation of resources and in more effective investment policies.

B. Economic Plan and Policies

The KRG has no full coverage economic development plan. The introduction of a four-to five- year plan is necessary to have a clear picture of the flow of resources and their utilization. Research on the design of such an economic plan and strategies and their evaluation is needed to guide the regional government in its economic and social policy decision-making and the implementation of its development policies. Lack of such a plan makes it difficult to have a clear water resources policy that needs coordination across several ministries/institutions such as oil and gas, agriculture, environment, municipalities, industries, construction and banking. For reasons such as oil prices, flow of oil export and revenue sharing outcome, most of which seem to be beyond the control of the regional government, the flow of financial resources is very irregular, making long-term decisions and investment in major water projects rather difficult. Some of the water projects are the obligation of the central government. This provides the central government with opportunity to implement water projects that are biased towards development of the downstream Iraqi areas.

There is little evidence of socially preferable project selection mechanism or any systematic cost benefit analysis conducted by the regional government to select projects that are socially preferable and give the largest net social benefits. The project proposals and their evaluation prior to a decision should be conducted by professionals across different disciplines and they should include deep analyses of the technology, economic, social, political, environmental, security, and legal aspects. National interest should be given the highest priority and no exception in the seven aspects listed above should be made.

The development policy of the region must aim to promote national competitive advantages and account for the landlocked condition of the region. The current import-oriented economy and liberal FDI-policy should be used to acquire technological capability. The recent years of intensive use of information technology ease technology transfer, joint venture business cooperation and formation of E-government. KRG must adopt a multi-channel development policy approach. Labor costs, administrative bureaucracy, corruption, transparency, accountability, security, risk, regulations and intellectual property rights are among sources of concerns mostly for foreign firms establishing business in the Kurdistan Region.

C. Capacity Building

Iraq has been subject to years of different sanctions, war and destruction, while the Kurdistan Region has enjoyed relative peace and high security in recent years. The production level of oil has been relatively high and stable. This, together with extremely high oil prices, has generated high oil revenues. The shared oil revenues have allowed the Kurdistan Region to start its reconstruction and development programs much earlier than the rest of Iraq. The KRG should take advantage of the existing peaceful conditions to promote the building up of capacity, not only to develop the Kurdistan Region, but also to undertake reconstruction of the cities of Kirkuk and Mosul. Such action is an obligation for the KRG and it will help the region's manufacturing and service sectors to develop.

The security situation in Iraq has been such that large corporations and NGO's with an interest in participation in the Iraqi reconstruction program steer clear of the country. The KRG for mainly political reasons has not been successful in attracting the majority of these firms and organizations to establish their headquarters at Hawler. One should have had taken better advantage of the presence of the Korean peace-keeping troops to facilitate the transfer of Korean technology to the region. Korea is the best partner for such cooperation, as the country has energy, communications, manufacturing, governance and institutional technologies to share, without imposing any political conditions on the receiving countries. In recent months certain steps have been taken to promote collaboration in the energy area. It is argued that a country's economic performance is to a great extent determined by its political, institutional and legal environment. The KRG should downsize and bring its institutions and governance to a higher standard by the intensive training primarily of its higher and medium level ranked civil servants.

A majority of public projects completed or yet incomplete are in the areas of development infrastructure. FDI is primarily in the areas of construction of housing, institutions and transportation, and services. This is due to the fact that natural resources are not yet exploited investment areas. An exploitation of natural resources including mining should have been undertaken as a part of the development process, based on domestic resources. The KRG through the new investment law has made serious efforts to provide official guidelines to investment activities. Various incentive measures in the form of land and other facilities and tax and duty exemptions have been introduced to promote investment activities. These incentive measures would certainly have had a positive effect on the development of industries in the area of development and the supply of domestic construction material.

D. Development Strategy

From the region's point of view, there are several weaknesses in the investment law. These include: a lack of emphasis on the transfer of technology, skills and management, possibility of misuse of land plot allocation, absence of modern business law and the negative trade balance (Heshmati and Davis, 2007). Several infrastructure factors are not optimal, such as the financial market and its functions, mismatch and low quality of education and skills, insufficient labor market training programs, high wage rates, low labor productivity and competitiveness in the region. In order to encourage inward and to discourage outward FDI, the KRG should undertake a number of proactive policy measures. Provisions of guarantees and securities, the dual currency, no devaluation risk and transaction cost must be better emphasized. The region is rich in unexploited natural resources. The signed oil contracts have not been properly investigated in respect with legal, economic, social, political and environmental aspects.

Despite weak and non-optimal development conditions, the Kurdistan Region can use the experience gained from several newly-industrialized economies as a model for its industrial development. Emphasis should be on the national capability as the result of intellectual and human capital; economic capital, social capital and political leadership to support the national interests. The KRG needs to have a development strategy, an economic plan and appropriate public institutions for implementing the plan. The path to development may involve the massive import of foreign technology to transform the economy structurally to a combined knowledge-intensive manufacturing-, agriculture- and service-based economy. The low education quality, the unacceptable practices of employment and nominations, manufacturing which hardly exists, the destroyed agriculture and an inability to develop a service industry are indications of the difficulty in predicting where the economy of the region is heading. All these in one or another way, directly or indirectly affect the water management and policies.

E. Firm and Household Taxation and Financial Markets

In addition to a development strategy and economic plan, the introduction of comprehensive firm and household taxation is necessary to smooth the flow of public revenues, to reduce inequality, to redistribute income and to create a strong financial base for continuous provision of public services. The policy should include a blend of macro-economic, micro-economic and industrial and social policies. The selection and effectiveness of policies will depend on the characteristics of the market organization, public institutions and the structure of political, educational and technological institutions. Public institutions should be supportive and not create problems in the form of bureaucracy, corruption and inefficiency. Changes in the current unsound politics-public-business relationships are preconditions for the successfulness in the mission.

The lack of an economic plan and basic national accounts and statistics do not allow the use of macro-economics policies and indicators to measure the performance and structure of the regional economy, to forecast the future and to evaluate policy outcomes. This is a necessary condition for regional planning that aims at balanced and sustainable economic development. The regional government spending consists of classic public activities. Taxation is either outdated or nonexistent. The Regional Government relies heavily on oil revenues. Other supplementary regional government revenues are raised from fees on building permission and vehicle registrations. The fiscal policy is limited to public employment programs, the provision of public utilities, recreation, and health care and education services and is not used in any stabilization policies.

The Iraqi banking system is characterized by a low level of savings, volume of credits and limited inter-bank relationships. The expansion of banks is not matched by a modern system of business laws and regulations which hinders the promotion of savings and credits. The Regional Central Bank is not independent in policy-making, but it should initiate policies to develop credit channels. Irregularities in the flow of revenues, a high dependency on hostile neighbors and a shortage of production factors may cause shocks and instability in the region's economy. There are no statistics available to compute the rate of economic growth in the different sectors of the economy to compare with those of the neighbors and trade partners.

7.8. SELF-SUFFICIENCY AND VULNERABILITY IN USE OF WATER

A. A General Perspective on Self-Sufficiency

Self-sufficiency is extremely low in the region in almost all areas of resources, products, services and technology. The living conditions, non-competitive wages, non-transparency of the market, and general employment conditions might affect the brain drain process and in parallel have prevented the repatriation of educated Kurds. Brain drain might be strong words and not really applicable for the unskilled and incapable Kurdish workforce. Their migration is more a result of desperation and unhappiness with their living conditions rather than demand for their unique skills elsewhere. The education system produces graduates that are not trained, creative or technologically upgraded to provide self-sufficiency in a skilled workforce. The low quality of the workforce together with low incentives, combined with low morale at work and in business and the dominance of private interests over national/regional interests are the responsible factors for the low levels of productive employment and negligible degree of self-sufficiency.

In the near future, reconstruction of the massively destroyed public infrastructure and the heavy indebtedness of Iraq will possibly limit the availability of further resources for development in the Kurdistan Region. The current and exceptional opportunity of peaceful governance and reconstruction in the region should be used in the best way to build up a strong and self-sufficient base for economic and social development and technology adoption in the region. An ineffective use of resources will endanger all achievements made in the past few years in unique regional self-governance. Intensive and specialized evening and weekend training programs should be organized for advisors in the regional government and public institutions like the Ministry of Water Resources to train public decision-makers, researchers, investigators and evaluators to learn about basic and effective organization structures and management.

A strong emphasis by the regional government should be placed on the transfer of technology, skills and management as basic conditions for the provision of investment incentives. These are vital for the capability to develop the region's economy and to attain a higher degree of self-sufficiency. The flow of oil revenues to the region inflated by recent years of high oil prices has raised the income level and consumption power of the regional government and a majority of the region's residents which has affected the trade balance negatively. The development has been destructive to local production, and in particular in the agriculture area. Kurdish society is very vulnerable concerning basic needs like food and textile products as well as access to clean water and in optimal quantity and quality to different locations with little inequality in provisions.

In the formulation of a model for industrial development the focus should initially be on the current policy and institutions, the conditions, and the resources available in the region and those needed. The development approaches in newly industrialized countries can serve as a base for development of an industrial model for Kurdistan and the establishment of appropriate infrastructure and organization as well as a selection of possible industrial policy instruments to improve security and self-sufficiency (Heshmati, 2007c). Among other existing negative factors to such development are high wages and low labor productivity. Efforts should be made to standardize wages to reflect the level of education, skills and abilities of the labor force. This will provide necessary tools for the government from a regional development perspective to support certain priority sectors like agriculture, electricity and water supplies from a self-sufficiency perspective.

Kurdistan as an underdeveloped region, but with the potential to develop, should industrialize as fast as possible, not only to catch up with its neighbors. Such rapid development is a precondition for continuity in enjoying the partial freedom it has gained. It should adopt an industrial strategy of self-sufficiency in particular in basic defense, security and economics. To industrialize in a short time, the KRG must draw up a series of economic plans. Initially, the regional government should build up effective service providing institutions, mobilize resources, protect infant industry, allocate credits, regulate technology flows, provide administrative guidance and publish forecasts seasonally. The establishment of science parks can serve for the purpose (Heshmati, 2007a)

Policymakers should provide general and sector-specific incentives to advance more rapidly and place more emphasis on building a strong base for indigenous sources of development. The creation of conditions for low and smooth bureaucratic controls is crucial for business development. Investment in technology support institutions and infrastructure must contain all the phases of import, application, assimilation, and modification of technology for the local needs. The policy process should shift by first promoting growth by direct intervention to promoting technological capabilities, self-sufficiency and competitiveness and then different subsidies and import barriers should be gradually removed. The measures for fighting corruption, reducing bureaucratic and unnecessary regulations should not be neglected. Sufficient and effective regulations and control mechanisms in the underdeveloped financial system are urgently required. Speculative and non-productive investment activities, concentrations of investment and creation of bubbles, for instance in the real estate market area in major cities, must be discouraged to avoid wasting scarce resources.

B. Self-Sufficiency in the Use of Water Resources

Kurdistan is rich in water resources in the form of rivers, springs and groundwater. The existing few major dams are used mainly for better management of water and for the generation of electricity and irrigation mainly downstream. Within the region, given poor resources and facilities, irrigation was facilitated to a desired level by traditional diversion techniques from small rivers. This was undertaken by farmers alone without much involvement from the government at any of the regional or central levels. Most land in plain areas is non-irrigated and farmed every second year and most land in locations far from urban areas is abandoned. This has led to the decline in agriculture and lower demand for irrigation water.

In recent years several factors have changed in regard to demand, supply and self-sufficiency in water resources. The changes include drought, diversion of water upstream, changes in population structure, declining production in agriculture and animal husbandry, establishment of new industries, changes in the dam capacities, and small shifts in the agriculture towards intensive forms such as greenhouse, aquaculture and recreation. The changes have resulted in lower demand for irrigation, but higher demand for urban consumption and recreation facilities, as well as an increased use of water in new and mainly construction and infrastructure-related industries. It is hard to produce estimates of demand and supply in pre- and post-change periods and to compute the actual changes and how it has affected the degree of self-sufficiency in the water area.

What are relatively new phenomena that affect strongly the degree of self-sufficiency are the water diversion and drought factors. The intensive water diversion activities upstream, in Turkey and Iran, are the most serious dangers, changes to and violations of international water laws. These two factors are considered to be a real danger to the Kurdistan Region's self-sufficiency, survival and maintenance of its social and natural population structure. These actions taken by neighbors have very likely multipurpose objectives such as long-term development of their economies by a better and effective management of water, as well as imposing political pressure on the Kurdistan Regional Government through the regulation of discharge of water from their dams. These countries have also suffered equally from the regional drought and low rainfall in recent years. Regardless of drought and water diversion activities, the rapid increase in the urban population in cities like Hawler and Sulaimanyah require a comprehensive investment in infrastructure to supply water to these locations through groundwater, pipelines, and the diversions of water undertaken.

7.9. A Proposed New Water Resources Plan and Policies

A. Data, Research and Publications

Data Collection and Processing

We have already elaborated on the fact that currently there are no reliable statistics available that cover different economic, social or environmental activities in the Kurdistan Region. A lack of basic statistics does not allow for the quantifying of the magnitude of demand and supply of water to analyze the needs, shortages and its socio-economic and environmental effects. In recent years the financial conditions have been optimal, so that different types of statistics required could have been collected and processed. During the preparation of this project we have noticed that a large amount of data at different places in the region is collected on a somewhat regular basis but they are not channeled to a central place for process, control and dissemination. A lack of qualified decision-makers and statisticians specialized in data management has been a limitation. Despite significant resources allocated, no or little data are available for professional and quality research and policy analysis.

In general a regional Center of Statistics should be responsible for the collection, processing and dissemination of statistics. In the absence of one and as previously we mentioned, in our view each ministry in the Kurdistan Region should have two directorates working in close cooperation specifically with statistics and research and development. These might already exist in the form of organizational units but the actual condition suggests that they are poor in performance. These units are not supposed to substitute the Center of Statistics but be a complement to it. In addition a local statistics unit at the Ministry will collect raw data and generate needed statistics at a disaggregate level which is not necessarily required or of interest at the regional level. These two directorates and their functions will be determinants for the achievement of the goals of the Ministry of Water Resources. If operated well, they will have a great impact on the organization, activities and performance of all directorates and also on the Ministry's creation of networks and collaborative external activities.

The Directorate for Statistics should plan and implement the collection of data and process and disseminate it on a systematic basis to relevant users. The data outcome should be published in the Ministry's periodical publications. Previously we have suggested as a publication outlet special research reports, monthly bulletins, quarterly and annual reports. The aims and objectives of each type of publication and type of data and indicators they will publish will be further described in detail. Furthermore, the directorate should on a regular basis organize in-house training programs for statisticians and conduct research covering its range of activities. The research, training and seminars should deal with, among others, the methods of data collection and processing of data to create suitable indicators covering all aspects of users and water sources and regulators' activities.

Research and Development

The Water Research and Development Directorate of the regional ministry should work with a systematic analysis of data collected by the Directorate of Statistics. It is through empirical research that the directorate and its researchers can assist in creating a regional strategy and plan for the ministry. Thus, this unit plays a central role and will be a determinant for the achievement of the goals of the Ministry. They will have a great impact on the function, organizational structure, activities and performance of the Ministry and likewise in the creation of networks and collaborative activities with external organizations, researchers and research institutes.

The Directorate of Research and Development, in addition to being a good example of the organizational form of a unit at the Ministry and capable of conducting tasks expected in the best way, must have its own research program and collaboration activities with external researchers. As a main objective it should to play an important rule in the publication of various forecast indicators on different aspects of water such as demand, supply and on investment and water quality issues. It should also take a lead as the main user of collected data and in identification of the water related research needs of the region, initiation of necessary research programs, and in establishment of external research collaboration and activities.

Seminars, Workshops and Conferences

The organization of seminars and conferences on water resources held on a regular basis and when appropriate should be another task of the Directorate of Research and Development. Annual conferences with coverage of all aspects of water could play an important role. They will enhance attention to water and the environment which have been neglected areas. One can call for papers on specific areas of preference such as construction of large dams, water quality and irrigation, and water-related health risks, management of water, pollutants, and regulations or alternatively allow researchers to conduct theoretical or empirical research on their preferred research topics. This approach, in addition to generating research, to satisfy short term needs, will help in capacity building which is important for satisfying the future and long term needs of society. The existing conditions with a low level of self-sufficiency and capability suggest that both long and short term perspectives seem equality important.

It can be noticed that in the region many meetings and conferences of different sizes are organized. There are excellent conference centers and hotels with the capacity to hold large conferences. There is experience in the organization of a few large conferences, but little or no effort is made to utilize the post-conference publication outcomes in a satisfactory way. For instance, there are no serious efforts made to generate selected post-conference publications based on the conference or conference summaries to guide institutions on new findings or to identify important topics for future meetings. Workshops and conferences are also an effective way of establishing external collaborative research activities. These will help the Ministry by leading to valuable research outputs that are not possible to conduct by using the in-house workforce capacity. In addition, the meetings will facilitate the identification of future potential employees and provide detailed information about their background and capabilities.

Statistics, Research and Their Dissemination

During the implementation of this project the research team, in collaboration with employees at the Ministry of Water Resources, visited several public institutions acquiring data on population, industry, hydropower generation, rain and snowfall and rivers and spring sources. The data has been written in excel format and collected in a small database. This database is expected to be expanded to include more data and made available to in-house and external researchers to utilize in their research. It also serves as a model for the development of similar small in-house databases which can be created at different ministries. Parts of these data bases that are of general interest can be collected and stored centrally at the established Kurdistan Region's Center of Statistics. An attempt has been made to establish such a center to manage the data collection, processing and dissemination at the regional level. The team is operating at the Ministry of Planning with little possibility of acquiring statistics from corporations and public institutions. Thus, due to lack of professional statisticians and a strong focus on the task, so far few outcomes in the form of published statistics has been made available. Their effort might be limited to and strongly biased towards the creation of databases used in the design of an economic plan.

The series of publications listed above should be made available online in soft format and free of charge at the Ministry's website. The Ministry currently has a website which provides basic statistics and information about water resources in the Kurdistan Region. The publication will help in enhancing public awareness on the importance of water resources. It further eases the monitoring of different public water-related projects and resources. It also serves as a tool to bring national and international researchers', universities' and research centers' attention to water problems in the Kurdistan Region. In a new globalized and connected world, an online publication is an important means of linking the Ministry and decision-makers, producers, consumers and national and international audiences. It informs people about the activities and policies of the Ministry and changes introduced in laws, new rules and regulations that affect the water market with implications for planners, households and industries.

The full collection of research and publications and unpublished statistics and reports should be kept in the Ministry's Library on water resources. In addition to the acquisition and collection of relevant published material and important documents and agreements linked to water, agriculture, industry and environment, the library should acquire important international literature on water resources and make it available to domestic researchers and decision-makers. The research data and library resources will encourage postgraduate students and researchers at different domestic and foreign universities to write their theses about water resources serving the Ministry and society's objectives and welfare. This type of collaboration will enhance the Ministry's research capacity.

B. Laws and Common Pool Relations

Water Plan and Policies

The Middle East is a region characterized by scarce water resources, rapid population growth and fast developing consumption-based economies. Water scarcity is increasing and expanding in the region. The scarcity of water is partially a result of neighboring countries divergence of water, changes in population structure and concentration, climate changes as well as the use of water in hydropower-based electricity generation. The increasing vulnerability suggests that it is important to investigate the current economic, social and water resources conditions and alternative sources of water. The investigation ideally will lead to measures proposed to enhance the effectiveness in the use of water resources to reduce the shortages in supply and the negative environmental effects.

Water is considered as a binding constraint on sustainable future economic and social development in the region. Improved efficiency in water use must be combined with the provision of new and additional water sources in the region to minimize the shortage of water. A comprehensive and detailed water and environmental law will be of great help in the design and implementation of strategies for regional cooperation, in the development and management of water resources, interregional trade relations, development of regional institutional arrangements, and in joint regional water planning among others reasons.

Water and Environmental Laws

Currently there are no water and environmental laws practiced in the Region of Kurdistan. The Iraqi laws which are mainly from the 60s and 70s are outdated and non-existing or not applicable to modern times. However, the Ministry of Environment has published a draft of Environment Law # 8 from 2008. It contains 5 chapters as follows:

1. Definitions and objective
2. Organization managing: planning, protection, recreation, evaluation, research, inspections, incentives, responsibility and compensations concerning environment
3. The laws of: protection and recreation of water, air, land, plants and animal, management of dangerous waste material, chemical, and environmental accidents.
4. Punishments
5. Conditions and factors affecting decisions made.

I would like to congratulate the Ministry of Environment for their new law. It is an important piece of work and certainly useful in their work.

The gap concerning water resources is expected to be filled through a project aimed at preparing a draft covering one of the most important laws in a modern economy, namely the Water Law.[36] It covers the specific water resources law, but when necessary it also deals with environment, production, consumption, investment, trade, business and health and education laws as well. In the preparation of the law account will be made for local conditions. Thus, the proposed law will serve as an example for the introduction of similar region-specific laws to be prepared for the Kurdistan Region. The project will focus on the following ten interrelated areas:

1. Review of the existing water and environmental law applicable in Iraq
2. Review of the European Water Framework Directive, European Water Initiative, and the Millennium Development Goals which serve as global water laws to identify future water policy directions
3. Identification of strengths, weaknesses and shortcomings of the related Iraqi laws
4. Preparation of a draft for the Water Law adapted to the specific characteristics of the Kurdistan Region
5. Investigation of the law's consistency with the Iraqi and related international laws

---

[36] This proposal with the title "Water resources law and its implementation in the Region of Kurdistan" initiated by Almas Heshmati and Chemen Bajalan was submitted to the Ministry of Water Resources in July 2008. If approved and financed, it is planned to be completed during September 2008 and June 2009.

6. Suggestions for necessary rules and regulations required to implement the newly introduced law successfully

7. Suggestions for different public investment and incentive programs to implement the law successfully

8. Estimation of the cost of implementation of the proposed investment and incentives programs

9. Suggestions for guidelines on locally organized training programs, organizational changes and structures, and activities to govern the water resources in the region effectively

10. Provision of guidelines on how to monitor and to evaluate the implementation of the law and to solve problems raised

There are a number of differences between the structure of the new draft of the Kurdistan Region Environment Law and the proposed Water Resources Law. The first and main difference is in the Water Laws linkage with the European Water Framework Directive, European Water Initiative and United Nations Millennium Development Goals which determine not only current but also future directions in water management. A second difference is that in the Water Law one gain is from experience in water areas in developed and transition countries in water areas concerning the planning, management, evaluation, monitoring, investment decisions, incentives, policy effects, rules and regulations. The third difference is that the Water Law project is not just a law but also a study of water laws in different country environments and development stages. A fourth contribution of the proposed study will be to identify the gaps and overlaps between the Water and Environment laws to prevent misuse or neglect in their implementation. Finally, since the original version will be written in English, it can also be used in the Ministry's communications with corporations and inter-state common pool water relations.

The project is to be financed by the Ministry of Water Resources of the Kurdistan Region. A part time local assistant and an expert in water resources nominated by the ministry will also help the researchers with data collection and its analysis and organization of the work. The work will start at the beginning of September 2008 and a preliminary report will be completed at the end of April 2009. The report will be revised following a workshop to be organized by the Ministry on May 2009 to get views, comments and suggestions by experts of water resources. The final revised report will be submitted to the Ministry of Water Resources at the end of July 2009. It will serve as a handbook for efficient use of water resources, for water policy analysis, in the region's cooperation with NGOs, and in the relationship with other users of common pool water resources in the region.

The report will contain five interrelated parts. The first part is a review of the International and Iraqi water and environmental laws and the Kurdistan Region's newly introduced Environment Law. The second part contains the draft of the Kurdistan Region Water resources law. The third part will be an examination of its consistency with Iraqi and International laws. The fourth part contains guidelines on rules and regulations, different policies and incentive mechanisms for the successful implementation of the law. Here gains are made from the review of experience from elsewhere and care is made to tailor those to be consistent with the region's conditions. In the fifth part suggestions are made on organizational changes, civil servant training and educational programs and various activities to facilitate the smooth and effective implementation of the law and incentive policy programs.[37]

Legal Team Setups

The Kurdistan Region and Kurds were in the past excluded from certain types of education, in particular those related to economics and industries and in particular petroleum technology. The restrictions were less in the legal area, although, the quality of education was and still is low and far from adequate to make the candidates able to deal with international laws and cross border relations. Currently there are at least five universities and several smaller universities and technical institutes providing higher education in the region.[38] Despite an education capacity in the interval of 55,000 to 60,000 university students, including around 1,000 enrollments in postgraduate programs there is no local capacity to deal with international law. Most universities in the region provide evening course programs in law aiming at middle and higher civil servants which is more or less to qualify them for promotion.

Given the shortage of capacity in the area of international law and the availability of resources and a development program that involves significant relationships with private foreign investors, multinational corporations, NGOs and foreign states, it is important to build up such local legal capacity. Legal capacity needs to be built up to cover a number of areas such as: the Iraqi government's use of weapons of mass destruction in Halabja where more than 5,000 were killed and 1000s still suffer from cancer as a result of the use of chemical bombs, the Iraqi government's Anfal massacre of more than 180,000 Kurdish civilians, the forced dislocation of Kurdish families in the Arabization campaigns, the destruction of nearly 4,000 of 4,500 villages in the Iraqi Kurdistan Region, the Kurds' rights to self-determination in the use of their own natural resources, oil and gas revenue sharing between central and regional governments, common pool water resources shared by Iran, Turkey, Iraq including the Kurdistan Region and Syria, and many other disputed areas.

Given the limited legal capacity and the urgent need to build it up, we propose the creation of a legal team. The legal team, in the capacity of a legal fire brigade, could best be composed of a number of experts in different fields covering: contracts in general and in particular business, environment, natural resources in general and oil and gas in particular, financial transactions, common pool water resources, military interventions, international law, the United Nations Security Council's work, The Hague Tribunal, European Court, minority rights, human rights, genocide, and knowledge about the position of countries protecting international law and minorities and collaboration with them. The team member experts could ideally be retired experts in the field who have no more regular employment and are free to allocate time to their new tasks and are able to travel. The non-experts part of the team should consist of local people with backgrounds in both national international laws and experience in diverse areas. The composition of the national part of the team should not be the traditional top-down, but should be ability-based and such that the capability is high in absorbing knowledge. Transfer of knowledge from the foreign expert members to local team members is

---

[37] Laws and incentives are needed to regulate the market. There are examples of regulations and their implementation.

[38] Salahadeen, Sulaimanyah, Duhok, Koya and Kirkuk are the five largest universities in the region. University of Kurdistan Hawler, American University of Sulaimanyah and Jihan University are among the smaller and recently established universities with education programs in social sciences.

crucial in building up local capacity. The establishment of such a team of national and international experts seems to be costly, but it is a national asset and it significantly reduces the cost of making mistakes and will be self-financed by claiming compensation from perpetrators for the harm and injustices they subjected the Kurds to in the past.

The work of the legal team could be related to past, current and future events. The first category, related to the past, includes systematic investigations, documentation and the preparation of cases for the regional government to submit cases to international courts concerning the violation of minority rights, genocide, massacre of civilian, destruction of properties, and forced migration exercised by the government of Iraq. The current cases could be related to oil and gas, common pool water resources, military intervention by foreign forces, reclaiming land and properties following forced migration, relocation of families subject to forced migration, oil revenue sharing, defense and security, implementation of the constitution and regional laws, the rights of Kurdish minorities in majority Arab-populated regions, discrimination of minorities, power-sharing at the central government level, aviation, transportation, diplomacy, etc. The future issues involve protection against all forms of violations encountered above, plus the Kurds right to self-determination and the formation of a Kurdish state in accordance with international law and the will of the Kurds if they so desire.

Monitoring Upstream and Downstream Water Activities

The upstream water sources in the Kurdistan Region are Turkey and Iran. In both countries in the last two decades a large number of dams have been built and the diversion of water sources like rivers has been intensive. The two countries' plans for intensive water diversion, dam construction and irrigation programs are comprehensive and especially harmful for the Kurdistan Region as a downstream user of water. There are international water laws on common pool water resources that regulate common water resources and unilateral and bilateral water activities. In the absence of a capable legal team to solve the problem through negotiations, the Iranian and Turkish governments in keeping with their political hostility towards the Kurdistan Regional Government use water diversion policy to increase the Kurds dependency and vulnerability as a minority. Thus, water is a new means of suppressing the Kurds and a shortage of water strangles their source of life and leads to their migration to politically designated areas.

Concerning downstream water activities, the central government through its Ministry of Water Resources is attempting to impose different kinds of pressure on the regional ministry to influence the water-related activities like hydropower generation, irrigation and diversion of water within the Kurdistan Region. Budgetary activities, financing water projects and employment relations are used to exercise such influence. The regional government aims to maintain control over water sources in its territorial authority, although this authority is weakened due to the KRG being tempted to use central government funds to finance water projects in places like the southeast of the Kurdistan Region. The KRG has also insufficient management and technological capability to undertake complex projects like the construction of large dams and irrigation projects. Thus, the higher the KRG's capacity, the stronger will be its position to exercise its authority in policy-making and the weaker is the Iraqi government's possibility of influencing the policies in the Kurdistan Region. The KRG should employ a policy that accounts for both realities of upstream and downstream as well as respect for international water laws, rules and regulations.

C. Project Evaluation and Collaboration

Cost-Benefit Analysis

In a modern economy, it is quite common that pubic projects, regardless of the investment amount, are evaluated in respect to their specific costs and benefits. The method is called cost-benefit analysis (CBA) which is a weighting scale approach for decision-making on whether the implementation of a project is worthwhile. A cost-benefit ratio is determined by dividing the projected benefits of a program by the projected costs. Thus the positive and negative elements are put on each side of the scale and the one with heavier weight wins. The costs and benefits are an aggregate of the net present or discounted values. The estimation of future risk and inflation rates has a strong impact on the predicted costs and benefits.

In the case of private projects, the net current value of benefits less the cost or profits determines investment decisions. However, in public or governmental planning and budgeting, the social benefits of a proposed project in monetary terms are measured and compared with the costs of the project. The procedure was first proposed in 1844 but not applied until the 1936 U.S. Flood Control Act. The calculation of the costs and benefits components was conducted by engineers. The Act required that the benefits of flood-control projects exceed their costs as a basic condition for the implementation of such projects. Later in 1950s the economists developed more consistent methods for measuring costs and benefits of projects.

A wide range of variables, including non-quantitative ones such as quality of life, preservation of nature, clean air, etc. are often considered because the value of the benefits or their accumulation may be indirect or projected far into the future. The costs and benefits are divided into two main categories: those which are observable and easily estimable (tangibles), and those which are not clearly observable or possible to estimate (intangibles). The observable costs include costs associated with people, machines and material for development and operation of the plants, while the tangible benefits are derived by estimating the cost savings of human, machine and other resources to run the new plant or system versus the old one. Intangible benefits, such as improved customer service, employee relations and health may provide the largest payback, but these items are harder to quantify in practice.

Priority Projects Based on Social and Economic Preferences

Examples of public projects where CBA is required to assist decision-makers in the water areas are: construction of dams, irrigation projects, diversion of water, production of hydropower, national parks, pollution control, wastewater management, and recreation and tourism projects. To each of these projects a different set of costs and benefits, with short and long-run horizons, tangible and intangible, qualitative and non-qualitative, measurable and non-measurable, etc. are associated. The ability of researchers and the degree of carefulness in the calculations determine how far one can go with the identification, quantification and accounting for different benefits and costs in relation to a public or private project's acceptance and implementation.

In a society with different needs and institutions the employees have different needs, skills and abilities. Thus, resources available for development are scarce and have multiple uses. Mechanisms are needed to deal with the multiplicity of needs and alternative projects as a solution to certain needs. In general for given resources different alternative projects are proposed. The projects have economic and social costs and benefits, as well as political, security, technology and environmental implications. Cost benefit analysis is used to rank projects and among alternative projects the ones with the highest benefits/cost ratios or simply those preferred by majority of voters are given high priority and selected for implementation.

Industrial Development of the Region

Industrial development of the region may seem to be out of the scope of water resources and the authority of the Ministry of Water Resources. However, it has to do with education, management, ability and technology which are crucial factors for the management of water resources, skillful project design, implementation and evaluation of project and interactions with other public and private institutions. Thus, the subject is highly relevant to the Ministry as industrial development impacts its operation.

S&T-Based Development

The region needs to have an economic plan and a development strategy. Industrialized and newly-industrialized countries without exception have all established a Ministry of Science and Technology (MST) as a necessary step to implementing their industrialization policy. Thus, it is important to establish an MST in the Kurdistan Region. The MST and Ministry of Planning should serve as a headquarters for the planning and implementation of its development strategy. It should initiate the first five-year plan with economic recovery and development as a priority. The plan must have a clear development strategy and be based on specific policies, such as import substitution and the promotion of exports and the import of technology-embodied capital. The policy will be successful at the time of the reconstruction of Iraq. Comprehensive investment in SandT institutions, education and other technology-enhancing infrastructure is a prerequisite for its success.

The economic policy should include a blend of macro-economic, micro-economic and industrial policies. The many dimensions should include employment creation, improved defense, economic and political security, a strong industry base, and rising firms' survival and productivity which are fundamental because of the landlocked situation of the region. The industrial policy should have multi-objectives and focus on key sectors, investment promotion, regulations and environmental controls, and minimize the investment risk and negative externalities. The policy instruments in general, some forms of tax incentives, import duties, RandD subsidies, import restrictions, export promotion, start-ups support and employment programs are all important policy measures.

Industrial Strategy of Self-Sufficiency

Kurdistan is an underdeveloped region with the potential to catch up with its neighbors in development. Such rapid development is a precondition for the continuity in enjoying the partial freedom it has gained. It should adopt an industrial strategy of self-sufficiency in particular in basic defense, security and economics. To industrialize in a short time, the KRG must draw up a series of economic plans. Initially, the regional government should build up effective service-providing institutions, mobilize resources, protect infant industry, allocate credits, provide administrative guidance and publish forecasts seasonally. The path to development may involve the transformation of the economy structurally to a combined manufacturing, agriculture and service-based economy.

The introduction of comprehensive firm and household taxation is urgent and necessary for a smooth flow of public revenues, reducing inequality in all its forms, redistribution of income and provision of public services. Demand promotion policies are available instruments to protect the home market and local production. The selection of sound policy measures in themselves do not determine the success of the policy. The effectiveness will depend on the characteristics of the market organizations, public institutions and the structure of political, educational and technological institutions. Public institutions should be supportive and solve rather than create problems in the form of bureaucracy, corruption and inefficiency.

Industrial Policy Orientation

Policymakers should provide general and sector-specific incentives and place more emphasis on building a strong base for indigenous sources of development. The creation of conditions for low and smooth bureaucratic controls is crucial for business development. Investment in technology-support institutions and infrastructure must contain all the phases of import, application, assimilation, and modification of technology for local needs Measures for fighting corruption, reducing bureaucratic and unnecessary regulations should not be neglected. Speculative and non-productive investment activities must be discouraged to avoid wasting scarce resources, concentrations of investment in certain sectors and the creation of bubbles, for instance in the real estate market in major cities.

There has been a major shift in reliance on local markets to an investment-driven development economy in the region. The economy has been rapidly modernized by the inflow of oil revenues and the promotion of development. The KRG's market intervention is minimal and the economy has become liberal and open and the private sector is relatively effectively operated. However, increased wages, inflation, the low work morale, discipline and productivity of the labor force, and irregularities in business practices have deteriorated the development and competitiveness of local production. The failure of the public employment program and the recent negative development in the form of the import of unskilled labor requires careful and serious measures to correct past mistakes. The universities have currently low academic standards. This is manifested in the massive import of consumer goods and the local engineers' lack of ability to produce the simplest products locally.

National Development Policy

The national development policy must aim at promoting national competitive advantages. The vision should build upon a national consensus to establish the basic directions and paradigms for sustainable economic development. After the initial goals and strategies are established, the regional government should construct a system to create the opportunities to strengthen capacity and to form an optimal environment to develop the economy. The current strong import-oriented economy and the opportunity for local firms to cooperate with foreign firms, despite it harmful effects, should be used to foster the rapid acquisition of technology and management capability. The recent years of the intensive use of information technology ease technology transfer and cooperation. The globalization of economic and technological activities also offers both challenges and opportunities requiring a higher social, technical and leadership competency.

It is better to adopt a multi-channel policy approach in obtaining new technology from external sources. Increased investment in education, to promote competition among the universities and to minimize state control and interventions in the administration of universities should be given a high priority. Other measures include investment programs to improve conditions for small and medium enterprises and to create an FDI-friendly business environment. Priority should be given to the information industry and its use not only in communication and production areas but also in the formation of E-government in the provision of public services. The KRG must succeed in its different reform programs, to reduce the outflow of capital, to increase the inflow of capital, to promote reliance on domestic resources, and to concentrate its capability in the key institutions and in the productive sectors.

D. Water Policies and Incentives

Pricing Water

Water is a utility that is not priced in the Kurdistan Region. However, the households pay on a monthly basis a symbolic sum that is far from covering the cost of the water supply. Pricing water can have a number of important functions.[39] First, it is expected to cover the cost of the supply of water. Second, it promotes incentives for reducing the excessive consumption of water, reducing the gap in water supply in urban areas. Third, the reduced consumption in turn leads to a reduced quantity and cost of wastewater management. Fourth, water saving technology will be developed that together with improved awareness is good for the environment. Fifth, reduced consumption of water combined with increased public awareness reduces the public cost of water provision and investment in provision capacity building. Finally, price is the main instrument in equating supply and demand and in particular reducing the costly excess supply for the state and municipalities. More benefits can be encountered linked to pricing water.

There is a desire to introduce a water price system to reduce the consumption of water and foremost to cover its production and distribution costs. Not-for-profit organizations supplying public goods often charge prices that cover their cost without expecting any profit, i.e. charging a price level that exceeds their production costs. However, the price in addition to covering production cost must be determined so that it covers necessary investments to improve upon the future supply of water. In for-profit organizations, price settings are different from the public producers and such that they maximize profits, as is their objective. Since water is a public good, so far no such market has existed in the Kurdistan Region.

In Iraq and the Kurdistan Region public utilities like fixed phone, electricity, water, health care and education were almost free and provided by the state. In recent years as a result of the privatization of several utilities and deregulations of the market segments, several services are priced like wireless telecommunications, private electricity, hospitals and

---

[39] There is comprehensive literature on pricing water. The research includes water pricing for sustainability (Grafton and Kompas, 2006), prices vs rationing (Grafton and Ward, 2007), water tariff and development (Lee, 2005), irrigation water policy in China (Hwang et al., 2008) and demand-price relationship (Xayavong et al., 2008).

university education. In the area of education, health and electricity the emergence of a private market is a result of the temporary or persistent shortage of public sector capacity. The state's inability as a supplier is taken advantage of by the private sector to utilize new business opportunities. The business sector, through its influence and participation in politics, has been able to influence economic policies and regulations. Lack of a corporate taxation system and strong regulations may explain the integrated nature of politics and business.

An effective pricing system has already been introduced in the telecommunications area where the suppliers are private companies. The telecommunications payment system and regulations could serve as a model to introduce a pricing system in the water area. In order to introduce prices and to account for the quantity of water consumed, investment in infrastructure for measurement and billing is required. In addition a trusted and well-functioning banking system is needed to operate the pricing and billing payments successfully.

The main consumers of water are the rural and urban household population, farms, industries and municipalities. The water sources are wells, springs, rivers and dams. It seems that it is not possible to apply a single pricing system to all categories of consumers and sources of water. The needs and water access conditions differ among the users. For instance households use treated water, while industry may use both treated and untreated water and the farmers use river water for irrigation and springs and groundwater for human and animal consumption. The dams are used for irrigation, hydropower generation and environmental concerns.

Here the aim is not to give any numbers concerning the pricing of water, but rather to elaborate on the determinants of water price and to bring the important factors to be taken into account to the attention of decision-makers. These factors are crucial in the design of a fair and environmentally-effective pricing policy of water resources and its sustainability in supportiveness to the regional development program. A water pricing team should be set up consisting of representatives of different consumer groups, suppliers including the state, municipalities and banking to work out a pricing system that is based on production costs and environmental concerns. The price should vary across users and be progressive and positively related to the level of consumption. Necessary investment in infrastructure and rules and regulation also need to be suggested. The payment system with discounts should be linked with opening an account like a salary account for public and private employees at a bank to encourage household-bank relationships.

Experience in Water Management

The water price team should take advantage of the experience in pricing policies and their impacts from other countries and in particular those in Australia with intensive research on water prices. Below we present a number of such studies investigating the impacts of water conservation policies and their impacts on water consumption, crop production, national food security, farmers' income and the extent of pollution. These can serve as a starting point for the consideration and selection of appropriate price policy measures for the Kurdistan Region and the indications about the Ministry's expectations about their impacts on consumers' water use behavior and environment.

For instance in the area of "irrigation externalities: pricing and charges" the report by the Australian Government, Productivity Commission is excellent guidance. In this report (Dwyer et al., 2006), the commission presents the results of research undertaken in 2005. It is water policy research including the modeling of regional economic impacts of changes in water trade within the southern Morray-Darling Basin. The research is aimed at assisting the implementation of the national water initiative, "rural water use and the environment: the role of market mechanisms". It focuses on water use efficiency and the feasibility of market mechanisms to address water-related environmental externalities. The key findings are: externalities associated with irrigation water supply and use are complex and the links with environmental changes and their effects are difficult to measure and understand, many factors influence the effect of a charge or tax on water on changes in water use, environmental externalities should be defined carefully, externality taxes make the costs of negative externalities transparent, a tax on water use may increase economic efficiency of water use, and finally the authors mention that challenges in implementing an externality tax are many.

Xayavong et al. (2008) is another study which provides insights into the importance of water price in promoting water conservation. The authors use Australian suburb data from 1995 to 2005 to estimate the water demand model and the elasticity of water demands in Perth. In the estimation of price, the marginal price is derived from the block tariff structure. The objective is to make the water price an effective tool for water demand management by increasing the price elasticity of demand. The key findings include: a higher price elasticity of demand than previously estimated and the non-price controls (sprinkler restriction, water wise rebate program and bores) have worked well in promoting water conservation. Several factors beyond the control of the water authority, such as the household income and size, housing characters and size, demographic factors and climate conditions also have influenced water use.

An economic analysis of water conservation policies in Texas, USA, is conducted by Taylor et al. (2007). It compares a range of scenarios from no restriction on irrigation for sixty years with three conservation policies: a 10% reduction in irrigated acreage, a 50% reduction in water pumped and used, and a 100% reduction in water use. The aim is to determine the effectiveness of each policy in conserving water and on the crop mix and outcomes. The effects are in the form of a shift from irrigation to non-irrigation heterogeneous by the location and extent of the reduction plan. In a similar study Schmitz (2002) measures the inefficiency in the presence of export taxes, import tariffs and state trading enterprises as domestic policy tools to regulate the Turkish cotton market through support programs like water, fertilizer and credit subsidies. Empirical results suggest that the inefficiency is small. Lee (2005), in studying water tariff and development in Malaysia, examines the extent of water subsidy and its impact to ensure affordable access by low-income households in rural areas at some states. Investments for upgrading or replacing the existing water infrastructure and organization reforms of the water sector are among other policy measures to improve the service quality.

Huang et al. (2008) studied the effects of irrigation water pricing in rural China. Results suggest that water pricing policies have great potential for curbing demand and addressing the emerging water crisis, but they also affect negatively food grain security and also have negative impacts on production and incomes. Thus an integrated package of policies is needed to achieve water saving goals without hurting rural incomes and national food security in the short run. The EU water framework directive has set up comprehensive criteria for water management, regulations, the pricing of full cost recovery, and polluter pays principles. Bazzani et al. (2002) quantify water demand and the optimal regulations and their impacts on water availability and prices of farm income in Italy. Results show that the adoption of a mix of pricing instruments related to crop rotation, water consumption and pollution improves the water policy efficacy.

The issue of urban water management including optimal price and investment policy under uncertainty and the role of urban water utility as a social planner is investigated in Hughes et al. (2008). Recent drought conditions across Australia have resulted in severe water restrictions in most capital cities. The current urban water shortages are indicative of a long-term trend of increasing urban water scarcity. This is deteriorated by the decline in inflows, increased demand driven by population growth and minimal addition to supply capacity. Effective demand management policies and optimal supply augmentation decisions are called for. The current demand management policy is predominately in the form of water restrictions to ration water in times of scarcity. It is inefficient and involves significant enforcement costs. The authors propose scarcity pricing as an alternative and more effective approach to the use of water restrictions. In the design of the model they account for extreme uncertainty surrounding future rainfall and dam inflows in a stochastic dynamic programming model of the urban water market.

Introduction of Recycle Deposits and Incentives

The Kurdistan Region faced a rapid change in the structure of the population and the process of urbanization. The comprehensive demographic changes and development programs resulted in a significant water shortage and also to the pollution of existing water resources. The social planners were not prepared for the changes and mismanagement of water resources was an unavoidable outcome. Inefficiency in the public sector, corruption, lack of knowledge and rules and regulations and the inability of policymakers to monitor the development led to massive polluting of nature. The lack of active national policies to manage the situation in an optimal way has given a free hand to businessmen to find their own way of providing drinking water. Even in the presence of marginal agriculture, water resources are highly polluted where the main contributor is the urban population.

The two main sources of pollution are the lack of a sewage system managed or, it would be more appropriate to say, not managed by the municipalities, and another is waste from drinking water and manufactured food packaging. The lack of a sewage system has led to the contamination of groundwater in the urban environment. The untreated groundwater is not likely to be safe as drinking water. The lack of education in managing waste (bottles, cans and packages) from drinking water and manufactured food has polluted the natural environment to a degree that is extremely unpleasant and the sign of a total failure by the public regulators. The Kurdish culture of picnic, dancing in the countryside and eating kebabs, combined with a lack of environmental consciousness have had a devastating effect on the countryside.

The policy-makers should introduce a system of recycle deposits around 20-25% of the value of drinking water, soft drink cans and bottles to encourage consumers to collect the waste. The amount, in addition to lowering the consumption of imported manufactured goods, will encourage the recycling of waste material with the help of both producers and consumers. The producers should be taxed to increase their incentives to use material more easily absorbed into nature. The recycling money can also be combined with fines for the violation of waste material regulations in public and private places. In Kurdistan it is prohibited to smoke in public places for health reasons, but not yet prohibited to pollute the countryside. It should not be a challenge to tax producers and encourage consumers to have a clean environment. Garbage collectors and signs are placed in all public places and managed by imported foreign unskilled labor, but the citizens are not yet accustomed to an urban life and consumption patterns.

Similar (importation tax and deposit added to price) incentives should be introduced to promote the collection and processing of other household and industry durable waste materials like cars, refrigerators, furniture, textiles, TV sets and computers and other electronic products, construction material, and the use of pesticides and fertilizers. These contaminate surface and groundwater sources with negative impacts on health and the environment. Waste material management and recycling policy has been difficult under the existing conditions of free trade which looks more like anarchy than free trade with clear regulations. The importing companies and exporters have no responsibility in the management of their production and distribution waste.

Media and Public Educational Programs

The Kurdish Media has developed quite fast without being combined with much active participation in public training and education. The main type of programs produced at the many satellite-based TV channels is entertainment in the form of Kurdish songs and dances and local news in the form of interviewing politicians and reporting about major regional government meetings with foreign visitors. The media channels lack social programs related to family, health, education, environment and public and social participatory activities. A similar situation is present in the areas of newspapers and magazines with low quality and effort concerning public educational programs.

The low education and skills in the production of socio-economic and environmental programs has its roots in the past when Kurds were excluded from all education that had to do with the media. The Regional Government has made comprehensive investment in media facilities such Hawler Media Center with different advanced functions to produce necessary educational programs with stronger and desired effects. However, the establishment is not yet complete and it is expected that it will host all media channels and having strong impacts on the skills and abilities to produce social and educational programs. The concentration of media in the Hawler Media Center will help in the transfer and spillover of technology to different media channels. It might be used for educational purposes as well as for a better environment.

Seasonal Neighborhood Cleaning Programs

In Scandinavia, it is a custom that on one Saturday in the Spring season and one in the Fall season all household members help in collecting waste material from public places and in their housing neighborhoods. This, in combination with general awareness on the advantages of having a clean environment and its maintenance, lead to an easy implementation of water and environment-related policies in a short time and with great perfection. This type of action could be implemented at no cost for the municipalities and include the teaching the citizens not to pollute their environment. The health and educational benefits of such actions especially for families with children, schools and the young generation could be enormous.

E. The Role of Water in Sustainable Development

Coordination of Water, Agriculture and Industry Activities

Water is an important resource in the current development program of the Kurdistan Region. In particular it is vital for household, construction, agriculture and segments of industry users. As mentioned previously, irrigation needs as a result of drought have increased but the size of farmed land has declined a lot, keeping the irrigation demands lower than before. A better coordination between the main users and stockholding public institutions and ministries should be a main objective of any future and successful water policies.

On the other hand the population increase and its concentration in urban areas has generated excessive and new demands for water and recreation, which to a large extent must be transported or diverted from distances to high population density areas. Lack of a sewage system and no or inadequate wastewater treatment plants have deteriorated the conditions for the groundwater usage in highly populated areas.

The industry, though still in its infant stage, has expanded very fast and diversified. Two of the main areas of industrial use of water are the industrial processing of drinking water and another is in construction. The expansion of the market for drinking water is due to the contamination of ground and surface water, the general increased income and better welfare, increased local production capacity for drinking water and soft drinks and population concentration in areas lacking clean spring, surface and groundwater.

Changes in the area of construction and the building up of public infrastructure are a result of increased population and its needs for housing and public services facilities. Increased oil revenues and their generous use in transfers and land allocation and public infrastructure investment in building roads, bridges, institutions, universities, hospitals, schools, housing blocks and recreation areas have all contributed to the increasing trend in the use of water and a greater imbalance in supply and demand.

Equality in Distribution of Investment Resources

The development in the Kurdistan Region in the areas of construction and development infrastructure has in recent years been enormous. The concentration has been in a few cities, primarily in Hawler, Sulaimanyah and Duhok. A few other places in relation to education investment like Koya have benefited from the boom. Many other smaller cities are more or less excluded from taking advantage of the situation.

There are several reasons for the inequality in distribution of development in the Kurdistan Region. One is the dual party system with headquarters in Hawler and Sulaimanyah where their main administration has been placed. The concentration of main offices in these two cities and attachment of defense, security and management to the two places has led to the expansion of needs for housing, offices and other development services to meet their needs. In addition on each side 21 ministries and the President's and Prime Minister's offices have been established. All these have led to the rapid expansion of the two cities at the cost of other cities' development. After their integration Sulaimanyah's development reduced in speed, while Hawler is expanding massively as all governance, organizations' and corporations' main offices has gradually moved to Hawler.

There is no doubt that an unequal share of the development budget is allocated to the rural areas and small cities. There are no studies which have been conducted about the distribution and development potential of rural areas in the aftermath of the decline of the agricultural sector and about how to reverse the negative development trend. Not many labor market institutions have been established in Kurdistan.

Such institutions are necessary to plan and implement active labor market policies, to evaluate their effectiveness and to initiate necessary reform programs. The institutions include inter alia, primary and other labor market organizations, research institutes, supervisory authorities, trade and investment promotion agencies, welfare, education and job market training-oriented authorities.

Thus, one possible area of creation of employment and development opportunities in smaller cities can be realized by the placement of job market training programs before they take off and like everything else are placed at Hawler. These smaller cities have the advantages of having plenty of low cost spaces for housing and education where different short and long term training programs for civil servants and private sector business can be easily organized.

Separation of Politics-Public-Private Relationships

Previously we emphasized that in addition to a development strategy and economic plan, the introduction of comprehensive firm and household taxation is necessary to smooth the flow of public revenues, to reduce inequality, to redistribute income and to create a strong financial base for the provision of public services. Such a system will also enhance the households' incentives and their awareness of the national interest. The taxation and redistribution policy should include a blend of different policies.

The selection and effectiveness of policies will depend on the characteristics of the market organization and the structure of different public institutions. Public institutions should be supportive and not create problems in the form of bureaucracy, corruption and inefficiency. In particular, changes in the current and unsound politics-public-business relationships are preconditions for the success in the mission and in the achievement of the expected positive policy impacts. Water policy must be equally subject to such relationships and their negative effects of policy outcomes.

It is amazing that a public sector consisting of so many employees and consuming a major part of the total public budget in salaries has been created without an assessment of need, and with job announcements, job descriptions, job interviews and competition. The system has led to the wrong people being placed in the wrong places and making the wrong decisions, adding to low capability in running the public sector and the provision of public services. The politics of the nomination of employees for the reason of trust and relationships rather than based on their working abilities is the main source of the inability, inefficiency, deteriorated self-sufficiency, disorganization and corruption in the public sector.

F. Capability and Skill Upgrading

Education, Wages and Productivity of Labor

Currently there are no labor market statistics available that cover the Region of Kurdistan. A lack of basic statistics does not allow for the quantifying of the magnitude of unemployment and to analyze its socio-economic impacts.

The high dependency of the Kurdish society on foreign labor in building up public infrastructure is a direct result of the low quality of education. Despite significant employment opportunities in the construction sector, local labor has been unable to seize the opportunities. Many of the main employers like construction companies, airports, hotels, restaurants and even municipalities are hiring foreign low-skilled workers in services where local labor is not willing to take jobs. The generous public employment policy has also resulted in a misallocation of resources, a low pay-off for education, encouraged laziness, raised expectations, and lowered the work morale and active participation in the development process.

The low quality of education is a result of a long period of a lack of resources, ineffective organizations, rapid expansion and the mismanagement of higher education. The education system produces graduates that are not trained, creative or technologically upgraded to provide self-sufficiency in a skilled workforce. The low quality of the workforce, together with low incentives and combined with low morale at work, are the responsible factors for the low levels of productive employment in the region. Since 2003 significant resources have been allocated to universities but the outcome of such investment in the form of production and administrative capability is negligible and has not been evaluated yet.

The wage levels should be determined by the labor productivity. Currently, the wage level is in non-parity with the labor productivity level. It negatively influences prices, employment and production. The informal employment procedures and generous sharing of oil revenue for wages are other factors that have contributed to the increase in the wage level and lowered competition. Since job openings are available mostly in the public sector, wage setting might be a reflection of favoritism rather than skills or education. In such a system, education is not a factor of qualification, rather a degree to legitimize the occupation of a job that the candidates have no skills for.

The labor productivity is very low because of low skilled labor, an inappropriate employment system, low morale at work, and misplacement of the workforce. Low labor productivity combined with a high public employment rate and wages is one of the main sources of the high inflation rate that negatively affects economic development. Thus, low labor productivity and a high wage rate are two main factors affecting negatively investment decisions. They not only prevent the inflow of FDI but also promote the outflow of domestic capital. The effects of the above factors on water resources is, among others, higher projects cost, delays in project implementations and a higher dependency on a foreign skilled and unskilled workforce.

Labor Market Policy Measures and Incentives

An active and effective labor market policy for the region should incorporate a number of policy measures. Here we limit ourselves to the measures that are deemed sufficient in the short-term to introduce major improvements to the function of the market. The most urgent step to be taken is to formulate a general labor market policy program for the region. A number of policies measures as part of such program are described below.

It is obvious that there is a shortage of experts at every stage of decision-making and levels of organization and institutions in the Kurdistan Region. The present higher education system is unable to train experts in different fields. There is a need to reform higher education to produce skills that correspond to society's needs. One could take advantage of the experience gained from the reform of education in transition economies.

The existing student aid program might have positively affected the enrolment rate in higher education, but has not necessarily enhanced working ability. Introducing elements of merit scholarships to promote and reward academic achievement and investment in human capital could improve this program. The higher education capacity in Kurdistan has also increased significantly in recent years. Given the shortage of skilled teachers, a workforce and experts, in the short-term repatriation of Kurdish experts from industrialized countries constitutes a main source to utilize.

In addition to the reform of higher education, significant investment in human capital should be made to improve the capability of creating new jobs. The process requires careful planning and enormous resources. Fortunately, sufficient resources have already been allocated to higher education. It is a matter of a change in attitudes and behaviors and a reallocation of resources to more needed education and training programs. More emphasis should be given to creativity and technology capability. Several incentives to promote a positive development in the private sector, such as youth training, placement programs, wage subsidies, tax rebates, credit guarantees and business startup support programs should be introduced.

It is necessary to establish the needed labor market institutions as soon as possible. Close cooperation between different institutions and the labor market actors is a prerequisite for the success of labor market programs. Care should be taken to minimize the risk that the established institutions result in a bureaucratic system, which develops into an expensive and complex project, binding most of the region's resources. A parallel reduction in the size of public employment is needed to reduce bureaucracy and for a better use of public resources in economic development.

Skill Upgrading and Training of Civil Servants

The job market in a modern economy is constantly facing a transformation process characterized by the destruction of old and the creation of new jobs. As a result, jobs in sectors with old technology producing goods not demanded, having low quality and being non-competitive are destroyed or outsourced to countries with productive but low cost labor. The rise of a knowledge-based economy has generated a new global infrastructure with information and telecommunications technology (ICT) playing an increasingly important role. In most countries the education system has expanded and new institutions have been established. Higher education must improve its administrative efficiency and competitiveness in response to demands from government, business and industry. Government plays a key role in enhancing the interaction between the government and the private and the education sectors.

Despite an increased number of universities, massive public investment in education and expanded capacity to produce education, the Kurdistan Region has never been more dependent on the import of human resources and imported goods previously produced locally.

Modernization of the education system and its competitiveness and compliance with a modern economy and world is thus a prerequisite for balanced and sustainable economic development. It is important to evaluate and discuss the issue of reform and modernization of the education system. It should be done by reviewing the reform process and evaluating the outcomes from the transition economies.

Nowadays, the standards are set by technologically capable and cost effective countries. No society can maintain competitiveness in the long run without the ability to import, understand, adopt, modify and create technology. In short capability, creativity, productivity, competitiveness and exchange are preconditions for a sustainable economic development. The Middle-East model of development, based on the massive export of oil and the import and distribution of commodities with simultaneous and systematic destruction of their own technology as an outcome, is not a sustainable approach to development.

The massive import of goods and labor is an indication of a significant mismatch in the education produced and skills needed in the labor market in the region. Thus an improved system, matching education and skills is necessary for the economy to function effectively. The educational system is expected to prepare the workforce in the Kurdish society for internal creation and external competition. An extended mismatch will result in the low competitiveness of the economy and increased unemployment and loss of welfare. Thus, policymakers and planners have a crucial role in the allocation of scarce resources.

The Ministry of Water Resources cannot be very different from other public institutions concerning the employees' capability and performance. They need to upgrade their skills to improve their abilities to do their job. Steps in a direction to face the challenges mentioned above can be taken in part through a training initiative from the Ministry of Labor and also in part by the Ministry of Water Resources through in-house training of its employees. This is crucial to the identification of society's needs and the formulation of water policies that satisfies those needs and in addition it maximizes the benefits and minimizes the costs associated with the implementation of the Ministry's policies.

7.10. RESOURCES NEEDED AND COSTS OF IMPLEMENTING THE POLICIES

We have elaborated in many places of this report on the importance of having a specific regional water policy. In this chapter we have discussed the components of a new water resources plan and policies for the Kurdistan Region. The new plan and policies are multi-dimensional and must fulfill the need and expectations of all users and sources as well as correspond to the socio-economic sustainable development of the region accounting for the balance in nature.

In the first part of the chapter we discussed public infrastructure and investment in development and water resources, followed by a presentation of the water laws and regulations in the past and now. The need for water resources statistics and quality monitoring are also elements that must be emphasized under the existing conditions of the intensive use of development resources and the harm that nature can be exposed to.

We have suggested a large number of measures for having a strong and effective water plan and policy. One group of measures involved the production of periodical and serial publications on water resources. Another important area of activities is that of the annual forecast of supply and demand for water using different methods incorporating all users and sources of water. The role of water prices and cost-benefit analyses of government interventions is crucial for the success of the measures.

The realities of economic development in the Kurdistan Region with reference to the job market and training, economic plan and policies, capacity building, development strategy and firm and household taxation and financial market functioning were discussed with reference to these factors' role in the design and implementation of the region's water plan and policies. We also discussed the issues of regional self-sufficiency and vulnerability in general and in the use of water resources in particular.

As elements of the new water plan and policies we pointed to several components. Firstly, data collection and management, research, publications and seminar activities are suggested. Secondly, laws and common pool relations referring to the proposed water law, setting up a legal team and monitoring the upstream and downstream water activities are mentioned. Third, concerning project evaluation and industrial development, we emphasize the importance and the cost-benefit analysis of public projects and their selection based on their social and economic impacts, as well as the policy of industrial development in general. Fourth, in regard to water policies and incentives we discuss the pricing of water, the introduction of recycle deposits and incentives, media and public educational programs, and seasonal neighborhood cleaning programs to reduce the pollutants. Sixth, the role of water in sustainable development is discussed by proposing a better coordination of activities of water, agriculture, industry and municipalities, as well as a more equal regional distribution of development resources. Finally, capability and skill upgrading are crucial measures in reducing the mismatch of education and skills needed, in increasing the productivity of labor and in skill upgrading and the training of civil servants to achieve the objectives.

In the design, selection and implementation of any of the above measures a comprehensive cost-benefits analysis should be conducted and the most preferred alternatives from a social point of view selected. This should include the use of government controls to soften the impact of policy measures like price changes. In any case, the benefit of government actions must exceed the costs.

To the best of our ability we have tried to point to a number of problems and limitations and suggest alternative approaches to solve them. Lack of data, time and capable human resources with field expertise to provide a detailed study of all policy measures suggested and incentives provided above makes it impossible for us at this stage to calculate any cost and benefits associated with each of the measures. Therefore we leave the choice of suitable measures among the suggested set and estimation of their possible impacts, benefits and costs to the Ministry of Water Resources to be undertaken by its engineers as they emerge at needed.

7.11. Summary of Water Resources Plan and Policies

As part of a new plan and policies we discuss a number of integrated areas. First, public infrastructure and investment in water resources area are discussed. Second, water resource laws and regulations concerning the past, present and those desired are discussed. Third, water resource statistics and quality monitoring is reported. Fourth, the introduction of periodical and serial publications on water resources is proposed. Fifth, these are used in the estimation and dissemination of the annual forecast for supply and demand for water. Sixth, the realities of economic development in the region are described. Seventh, the issue of self-sufficiency and vulnerability in the use of water resources is elaborated on. Eighth, elements of a new water resources plan and policies are proposed, and finally the resources needed and costs to implement the policies are discussed.

Public Infrastructure for Development

Development in the areas of infrastructure in general and investments in water resources in particular in the Kurdistan Region has been impressive. This is true concerning the development in the last two decades as a result of increased local self-governance, globalization of knowledge, technologies and economies. The regional government paid special attention to attracting foreign direct investment to the region. The inflow has been different in distribution among locations and sectors. Investment in services, recreation and tourism has been significant which concerns water resources. In parallel these foreign investments have promoted public complementary investment by the regional government in airports, dams, irrigation and water supply projects and education as the infrastructure for development.

The establishment of the Ministry of Water Resources in 2006 is to be considered as an important investment in development infrastructure. It reflects the desire of the Regional Government to address the severe problems of water resources facing the region. The most important challenges are the problem of water scarcity, providing clean drinking water to communities, the creation of a sewage system network in urban areas, sewage treatment and the overall management of water resources including combating the environmental degradation of the depletion of water resources.

Existing Water Laws, Regulations and Monitoring Quality

Water is a vital resource and managing water resources and the way of using them is very important for human beings. It is important to promote the high quality of water and to prevent a shortage of water in the future, especially taking into account factors impacting global water resources. Most countries have different laws such as those of environment and water. In Kurdistan these two institutions are separated. The laws of water are to regulate all issues related to supply and demand, the relationship between consumer and providers, and the obligations of the regulators. Few objectives of these laws are listed in this chapter.

There are several general goals and strategies of water resources which are to enhance the efficiency in the use and management of water. These include: increasing the rate of water, improving the quality of water, assuring the availability and continuity in the flow of water resources, improving irrigation techniques, and finally flooding prevention and management. Irrigation is one of the most important topics in research on water and is heavily regulated. Concerning the content of the Iraqi laws of irrigation and the role of the Ministry of

Agriculture, the regulations and guidelines are old and not modified to correspond to current conditions and needs.

Databases are fundamental to the regulation and development activities of established institutions and their functions. The availability of specialized databases is necessary in each ministry in the region. Most of the ministries are attempting to establish data collection and analysis sections. Ministry of Water resources is one of the ministries that need to create databases to monitor and evaluate factors and events that affect water resources. Thus access to data is necessary to have good management of water. Updating statistics is another step toward regulation. Data is also a precondition for forecasts.

Basic water quantity monitoring activities in the region are performed for the groundwater and drinking water distribution systems. Water quality sampling collection must be run continuously using proper methods and advanced laboratories. Financial resources are available to purchase such equipment to prevent epidemics. A water quality network should be established in the region for different types of monitoring. These networks must be developed for each source of water. After the specific monitoring plan is established, water quality data should be collected and evaluated.

Utilities are developing new water-saving equipment which is extremely important in drought years. There are several potential benefits of water and cost saving equipment including: energy saving, wastewater reduction, cost reductions, and protection of environment. In addition attempts should be made to identify the nature and extent of supply and demand problems. Wastewater conservation methods should be given priority. The water conservation methods are applicable to a variety of urban residential, industrial, commercial, and government users. Recently, the General Directorate of the Ministry of Water Resources has presented suggestions to regulate water use.

Data, Research and Conference Activities

One of the main tasks of the Ministry of Water Resources should be the production of research, reports and statistics for multiple purposes. It is important to inform investors, the public and private sectors and the general population about the state of water resources in the region. Ideally the annual report should be complemented with publications on a regular basis. We have proposed publications of special research reports, monthly bulletins, quarterly reports, annual reports, and establishment of an informative web-site, research and statistics directorates, a library, and research funds as necessary measures to achieve these goals.

The water market in Kurdistan is still traditional and subject to little regulation. Here, like the goods market, the emergence of a market for water services is the process by which often public providers and buyers determine price and quantities and terms for its distribution. The public sector water agencies play a major role in the market. In the context of public policy application two general observations are that: water resources are limited and consumers may face water scarcity.

Public Water Project Procedures

This study is an economics-oriented study on how to cope with water scarcity and how to allocate limited water resources among competing requirements in Kurdish society. We use economic theory to explain behaviors in the market and to design models to provide the basis for predictions of supply and demand for water. The typical question is what determines the general price of water, supply, revenue and the effects of government policies on the market. Good water management depends on incentives to make people rational in their behavior. Thus economic principles can be used to assess access and use of water and to evaluate the effects of policies.

Cost-benefit analysis is a calculation and comparison of all costs and benefits associated with a given course of action like a water project. If benefits are greater than the costs, choices are made. Time and risks affect the costs and benefits of a choice. The method is useful in public project selection and decision-making. Water is a public good where the benefit is received by all members of the society. Government controls like excise taxes in the context of water is some form of water ransom. It also has social effects in the form of increased negative health effects, but also positive effects since it stabilizes the consumption and economy of households by reducing wastewater discharge.

Almost all economic activities have at some time been subject to some types of government regulations. Examples of regulatory agencies are various utility commissions, while examples of regulated industries are electricity, water and sewage. In the literature there is little research on why and how regulations happen, but the two strands of theories are public interest and economic theory of regulations. The public interest theory suggests that regulations improve the efficiency of the market. Improved managerial efficiency, increased competition, downsizing, and a cost-benefit analysis of public programs are measures to make the bureaucracy more efficient.

Forecasts of Supply and Demand for Water Resources

In order to forecast supply and demand for water resources we need information about the main sources and users of water resources. There are different ways that demand and supply can be predicted. These can be classified into parametric and non-parametric approaches. A simple non-parametric approach is where the supply of water resources is computed by adding the water sources, while the demand is a simple aggregation of the water users. The aggregation should be based on the latest information and adjusted for a number of factors like changes in population, land size, industry structure, uncertainties and risks, and the possible effects of water policies.

The two methods have their benefits and limitations. The non-parametric is simple and requires less data to predict supply and demand for water. It requires only the quantity of water by user and sources and an accounting for expected changes. The parametric approach has a number of benefits including: it allows the estimation of effects of policies on the demand and supply of water, it accounts for causation and direction of effects, it allows for identification of factors and their effects, and it uses statistics to construct confidence intervals for estimated effects and predicted values.

Self-Sufficiency and Vulnerability

The current states of a number of factors that are vital to the development of Kurdistan Region are investigated. These include the labor market, mismatch of education and skills, technology resources and several other factors like an economic development plan and policy, reconstruction capacity building, inflow of investments, the industrial development model and macro-economic policy These factors directly or indirectly affect the water policy of the regional government. A lack of basic statistics does not allow quantification of the magnitude of any indicators to analyze the socio-economic effects of public water policies. Most of the data used for completion of this project are raw data, of a multipurpose nature, but not properly classified or checked for consistency.

Self-sufficiency is extremely low in the region in almost all areas of economics, technology and management. The education system produces graduates that are not trained, creative nor technologically upgraded to provide self-sufficiency in a skilled workforce. The low quality of the workforce together with low incentives, low morale at work and in business, and the dominance of private interest over national/regional interests are the responsible factors for the low levels of productive employment and negligible degree of self-sufficiency.

A strong emphasis should be placed on the transfer of technology, skills and management as basic conditions for the provision of investment incentives. These are vital for the capability to develop the region's economy and to attain a higher degree of self-sufficiency. The flow of oil revenues to the region has affected the trade balance negatively. The development has been destructive to local production and in particular in the agriculture area. Kurdish society is very vulnerable concerning basic needs. Development approaches in newly industrialized countries can serve as a base to improve self-sufficiency. Policymakers should support indigenous sources of development. The creation of conditions for low and smooth bureaucratic controls is crucial for business development.

New Challenges in Management of Water Resources

Kurdistan is rich in water resources. The existing few dams were used mainly for the better management of water and for the generation of electricity and irrigation downstream. Within the region, irrigation was facilitated by traditional diversion techniques. In recent years several factors have changed in regard to water demand, supply and self-sufficiency. The changes include drought, diversion of water upstream, changes in population structure, declining production in agriculture, the establishment of new industries, old dams, and small shifts in agriculture towards an intensive form, such as greenhouses and aquaculture and recreation. The changes have resulted in a lower demand for irrigation, but a higher demand for urban consumption, recreation facilities and construction. It is hard to produce an estimated demand and supply and to compute changes in self-sufficiency.

What is a relatively new phenomenon that affects the degree of self-sufficiency is the water diversion and drought. The intensive water diversion activities upstream, in Turkey and Iran, are the most serious changes and violations of international water laws. These are very likely to be multipurpose such as for the long-term development of their economies by a better and effective management of water, as well as imposing political pressure on Kurdistan by limiting the discharge of water. Regardless of drought and water diversion activities, the rapid increase in the urban population in cities like Hawler and Sulaimanyah requires comprehensive investment in infrastructure to supply water to these locations.

New Water Plan and Policies

In the proposal for a new water plan and policies we are able to propose the key elements, namely data, research and publications, laws and common pool relations, project evaluations, water polices and incentives, the role of water in sustainable development and capability and skill upgrading. Each ministry in the Kurdistan region should have two directorates working with statistics and research. Their functions will be determinants for the achievement of the goals of the Ministry of Water Resources. The research produced can assist to create a regional strategy and plan with a great impact on the organizational structure, activities and performance of the ministry and its collaborative activities.

The Middle East is a region characterized by scarce water resources and rapid population growth. Water scarcity is increasing and expanding in the region. The scarcity in Kurdistan is a result of neighboring countries divergence of water, changes in population structure and concentration and climate changes. It is important to investigate the economic, social and water resource conditions to propose measures to enhance the effectiveness in water use to reduce the shortages and their effects. Water is considered as a binding constraint on sustainable future economic and social development in the region. A water law will be of great help for strategies to manage water resources and joint regional water planning.

Legal Water Resources Team

The Kurdistan Region and Kurds were in the past excluded from certain types of education. Given their limited capacity in the areas of international law it is important to build up legal capacity. Legal capacity is needed to cover a number of areas such as in the use of weapons of mass destruction, the Anfal massacre, forced migration, the massive destruction of villages, the rights to the use of one's own natural resources, oil and gas revenue sharing and common pool water resources. The best legal team could be composed of a number of experts in different fields covering: contracts, business, environment, natural resources, finances, common pool water resources, military intervention, international law, the UN Security Council's work, international tribunals, the European court, minority rights, human rights and genocide. The team members could be foreign experts assisted by local experts. The establishment of such a team reduces the costs of making mistakes.

The work of the legal team could be related to the past, present and future. The first category is in the form of systematic investigation, documentation and preparation of cases for the regional government to submit cases to international courts concerning violations of minority rights, genocide, massacres of civilian, destruction of properties, and forced migration exercised against Kurds. The current cases could be related to oil and gas, common pool water resources, militarily interventions, reclaiming land and properties following forced migration, relocation of families subject to forced migration, oil revenue-sharing, implementation of the constitution and laws, the rights of Kurdish minorities in majority Arab populated regions, power sharing at the central government level, aviation, transportation, etc. The future issues involve protection against all violations encountered above plus the Kurds right to self-determination in accordance with international law.

Governance and Water Resources

Public projects regardless of the investment amount should be evaluated in respect to their costs and benefits. The method is called cost-benefit analysis for decision-making in the worthwhile implementation of a project. The costs and benefits are an aggregate of the net present or discounted values. Examples of public projects in the water areas are: the construction of dams, irrigation projects, production of hydropower, national parks, pollution control and wastewater management. To each of these projects different sets of costs and benefits are associated. The ability of researchers and the degree of carefulness in the calculations determine how far researchers can go along identification, quantification and accounting for different benefits and costs.

Kurdistan is an underdeveloped region with the potential to catch up with its neighbors. It should adopt an industrial strategy of self-sufficiency. To industrialize in a short time, the regional government must draw up a series of economic plans. Initially, the government should build up effective service-providing institutions, mobilize resources, protect infant industry, allocate credits, provide administrative guidance and publish forecasts seasonally. The introduction of firm and household taxation is necessary for a smooth flow of public revenues, reducing inequality, redistribution of income and provision of public services. Demand promotion policies are available instruments to protect the home market and local production. Public institutions should be supportive and solve rather than create problems in the form of bureaucracy, corruption and inefficiency.

Region-Specific Water Policies and Incentives

Water is a utility that is not priced in the Kurdistan Region. However, households pay on a monthly basis a symbolic sum that far from covers the cost of the water supply. Pricing water can have a number of important functions: to cover the cost of supply, to promote incentives for reducing water consumption and water gap, it reduces the quantity and costs of wastewater management, water saving technology will be developed, the investment in capacity is reduced, and price is the main instrument in equating supply and demand. A pricing system implemented elsewhere could serve as a model for introducing a pricing system in the area of water. In order to introduce prices and to account for the quantity of water consumed, investment in infrastructure for measurement and billing is required. In addition a well functioning banking system is needed to operate the policy reform successfully.

The Kurdistan Region has faced a rapid change in the structure of population and urbanization. The comprehensive demographic changes and development programs resulted in the shortage and pollution of water resources. Inefficiency in the public sector, lack of knowledge, rules and regulations and the inability to monitor the development has led to massive pollution of nature. The two main sources of pollution are the lack of a sewage system and waste from drinking water and manufactured food packaging. The policy-makers should introduce a system of recycling deposits to encourage the consumers to collect the waste. The producers should be taxed to increase their incentives to use material friendly to the environment. Import tax incentives should be introduced to promote the collection and processing of other household and industry waste materials. Media could be used for educational purpose and a better environment and the public should participate in seasonal neighborhood cleaning programs.

Water is an important resource in the current development program of the region. In particular it is vital for the household, construction, agriculture and industry users. A better co-ordination between the main users will be one main objective of any future and successful water policies. The development in the Kurdistan Region in the areas of construction and development infrastructures has been enormous. The concentration has been in a few cities, primarily in Hawler, Sulaimanyah and Duhok. Many small cities are excluded from taking advantages of the development. There is inequality in the distribution of development and there is no doubt that an unequal share of the development budget is allocated to the rural areas. One possible area of creation of employment and development opportunities in smaller cities can be placement of job market training programs and water projects.

The labor market, its institutions and training programs in the region is not developed. The job market in a modern economy is constantly facing a transformation process characterized by the destruction of old and the creation of new jobs. Government plays a key role in enhancing the interaction between the government and the private and the education sectors to smooth the transformation. Despite an increased number of universities, massive public investment in education and expanded capacity, the Kurdistan Region has never been more dependent on the import of human resources and imported goods previously produced locally. The Ministry of Water Resources cannot be different from other public institutions concerning capability and performance. Employees need to upgrade their skills to improve their ability to provide services.

We have elaborated in many places of this report on the importance of having a specific regional water policy. We have discussed the elements of a new water resources plan and policies for the region that are multi-dimensional and fulfill the need and expectations of all users and sources and correspond to the socio-economic sustainable development of the region. As elements of the new water plan and policies we pointed to several components such as: data collection and management, research, publications and seminar activities; laws and common pool relations; setting up legal teams and monitoring the upstream and downstream water activities; project evaluations and industrial development; suggested water policies and incentive; the role of water in sustainable development; coordination of activities of users of water; a more equal regional distribution of development resources; and capability and skill upgrading to achieve the objectives.

In design, selection and implementation of any of the above measures comprehensive cost-benefit analyses should be conducted and the most preferred alternatives from a social point of view selected. This should include the use of government controls to attain the desired impact of policy measures like price changes. Lack of data, time and capable human resources did not allow at this stage for the calculation of any costs and benefits associated with each of the measures. Therefore we left the choice of measures and the estimation of their impacts, benefits and costs to be undertaken as needed by the Ministry as they emerge.

Chapter 8

SUMMARY AND CONCLUSIONS
OF THE INTEGRATED WATER RESOURCES
MANAGEMENT IN THE KURDISTAN REGION

8.1. THE BACKGROUND AND OBJECTIVES

The Middle East is a region characterized by scarce water resources and a rapidly growing population. Water scarcity is increasing and expanding which makes water a binding constraint on the sustainable future economic and social development in the region. Improved efficiency in water use must be combined with the provision of new and additional water to minimize the shortage of water. In addition to being a source of conflict due to interconnected water resources, water is also a factor for promoting interstate co-operation. Economic, technical and regional water-sharing agreements can serve as instruments for conflict avoidance. Therefore, management of common pool water resources of the Middle East should be given more attention.

A comprehensive strategy for regional co-operation in the development and management of water resources, exchange of agricultural products, development of regional institutional arrangements, and joint regional water planning is both necessary and beneficial to all regional parties. The logic of collective action has already in several cases, like Israel-Jordan-Palestine, made it possible to develop co-operation in water issues. Institutional development is a binding constraint on the capacity to respond effectively to the water problem, but the energy-rich countries in the Middle East can afford to finance necessary water development projects.

The Kurdistan region in Northern Iraq is not an exception from the rest of the Middle East. Similar conditions apply to this region as well. Water scarcity is increasing and a is a binding constraint on economic and social development. The scarcity of water is a result of the neighboring countries' divergence of water, changes in population structure and concentration, climate changes, as well as the use of water in hydropower-based electricity generation. It is important to investigate the current economic, social and water resource conditions and alternative sources of water. Different measures are proposed to enhance the effectiveness in the use of water resources to reduce the shortages in supply and negative environmental effects.

This study examines the current economic practices of integrated water management in the Kurdistan region and suggests ways to change conditions to encourage the region's decision-makers to pursue sustainable resource development through interstate-KRG-consumers' co-operation. The project focused on:

- Making a comparative study of water resources in Iraq and its neighboring countries with the Middle East and North Africa (MENA) and the world averages.
- Conducting a sector analysis to identify and quantify available water resources, the needs and sub-optimality in their uses,
- Analyzing current allocation and quantifying and suggesting necessary reductions in the wasteful use of water resources,
- Designing water policies and suggesting measures that improve regional water planning and management practices,
- Developing techniques and models in the projection of demand, supply and future utilization patterns and quantification of the water gap,
- Suggesting alternatives for provision of water to areas facing scarcity on the basis of long-term and minimum cost solutions,
- Proposing economically and environmentally optimal practices of co-operation and resource management, and
- Suggesting opportunities for increased regional government investment in development of the water market.

This project is supported by the Kurdistan region's Ministry of Water Resources (MOWR). The University of Kurdistan Hawler (UKH) has supported the project by providing access to the university's research facilities and a number of its graduate students assisted, mainly with data collection. In addition to financial support, the MOWR has provided statistics, professional staff and other infrastructure resources. A preliminary version of the report was completed during July and August 2008 and presented at a workshop organized by the MOWR, but held at UKH on August 25 2008. The aim was to get views, comments and suggestions by experts in water resources. Several reviewers provided comments which are reflected in this revised version. This final report is to be used by the MOWR as a handbook for the efficient use of water resources, for policy analysis and in co-operation with Non-Governmental Organizations (NGO's) and in relationship with other users of common pool water resources in the region.

This report contained a number of chapters. Chapter 1 is an introduction to water resources and it states the objectives of this study. Chapter 2 is a comparative regional study of water resources. The performance of Iraq and its neighboring countries is compared with those of MENA and world averages. Chapter 3 is a review of the literature on water resources with a focus on planning, management, regulations and water policies. Chapter 4 is about the Kurdistan Region water resources in historical and regional perspectives. Chapter 5 is on the current state of water resources in the region. The emphasis is on the sources and quantities available. Chapter 6 presents the users of water resources. Finally, Chapter 7 presents a new water resources plan and policies. Here the focus is on factors crucial to the efficient management of water resources. Due to limited data resources and time, not all the objectives have been fulfilled, but necessary guidelines are provided to complete those in future. Each of the chapters is summarized below.

8.2. PREVIOUS RESEARCH ON WATER RESOURCES

One objective with this part of the study was to review international research on water resources. In particular it investigated the state of water resources at the regional level and the water management policies applied in the MENA region. The European Union (EU) water and landscape policy and efforts for a global agenda are reviewed and experience gained is used in the design of water policies for the Kurdistan region. Through studies of legal and common pool aspects, water policies, the determinants of a set of effective policies for water management are identified. Special attention is made to policies targeting major sources and users of water resources such as urban population, agriculture and industry. The areas studied are hydro-politics and water-sharing conflicts resolution, urban water management, price and investment policies, irrigation, and advantages of wastewater re-use. Alternative policies are suggested to remedy a number of problems facing the region.

The Water Framework Directive (WDF), which is European legislation designed to preserve, restore and improve the water environment, establishes a framework for managing the water environment by taking into account environmental, social and economic aspects. The directive uses an integrated multi-disciplinary approach based on geography, ecology, economics and sociology. The WDF was followed by the World Summit on Sustainable Development (WSSD) where the EU water initiative was launched. The initiative is designed as a model for future actions to contribute to meeting the Millennium Development Goals (MDGs) for drinking water and sanitation within the context of an integrated approach to water resource management. Addressing the water challenge is a key to sustainable development and reducing poverty. The complexity in EU water planning decisions is addressed by the MULINO project.

The review showed that the politics of water scarcity in relation to the few great waterways like the Nile, the Jordan and the Tigris-Euphrates in the Middle East is vast. The intensity of water conflicts can be exacerbated by the region's geographic, geopolitics or hydro-politic landscape. However, the region's ongoing multilateral peace negotiations show the principles for co-operative regional water management. The hydro-political tensions surrounding the Euphrates basin between Turkey, Syria and Iraq in the 1960s and 1970s and Turkish GAP project has been high. The measures in water resource disputes are divided into international water law, needs-based equity, and economic equity. The water laws only concern themselves with the rights and responsibilities of states. Political entities with water right claims like Kurds and Palestinians are not represented. In practice, claims for shared water rights are often based on geography or chronology.

The urban water supply in the region is often provided by a public supplier and the demand for the service is inelastic in price level. This characteristic of the market may encourage inefficient allocation of water. The regulator or social planner introduces water availability constraints due to shortages. The policy tools available are demand management and supply augmentation. The former involves prices, rationing, awareness campaigns and incentives for improving water use efficiency by restricting or reducing water use in times of scarcity. The latter policies are concerned with the nature and timing of additions to water inflows and storage capacity infrastructure. In the short-run the supply infrastructure is fixed and water consumption has an essential and a non-essential component. In the long run, it is possible to alter the supply infrastructures and there are possibilities to determine simultaneously both demand management and supply augmentation policies.

Agriculture accounts for a large total share of water use. There is large heterogeneity in the quantity and timing of water use by location and specialization. Irrigation has several externalities which change the environment. Many of the changes are associated with the intensive use of water in agriculture. Frameworks are developed for analyzing the characteristics of externalities incorporating its sources, how it is transmitted and its effects. These characteristics affect the solutions and the effectiveness of policy instruments. Government actions are costly in the form of policy development, administration, monitoring, enforcement and compliance with regulations. Government should intervene in the market only when the benefits from intervention outweigh the costs. The options for intervention include using or creating new markets, regulations and education, information, and price instruments such as taxes, charges and subsidies.

The use of fresh water in agriculture is becoming restricted and at the same time the supply of reclaimed sewage and other alternative sources from urban consumption is increasing. Agriculture, as a main user of water, is subject to competition with other users. Therefore, farmers have to rely on marginal water sources like recycled and saline water. One possible source of additional water is the use of wastewater. With minor environmental restrictions, urban wastewater can be utilized for agricultural irrigation and river rehabilitation. Regional planning models are developed to describe the economic, environmental and organizational aspects of sharing fresh and recycled wastewater among entities. The planning model determines the optimal crop mix and the optimal allocation of limited water and land resources among users.

Water models and methods are designed to solve problems that are often of a multi-disciplinary character, covering several disciplines such as agriculture, biology, technology, politics, economics, sociology, mathematics, statistics and information technology. The alternative sources are in general ground, surface and wastewater, while their uses are for household, agriculture and industries. The players in the market are mainly municipalities, consumers, farmers, business and regulators. There are a number of areas that the water economics literature emphasizes. The literature on irrigation is a main component. It elaborates on several sub-areas such as: irrigation technology adoption, groundwater conservation, drip irrigation, forecasting irrigation, agricultural sustainability and irrigation, and an estimation of the potential to reduce water demand for irrigation.

Among incentives and policies worth mentioning are: subsidized irrigation programs, irrigation system management, water management and water conservation policies, sewer surcharges and pollution control. The economic evaluation of the different aspects of water, technology adoption and effects of policy measures are intensively studied. Models are designed to estimate the optimal use of irrigation water, groundwater, irrigation and nitrogen, optimal and priority-based allocation of water sources to alternative uses. In addition the economic evaluation concerns an analysis of investment in alternative irrigation, diversion and distribution systems.

8.3. THE MENA REGION'S WATER CONDITIONS

Since a study of water resources in the Kurdistan region cannot be conducted without a linkage to the water resources in Iraq, a comparative study of the Iraqi and its neighbors' water resources was undertaken. The linkage to the rest of Iraq and neighboring countries is due to statistics, legal and common pool aspects, water policies as well as water management. The state of water in Iraq and among the neighbors (Turkey, Iran, Syria, Jordan, Kuwait and Saudi Arabia) is further compared with the averages for Middle East and the world.

The data used to illustrate the water resource conditions were obtained from the World Development Indicators Database 2006. The data covers the period 1960-2005 and it contains 39 economic indicators linked with water resources and environment. These are used for the general comparative analysis during the period 1981-2005. The indicators are grouped into several groups including: the major sectors' share of GDP, the arable land area and its utilization, population structure and its distribution, hydro-based electricity generation, international tourism, improved water sanitation and water resources, CO2 emissions and organic water pollutants, and different industrial sub-sectors' water pollution.

The results of the comparison suggest the presence of significant differences among the sample countries and changes over time. The heterogeneity is related to the land and population sizes of the countries and their agriculture, industrial and population structures. The countries' economies differ by the combination of population, agriculture, industry and services. Each of these sectors requires access to water resources differently. Agriculture uses water mainly for irrigation, industry for different production processes, while services use it for tourism and recreational activities. Turkey and Iran have economies based on a better balanced combination of industry and agriculture, while in Saudi Arabia and Kuwait oil-related industries dominate. The service sector in Turkey and Jordan are large. Ideally one should create a composite index to rank the countries in one single way.

The Iraqi economy is different from other economies in the region due to the decades of wars, sanctions, invasions and the lack of statistics. The data for Iraq, if available, covers mainly the period before the 2003 invasion period. It is reasonable to expect a significant deterioration in the living and water resource conditions in recent years. The general changes in the structure of the economy, major changes in the population structure, negligence of water resources and in particular the deteriorated water sanitation facilities and water pollutants are among causal factors to the deteriorated environmental and living conditions. Old and lacking regulations have not been helpful in improving the situation.

8.4. THE REGION'S WATER CONDITIONS
IN A HISTORICAL PERSPECTIVE

The Kurdistan region is rich in water resources and has highly fertile land. It has several sources of water that are used foremost in households and agriculture. The sources are classified according to four traditional categories: groundwater, surface water, dams and treated wastewater.

Groundwater is one of the most used water resources in Kurdistan. It is the major resource for drinking water and for other urban and rural life uses and is easily available in all parts of Kurdistan. Wells are the most used types of groundwater and are used by all the sectors in the Kurdistan Region. Hawler has the largest number of wells compared to other governorates. Using wells is not optimal environmentally but it is an easy and cheap method of providing water and permission is given generously. However, the groundwater resources in many places have been polluted by the household sewage system which has caused a great risk to public health.

Surface water is another common source of water in the Kurdistan Region. It is in the form of rivers and springs. The two main rivers are the Tigris and Euphrates. There are also several other smaller rivers and springs in the region. These are classified according to the governorates. Rain and snowfall is the main factor behind variations in the water levels in the rivers and springs. It affects their discharges. Lack of rain and snow in recent years has caused serious problems in the form of water shortages for the population.

A History of building dams dates back to early times. People created basins and reservoirs to meet their needs. Dams were used of save water in one season and use it in another season. Kurdistan is a mountainous region which means that it is suitable for constructing dams to preserve water. A number of dams were built in the past but existing dams are not constructed so as to cover all parts of the Kurdistan Region. There are only three large dams in Kurdistan which provide water to very limited areas. The capacity will be strengthened by another 8 uncompleted dams in the region whose construction is in progress. Dams are important for increasing domestic products and can be used for meeting the needs of different sectors and agriculture. Despite their positive effects, dams have negative environmental impacts on the landscape.

Treated wastewater is a fourth source of water. This method has not been developed yet in the Kurdistan Region. The government has a plan for saving wastewater that is used by households and in business and cleaning it to be reused. In addition, the treated water can be used for many different purposes, directly or indirectly. Using treated water has the advantages that it will reduce the groundwater usage. This method can help the region to solve partially its water shortage problem. The Kurdistan Region has faced a shortage of water due to the drought and use of treated wastewater in addition to being good environmentally it is an additional source of water for irrigation and groundwater recharge.

8.5. CURRENT STATE OF WATER RESOURCES IN THE REGION

The aim was to analyze the current state of allocation of water resources by water sources and water-using sectors. The focus is on the sources and the quantity available, the current allocation among users, the optimal or desired allocation, and estimation of in-optimal use or disequilibrium by each sector and its underlying causal factors.

The sources of water are divided into three main parts. The first source is dams. Despite their small number, they are considered to be one of the main sources of water by the restoration of water that can be used for different purposes. Other water resources are surface water and groundwater. Surface water includes rivers and springs and their quantities are measured through the discharge of the water. We have presented the quantity of rain and snowfall in each governorate over a 10-year period. The groundwater is from wells, the quantity of which is affected by the rate of rain and snowfall.

The users of water are households, industry, agriculture and municipality and services. The largest consumer of water is the household sector. Surface and groundwater are used by households. Irrigation in agriculture is not well-developed in Kurdistan and this is why agriculture is not the major consumer of water resources that it was. Improved irrigation will promote the degree of self-sufficiency in the region. The industry is another main category of consumer. It generally uses groundwater in production but the industrial sector is still at an infant stage and not very developed.

The optimal allocation of water differs from one sector to another. It is difficult to measure the optimal water use of agricultural and industrial sectors. In agriculture, we have only information about the land used for agriculture and potential land not yet farmed. Meanwhile, in the industrial sector, there is no optimal allocation as details about production capacity and plans are missing. We have only information about the maximum rate of water set for the industries. The optimal distribution to households is easier to compute and it depends on the size of population in each governorate.

The in-optimal distribution of water by sectors can be estimated as the gap between the optimal and current allocations of the sources by users. The degree of in-optimality can vary across users and over time. In other words, it indicates shortage or excess of supply of water resources faced by consumers. In the Kurdistan Region many factors affect the disequilibrium in water resources. These imbalances in water resources affect differently the different sectors such as households, agriculture, and industry. The quality of water in the Kurdistan Region is relatively high compared to other parts of Iraq. This is related to the geographical structure of Kurdistan.

8.6. MAIN CONSUMERS OF WATER RESOURCES IN THE REGION

The main consumers of water (households, industry, agriculture and municipalities and services) in the Kurdistan Region differ by characteristics and their share of total consumption and by the outcome of their uses of water in the form of negative direct and indirect externalities. The direct effects are in the form of the difference in quality of water before and after its consumption while the indirect effects are in the form of pollutants resulting from using water and crowding out other potential users.

The largest user in terms of numbers is households who use water for drinking, cooking, hygiene and other household activities. Households' consumption differs by location and is grouped into urban and rural areas. The rural inhabitants are closer to the source of water and unlikely to have access to water distribution and treatment systems. Despite the closeness to water sources and access to a greater quantity the quality of drinking water is often much lower than that in urban areas due to contamination and the lack of treatment facilities.

The agricultural sector is the second largest group in terms of number, but the sole largest in terms of water quantity usage. The sector uses water for drinking, animal husbandry and irrigation. The Kurdistan Region was mainly an agricultural society. The central government policy in the 70s and 80s led to a systematic destruction of rural life and speeded up the urbanization process. Thus there has been a rapid change in the agricultural sector and in the demography of the region. High wages, long-term investment perspectives, low-short term profitability, and speculative investment behavior in the booming construction sector, makes it impossible for agriculture to attract productive investment to the rural areas.

The industrial sector in the Kurdistan Region is small and in its infant stage but it is the third largest group which uses water in various production processes. The development of such an industry has been one of the priorities of the KRG whose activity, through its investment law and various incentive policies, promotes its growth. The main users of water resources related to industrial processes are those of cement, drinking water, construction and food processing. The construction industry might be the largest group. There is hardly any manufacturing industry in the region. Local production of materials used in construction and agriculture should be produced locally.

The last category of consumers, classified as the municipalities and other services like hotels and restaurants, is also a major consumer of water. The water by this category is used for the preservation of nature, for water security reasons, for recreation and tourism as well as for production of electricity. The first types of uses are related to environmental public investment. There have been comprehensive public and private investment programs in building up the necessary infrastructure for the development of the tourism industry. The capacity exists but the services are not utilized in an effective way. The reason might be a lack of experience, ineffective advertising and organization, excessive investment in an unknown area, and the issues of security and expensive service and transportation costs. The production of hydropower-based electricity is, however, a major user of water.

Different measures as part of public water policy to prevent or to reduce the magnitude of negative externalities and the role played by gender and its relationship with water management were also reviewed. Gender plays a major role in relation to the water supply, sanitation and activities that promote awareness of environment risks and protective actions taken to enhance the health of the family. Women's involvement in the decision-making process on water management in the Middle East is underrepresented due to cultural complexities and the limited influence by different society organizations.

8.7. WATER PLAN AND POLICIES AND RECOMMENDATIONS

As part of a plan and associated policies we discuss a number of integrated areas. First, public infrastructure and investment in the water resource area is discussed. Second, water resource laws and regulations concerning the past, present and those desired are discussed. Third, water resources statistics and quality monitoring is reported. Fourth, the introduction of periodical and serial publications on water resources is proposed. Fifth, these are used in the production and dissemination of annual forecasts for supply and demand for water. Sixth, the realities of economic development in the region are described. Seventh, the issue of self-sufficiency and vulnerability in the use of water resources is elaborated on. Eighth, a new water resources plan and policies are proposed, and finally the instruments and resources needed to implement the policies are discussed.

Development in the areas of infrastructure in general and investment in water resources in particular in the Kurdistan Region has been impressive. This was facilitated during the last two decades as a result of increased local self-governance. The regional government paid special attention to attracting foreign direct investment to the region. The inflow in services, recreation and tourism has been significant and this concerns water resources. In parallel complementary public investment has been undertaken by the regional government in dams, irrigation and water supply projects and education as the infrastructure for development. The establishment of the Ministry of Water Resources in 2006 is an important investment in development. It reflects the desire of the Regional Government to address the severe problems of water resources facing the region. The main problems are water scarcity, the provision of clean drinking water, the creation of a sewage system network, sewage treatment and the overall management of water resources.

One of the main tasks of the Ministry of Water Resources should be the production of research, reports and statistics for multiple purposes. One main purpose would be to inform investors, the public and private sectors and the general population about the state of water resources in the region. Ideally the annual report should be complemented with other publications. We have proposed the publication of special research reports, monthly bulletins, quarterly reports, annual reports, and the establishment of an informative web-site, research and statistics directorates, a library, and research funds.

Kurdistan is rich in water resources. The few existing major dams were used mainly for better management of water resources, for the generation of electricity and irrigation downstream. Within the region, irrigation was facilitated by traditional diversion techniques. In recent years several factors have changed in regard to water demand, supply and self-sufficiency. The changes include drought, diversion of water upstream, changes in the population structure, declining production in agriculture, the establishment of new industries, changes in the dam capacities and life expectancy, and small shifts in agriculture towards intensive forms such as greenhouses and aquaculture and recreation. The changes have resulted in lower demand for irrigation, but higher demand for urban consumption, recreation, construction and infrastructure. Given unavailability of statistics, it is hard to estimate demand, supply and shortages.

What is a relatively new phenomenon that affects the water conditions is diversion and drought. The intensive water diversion activities upstream, in Turkey and Iran, are the most serious changes and violations of international water laws. These are very likely to be multipurpose, such as in the long-term development of their economies by a better and effective management of water, as well as imposing political pressure on Kurdistan through the discharge of water from their dams. Regardless of drought and water diversion activities, the rapid increase in the urban population in cities like Hawler and Sulaimanyah requires comprehensive investment in infrastructure to supply water to these locations through groundwater, pipelines, and diversion techniques.

As a proposal for a new water plan and policies we are able to propose the key elements of such namely the issues of data, research and publications, laws and common pool relations, project evaluations, water polices and incentives, the role of water in sustainable development and capability and skill upgrading. Each ministry in the region should have two directorates working in close co-operation, specifically with statistics and research. Their function will be determinants for the achievement of the goals of the Ministry of Water Resources. The empirical research produced can assist to create a regional strategy and plan for the Ministry. It will have a great impact on the organizational structure, activities and performance of the Ministry and its external collaborative activities.

The Kurdistan Region and Kurds were in the past excluded from certain types of education. Given the limited capacity in the area of international law and the availability of resources and development programs it is important to build up such legal capacity. The work of the legal team could consist of issues related to the past, present and future. The first category is in the form of systematic investigation, documentations and preparation of cases for the regional government to submit cases to international courts concerning violations of minority rights, genocide, massacres of civilian, destruction of properties, and forced migration exercised against Kurds. The current cases could be related to oil and gas, common pool water resources, militarily intervention, reclaiming land and properties, the relocation of forcibly migrated families, oil revenue-sharing, implementation of the constitution and federal laws, power-sharing at the central government level, aviation, transportation, diplomacy, etc. The future issues involve protection against all violations encountered above, plus the Kurds right to self-determination and the formation of a Kurdish state in accordance with international law and the Kurds desire.

Water is a utility that is not priced in the Kurdistan region. However, the households pay on a monthly basis a symbolic sum that is far from covering the cost of the water supply. Pricing water can have a number of important functions: to cover the cost of its supply, to promote incentives for reducing the consumption and its gap, it reduces the quantity and costs of wastewater management, water saving technology will be developed, the public investment in capacity is reduced, and price is the main instrument in equating demand and supply. An effective pricing system has already been introduced in the telecommunications area, which indicates the feasibility of water pricing system. In order to introduce prices and to account for the quantity of water consumed, investment in infrastructure for measurement and billing is required. A well functioning banking system is needed to operate pricing successfully.

The Kurdistan Region faced a rapid change in the structure of its population and urbanization. The comprehensive demographic changes and development programs resulted in the shortage and pollution of water resources. The inefficiency in the public sector, lack of knowledge, rules and regulations and the inability of policymakers to monitor the development has led to massive polluting of nature. Even in the presence of marginal agriculture, the water resources are highly polluted where the main contributor is the urban population. The two main sources of pollution are the lack of a sewage system and waste from mineral water and manufactured food packaging. The policy makers should introduce a system of recycling deposits to encourage consumers to collect the waste. The producers should be taxed to increase their incentives to use material more easily absorbed in nature. Similarly import tax incentives should be used to promote the collection and processing of other durable household and industry waste materials. The media could be used for educational purposes and a better environment. Public participation in seasonal neighborhood cleaning programs is another recommended measure.

We have elaborated in many places of this report on the importance of having a specific regional water policy. We have presented a water resources plan and policies for the region which is multi-dimensional and fulfills the needs and expectations of all users and sources and corresponds to the socio-economic sustainable development of the region. As elements of the plan and policies we pointed to several components including data collection and management, research, publications and seminar activities; laws and common pool relations; legal teams and monitoring the upstream and downstream water activities; project evaluations and industrial development; suggested water policies and incentives; the role of water in sustainable development; coordination of activities of users of water; a more equal regional distribution of development resources; and capability and skill upgrading to achieve the objectives.

In the design, selection and implementation of any of the above measures a comprehensive cost-benefits analysis should be conducted and the most preferred alternatives from a social point of view selected. This should include the use cf government controls to enhance the desired impact of policy measures. Lack of data, time and capable human resources did not allow at this stage for the calculation of any costs and benefits associated with each of the proposed measures. Therefore we leave the choice of measures and estimation of their effects and costs to be undertaken by the Ministry's research staff as needed as the measures emerge.

Chapter 9

AN INTRODUCTION TO THE
MINISTRY OF WATER RESOURCES[*]

9.1. BACKGROUND HISTORY

The establishment of the Ministry of Water Resources (MOWR) and its introduction in the new regional government formed in May 2006 was to reflect the desire of the Kurdistan Regional Government (KRG) in the new institutional arrangements to address the problems of water resources throughout the Kurdistan Region.

The Ministry of Water Resources is working with one of the most complex problems of development in the Kurdistan Region and the most important challenges namely, the problem of water scarcity and the challenge of providing clean drinking water for residents in urban and rural communities, the creation of an integrated sewage system network in urban areas, sewage treatment and management of water resources planning and utilization. It is known that the importance of water is not only for drinking and food production but is also a basis for sustainable development. There is great emphasis on the strong interrelationship between the availability of water on one hand and public health, unemployment, poverty and education and overall development on the other.

The Ministry has another challenge which is to confront the problem of combating environmental degradation, the depletion of water resources and the pollution of the basic plants, soil, air and water. It aims to take appropriate measures to protect these resources and preserve them because its great importance as a community activity underlying economic, development and stability depends upon the population (especially in the countryside).

9.2. THE MINISTRY OF WATER RESOURCES

The mission of the Ministry of Water Resource (Figure 9.1) is to provide Integrated Water Resources Management to the citizen of the Kurdistan Region. As the steward of this vital resource, the Ministry strives to balance the competing demands of households,

---

[*] This chapter was prepared by Nabaz T. Abdullah, Ministry of Water Resources, Kurdistan Regional Government.

irrigation, municipalities and industries, hydropower generation, flood control and environmental requirements with the supply of water. The goal of the Ministry is to transform and modernize the MOWR into a dynamic and efficient organization that meets current requirements and optimizes the future utilization of the diminishing water resources of the nation. The focus is on areas of improvement including the improved operation and maintenance of water control structures and pump stations, efficient management of water through conservation and optimization, and a comprehensive approach to project approval that considers technological, economic, social, health and environmental impacts, competing demands, and public involvement.

MOWR aims to contribute to the development of water resources based on the methodology of integrated management of water resources and to provide clean drinking water and sanitation services as well as the optimal allocation of water for other uses. It protects the environment from pollution and desertification and promotes natural resource conservation and rational use, through the building and activation of the relevant legislation and implementation awareness and incentives programs. It encourages the participation of local communities, NGOs and other institutions of civil society and the private sector and women and their organizations in efforts to reform the water and environmental conditions. MOWR aims to lead the contribution to the promotion of sustainable development and improvements in public health and the alleviation of poverty and unemployment. The goals, in addition to being region-specific, are consistent with the United Nations Millennium Development Goals.[40]

9.3. THE OBJECTIVES TO BE CARRIED OUT

The Ministry and its bodies and institutions aim to achieve their goals through the exercise of the powers granted to them in legislation and to implement the plans for water and environmental reform, according to the water sector reform strategy and policy of the KRG and to carry out the following objectives:

1. Develop and review strategies and policies for the development and management of water resources and develop water and sanitation services in rural and urban areas, environmental protection, as well as polices and controls the administration, operation and maintenance of dams and water installations, in line with the scientific underpinnings and economic feasibility and in the light of existing legislation and government programs, and submitted to the Cabinet when necessary for approval.
2. Work to develop laws and regulations, related bodies and institutions of the Ministry and review and approve the proposed amendments and take necessary action for their adoption.
3. Promote an integrated approach to water resources management and environmental work to streamline the demand for water and natural resources in general.

---

[40] The MDGs represent a global partnership that has grown from the commitments and targets established at the world summits of the 1990s. The goals promote poverty reduction, education, maternal health, gender equality, and aim at combating child mortality, AIDS and other diseases. Set for the year 2015, the MDGs are an agreed set of goals that are expected to be achieved. For full description of the goals and evaluation of progress in their achievements see http://www.undp.org/mdg/

4. Develop traditional harvest rain and non-traditional resources such as water desalination, sewage treatment and determine criteria for their development and use.

5. Work to strengthen the role and contribution of local communities in the overview of the costs of operation and maintenance and management of water and sanitation projects in the countryside and in the management of water basins and environmental resources and natural reserves and strengthen the role of NGOs and private sectors in these areas.

6. Work to develop water and sanitation services in rural and urban areas and expansion as that achieves the objectives of the ministry and ensure the sustainability of these services in the long run.

7. Adopt rules for the governing partnership between the government and the private sector in water and sanitation services, environment and refer them to the Cabinet for approval, and encourage private sector investment in this area in the light of the legislation in force.

8. Develop policies that help to understand the situation of water and sanitation in the light of technical, economic and social data, and according to the laws in force.

9. Act to implement the policies of water reform and the sanitation sector and agree on proposals to establish local institutions for water and sanitation controls in the light of the organization and approved plans.

10. Work to protect the environment and preserve its integrity and balance, the maintenance and development of natural systems so as not to compromise the rights of future generations, preserving biodiversity and establish national nature reserves and encourage NGOs, private sectors and local communities to contribute to this work.

11. Develop the Ministry's policy to protect the national environment from harmful influences resulting from the activities that take place outside the borders and work to implement this policy in coordination with the relevant agencies.

12. Contribute with the relevant agencies to developing public policy in the field of eco-tourism.

13. Determine the quantitative and qualitative targets in the areas of the Ministry and adopt the basis for detailed plans for water bodies, institutions and the environment.

14. Prepare annual and five-year work plans and coordinate projects with plans filed by the bodies and institutions of the Ministry and adopt a unified plan for the Ministry and work to overcome the difficulties of implementation.

15. Receive and review all the investment needs of the bodies and institutions of the Ministry and identify priorities and co-ordinate funding with the Ministry of Planning and International Cooperation and the Ministry of Finance in the light of approved policies and strategy for poverty alleviation.

16. Build model pilot projects in various areas of environment, water and sanitation co-ordination with agencies and related institutions.

17. Review and approve the annual budget of water at the region and the level of each basin, and identify the outstanding shares of each sector in each basin, according to priority in employment.

18. Adopt protection and quarantine zones in the water basins in areas of water proposed by the General Authority for Water Resources and submitted to the Cabinet for approval.

19. Draw up plans to cope with environmental disasters and water and in co-ordination with relevant agencies.

20. Develop action plans and methods to fight pollution in its various forms and to avoid any adverse effects or damage directly or indirectly which may result from urgent development programs and pay for an environmental impact assessment studies operational tool to confront environmental degradation and reduction and to achieve environmentally sustainable development.

21. Develop relations with international organizations and donor countries and co-ordinate their activities in the areas of water resources and the environment regarding water and sanitation services in cooperation with the relevant agencies.

22. Prepare draft conventions, loans and international aid for water resources, water and sanitation, environment and refer to the competent authorities for approval and ratification.

23. Develop information systems for water and the environment in the Kurdistan Region.

24. Co-ordinate a policy of water and environmental monitoring and assessment of the commitment and take the necessary action.

25. Co-ordinate plans and investment programs for the bodies and institutions of the Ministry.

26. Work to co-ordinate development projects related to water, sanitation and the environment implemented by ministries and other funds and make recommendations thereon in the context of inclusion in development plans and the investment budget for the Kurdistan Region, under laws in force.

27. Supervise the institutions and bodies and projects of the Ministry and co-ordinate their activities, monitoring and evaluation of performance, direction, according to the legislation in force and in the light of policies and plans approved.

28. Control the level of implementation of existing legislation on water resources and water services and sanitation and the environment and take the necessary measures to enforce cooperation with the relevant agencies.

29. Ratify the draft contracts and agreements relating to the activities of bodies, institutions and various projects of the Ministry in accordance with the legislation in force, including the contracts of partnership with the private sector.

30. Carry out projects related to international and regional conventions on water and the environment in order for the Kurdistan Region to be part of regional water authorities and their ratification activities. In addition, work on the implementation of international commitments and those according to the country legislation in force.

9.4. THE MINISTER'S FUNCTIONS AND POWERS

1. Implementation of government policy with regard to the Ministry in accordance with the legislation in force.

2. Overseeing the development of the overall plan of the ministry within the cabinet and monitoring its implementation and reporting on the level of implementation of decisions and orders Cabinet to the Council by the system and developing

operational plans and programs for the realization of the ministry and bodies, institutions and facilities of the ministry.

3. Co-ordination with the ministers concerned in the planning or execution when it comes to the active work of the Ministry.

4. Supervising the Ministry and guidance departments, offices and facilities, concerning tasks administered in accordance with the principle of individual responsibility and collective consultation and be responsible for their activity before the Council of Ministers.

5. Making the necessary decisions concerning the management and co-ordination and organization and assessing the level of implementation of the functions and powers of the Ministry under the terms of reference in accordance with the legislation in force.

6. Formation of the Ministry and committee-run projects and co-ordination of these committees and any other committees formed for the functioning of the Ministry and carry out their tasks in accordance with the provisions of these Regulations.

7. Supervising bodies and institutions of the Ministry, according to the legislation in force.

8. Adoption of the budget and the annual water quota for each sector according to the priority in employment in each basin and referring them to the Cabinet for approval.

9. Adoption of rules, standards and regulations governing the participation of local communities and grassroots organizations in the protection and management of water resource management projects, water and sanitation and the environment, according to the legislation in force.

10. Adoption of rules and standards and national regulations to protect the environment from pollution and conserve natural resources as well as the specifications and technical standards in water and sanitation, and referring them to the Cabinet for approval.

11. Adoption of a regulations and conventions partnership with the private sector in water services, sanitation and the environment in accordance with the legislation and policies in force, and referring them to the Cabinet for approval.

12. Informing the Council of Ministers of international and regional conventions on the areas of work of the Ministry to which the Kurdistan Region is party, as well as bilateral agreements in these areas, for their approval in coordination with the competent authorities.

13. Co-ordination with the Minister of Planning and International Co-operation agreements on loans and international aid work in the areas of the Ministry.

14. Nomination and appointment of leading cadres in the Ministry and its facilities, and their promotion, rehabilitation and release in accordance with the regulations and laws in force.

9.5. Some Strategic Objectives of MOWR

1. To develop regulations for water law and its strict application and awareness of its importance to reduce the indiscriminate drilling and rational use of water resources and modernization of legislation on environmental protection.
2. To modernize the national strategy for water, and work to implement policies through the preparation of a national water plan and a scheme at the level of water basins and regions with a focus on completing the maps and plans of water basins in their critical first stage.
3. To develop and implement a master plan for water installations to enhance groundwater recharge and provide for different uses including irrigation in the light of technical studies and determines their bases of operation and maintenance.
4. To develop a unified investment plan for water, the environment and programs required for implementation and monitor the implementation, evaluation and promotion of transparency in program implementation.
5. To continuing the policy of decentralization in the management of water and sanitation facilities in urban and rural areas and strengthen the participation of the local authority and users in the establishment and management of these facilities.
6. To overseeing all facilities operating in water and the environment and monitor their performance and evaluate them periodically.
7. To support institutions and bodies operating in the area of water and sanitation in rural and urban areas and improve their performance and increase the number of beneficiaries in the light of a master plan.
8. To investigate environmental issues linked to sustainable development and work to complete the map of environmentally sensitive areas and rich biodiversity and develop plans and the legislation necessary for the declaration and management of a number of natural reserves.
9. To carry out a comprehensive assessment of the management of hazardous waste and landfill.
10. To further implement the Kurdistan Region's obligations towards global environmental issues.

9.6. Problems Facing MOWR and Their Possible Remedies

The formation of the Ministry of Water Resources was also vested with the authority and the responsibility for planning and managing water resources, environmental protection and biodiversity conservation in the Kurdistan Region (see Table 9.1). Formation of the Ministry has helped to bring to public attention, and acknowledge a matter of great embarrassment, the current status of this resource and the environments and habitats suffering from an imbalance between the available and the depleted and those vulnerable to depletion. The increasing trends in pollution, degradation and desertification are a heavy additional burden on the Ministry. MOWR aims at the precise co-ordination and integration of all stakeholders in these components and is working towards the development of decision-making and executive bodies. Focus is made on the roles played by the general public and individual social responsibility towards environmental protection and conservation of resources. The objective is to transform the negative trends among these actors to positive trends and a constructive manner.

Table 9.1. Problems facing MOWR and their possible remedies

Problem	Remedy
The indiscriminate drilling of water wells and groundwater depletion and encroachment on the campus fields of drinking water, tolerated irregularities in drilling without licenses, encroachment on the powers of the Water Resources Ministry and the issue of permits by some local Councils before drilling.	-Control the movement of drilling rigs and in particular between provinces. -Deal firmly with irregularities and move security forces to deter them (as they are moved for other security issues). -Stop local councils from issuing permits for drilling without prejudice to their right to receive fees, and refer requests for drilling wells to the authorities.
Water pollution with negative impact on environment because of the spilling of the remnants of the indiscriminate burning of oil and diesel mixed with water at car washes.	Work to change the oil pools in the cities and district centers to collect oil reservoirs in particular. Require employers to collect oil changed in barrels. Prevention of car washes from sinking their waste away from watercourses.
The presence of garbage dumps and fields within water basins and poor management and random selection of landfill sites. Burning garbage and air pollution, and its impact on the environment and public health.	Linking municipalities' budget to their environmental concern. Payment of taxes on soft drinks and bottled water to cover their collection and recycling. Penalizing offending consumers, producers and municipalities
Links to illegal water connections and the impact on higher rates of wastage of water and low income and lack of services and reluctance of donors to continue providing support.	Support institutions and their water branches to remove the irregularities and penalize offenders and transfer meters away from homes.
Indiscriminate discharge of wastewater to the sewer system by industrial and commercial enterprises (workshops, hospitals, photography studios, slaughterhouses and supermarkets, oil changes, etc.)	Co-operation to deter violations and compel them to deal with offal prior to its disbursement in the sewer system.

See :Oranzational Chart of the MOWR

Ministry of Water Resources

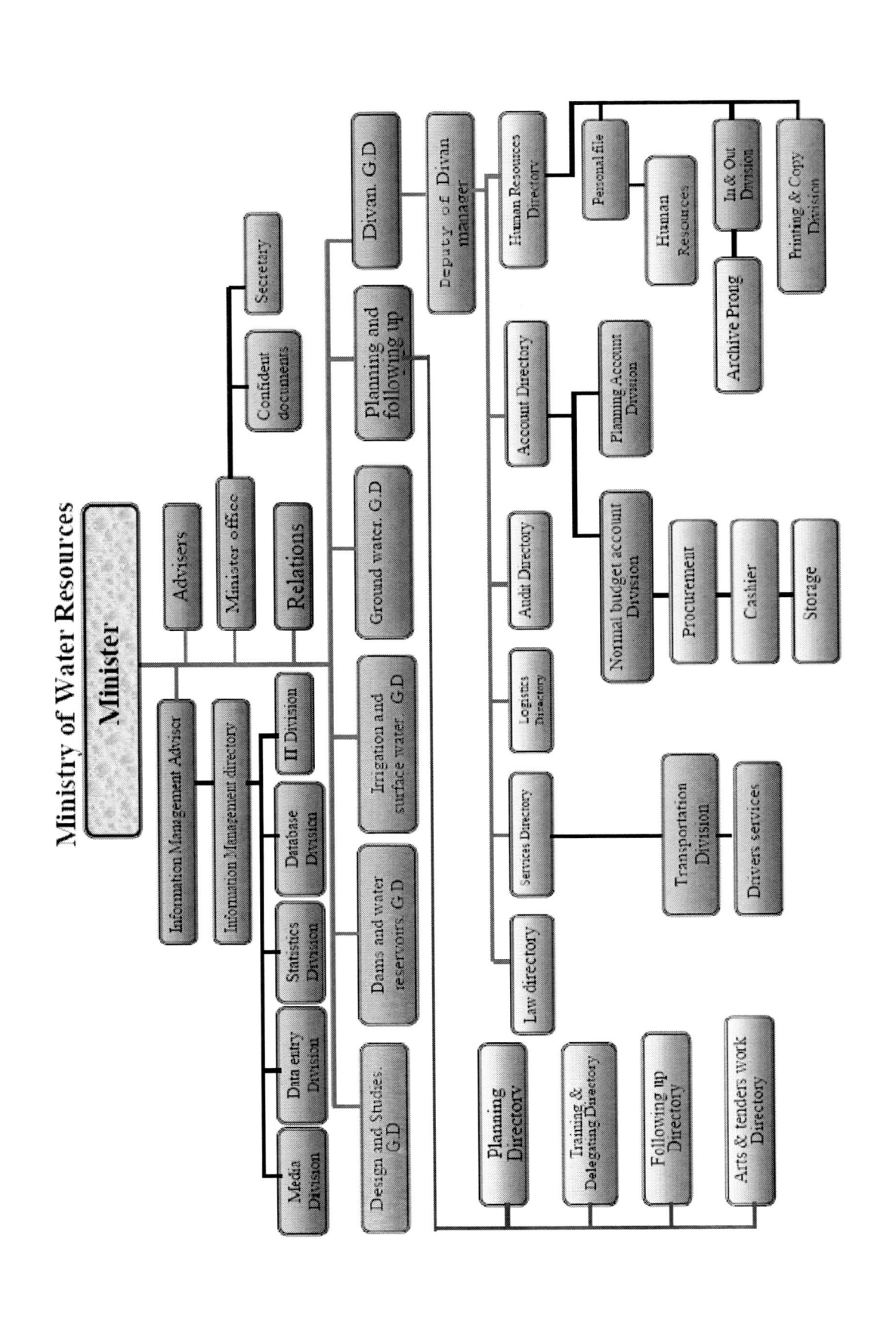

REFERENCES

Amery H.A. (2002), Water Wars in the Middle East: A Looming Threat, *The Geographical Journal* 168(4), 313-323.

AusAid (2000), Gender Guidelines Water Supply and Sanitation: Supplement to the Guide to Gender and Development, Australian Aid, March 2000.

Axelard, G. and E. Feinerman (2007), Regional Planning of Wastewater Reuse for Irrigation and River Rehabilitation, Department of Agricultural Economics and Management, The Hebrew University of Jerusalem, Israel.

Banerjee, S., Gunter, L., Bramblett, J., and Weszstein, M. (2004), Alternative Methods of Forecasting Agricultural Water Demand: a case study on the flint river Basin in Georgia, Paper for the 2004 SAEA annual meeting in Tulsa, Oklahoma.

Banerjee, S.B., Martin, S.W. (2008), Econometric versus Engineering Prediction of Water Demand and Value for Irrigation, Paper presented at the American Agricultural Economics Association Annual meeting, Orlando.

Bartolini, F., Bazzani, G.M., Gallerani, V., Raggi, M., Viaggi, M. (2005), Water Policy and Sustainability of Irrigated Farming Systems in Italy, Paper presented at the XIth of the EAAE, Copenhagen, Denmark.

Bazzani, G., Pasquale, S.D., Gallerani, V., Viaggi, D. (2002), Water Regulation and Irrigated Agriculture under the EU Water Framework Directive, Paper presented at the Xth EAAE congress 'exploring diversity in the European Agri-Food system', Zaragoza, Spain.

Bilgic, A., Eren, G., and Florkowski, W.J. (2008), Willingness to Pay for Potable Water in the Southeastern Turkey: An Application of Both Stated and Revealed Preferences Valuation Method, Paper presented at the Southern Agricultural Economics Association Annual meeting, Dallas, TX.

SBEC (1982), The Complete Plan of Water Resources and Land Development in Iraq, 8 Volumes 1972-1982, Silkhom Brom Export Company, Soviet Union.

Cano, G. (1989), The Development of the Law in International Water Resources and the Work of the International Law Commission, *Water International* 14, 167-171.

Cankurt, M., Miran, B., Gunden, C., and Shahin, A. (2008), Awareness to Environmental Pollution in Turkey, Paper presented at the Southern Agricultural Economics Association Annual meeting, Dallas, TX.

Caponera, D.A. (1985), Patterns of Cooperation in International Water Law: Principles and Institutions, *Natural Resources Journal* 25, 563-588.

Davies, D.H. (1957), Observation on Land Use in Iraq, *Economic Geography* 33(2), 122-134.

Deller, Steven C., Tsung-Hsiu (Sue) Tsai, David W. Marcouiller, and Donald B.K (2001), The Role of Amenities and Quality of Life in Rural Economic Growth, *American Journal of Agricultural Economics* 83(2), 352-365.

Devi, M.G., Davidson, B., Boland, A.M. (2007), Economics of Wastewater Treatment and Recycling an Investigation of Conceptual Issues, Faculty of land and Food Resources, University of Melbourne.

Dinar, A. and A. Wolf (1997), Economic and Political Considerations in Regional Cooperation Models, *Agricultural and Resource Economics Review* 26(1), 7-22.

Dinar, A. and D. Yaron (1986), Treatment Optimization of Municipal Wastewater and Reuse for Regional Irrigation, *Water Resources Research* 22(3), 331-338.

Duda, A.M. (2003), Integrated Management of Land and Water Resources Based on a Collective Approach to Fragmented International Convention, *Philosophical Transaction: Biological Sciences* 385(1440), 2051-2062.

Dwyer, G., Douglas, R., Peterson R., Chong J. and K. Maddern (2006), Irrigation Externalities: Pricing and Charges, Productivity Commission Staff Working Paper, Melbourne, March.

Dwyer, G., Loke, P., Appels, D., Stone, S., and D. Peterson (2005), Integrating Rural and Urban Water Markets in South East Australia: Preliminary Analysis, Paper Presented at the OECD Workshop on Agriculture and Water: Sustainability, Markets and Policies, Adelaide.

Edwards, G. (2006), Demand Management for Melbourne's Water, *Economic Record* 82, 54-63.

Evans, D., Fullilove, M. TH., Green, L., and Levison, M. (2002), Awareness of Environmental Risks and Protective Actions among Minority Women in Northern Manhattan, *Environmental Health Perspectives* 110(supplement 2), 271-275.

Ethelston, S. (1999), WATER AND Women: The Middle East in Demographic Transition, Middle East Report, No. 213, Millennial Middle East: Changing Order , pp.8-12+44.

Fang, X., Roe, T., and Smith, R.B.W., (2006), Water Shortage, Water Allocation and Economic Growth: the case of China, Center for disease control, Atlanta, University of Minnesota.

Farolfi, S., Mabugu, R.E., Ntshingila, S.N., (2007), Domestic Water Use and Values in Swaziland: A Contingent Valuation Analysis, *Agrekon* 46(1), 157-170.

Galston, William A., and Karen J. Baehler (1995), Rural Development in the United States: Connecting Theory, Practice, and Possibilities. Washington, DC: Island Press.

Giannoccaro, G., Prosperi, M., Zanni, G. (2008), DEA Application to Evaluate the Technical and Ecological Efficiency of Water Pricing Policies, Paper presented at the 107th EAAE seminar "modeling of agricultural and rural development policies". Sevilla, Spain.

Gibson, Lay James (1993), The Potential for Tourism Development in Nonmetropolitan Areas, in David L. Barkley, ed., *Economic Adaptation: Alternatives for Nonmetropolitan Areas*, Boulder, CO: Westview Press.

Giordano, M., Giordano, M., Wolf, A. (2002), The Geography of Water Conflict and Cooperation: *Internal Pressures and International Manifestations* 168(4), 293-312.

Giupponi, C., Cogan, V., and I.L. Jeunesse (2002), EU Water Policy: Research Developments and New Management Tools, Center for International Food and Agricultural Policy, University of Minnesota.

Giupponi, C., Mysiak, J., and J. Crimi (2006), Participatory Approach in Decision Making Processes for Water Resources in the Mediterranean Basin, Fondazione Eni Enrico Mattei, Nota di Lavoro 101.2006.

Gleick, P.H. (1993), Water and conflict: Water Resources and International Security, *International Security* 18(1), 79-112.

Goldfarb, O., Kislev, Y. (2002), Water Management in Israel: Rules vs. Discretion, the Hebrew University of Jerusalem, The Center for Agricultural Economic Research, Discussion Paper No. 12.01.

Grafton, Q. and T. Kompas (2006), Sydney Water Pricing for Sustainability, Paper Presented at the 50th Annual Conference on the Australian Agricultural and Resource Economics Society, Queenstown, Sydney, 8-10, February 2006.

Grafton, Q. and M. Ward (2007), Prices versus Rationing: Marshallian Surplus and Mandatory Water Restrictions, Working Paper, Economics and Environment, Australian National University, Canberra.

Grove, B., Nel, F., Maluleke, H. (2006), Stochastic Efficiency Analysis of Alternative Water Conservation Strategies, *Agrekon* 45(1), 50-59.

Haddadin, M.J. (2002), Water in the Middle East peace process, *The Geographical Journal* 168(4), 324-340.

Haruvy, N. (1998), Wastewater Reuse – Regional and Economic Considerations, *Agriculture Ecosystems and Environment* 23, 57-66.

He, L., Tyner, W.E., Doukkali, R., and Siam, G. (2005), Strategic Policy Options to Improve Irrigation Water Allocation Efficiency: Analysis on Egypt and Morocco, Paper presented at the American Agricultural Economics Association Annual Meeting.

Heshmati A. (2007a), Labour Market Policy Options of Kurdistan Regional Government, IZA Discussion Paper 2007:3247.

Heshmati A. (2007b), Establishment of Sciences Parks in the Federal Region of Kurdistan, IZA Discussion Paper 2007:3252.

Heshmati A. (2007c), A Model for Industrial Development of the Federal Region of Kurdistan: Science and Technology Policy, Instruments and Institutions, IZA Discussion Paper 2007:3213.

Heshmati A. (2008a), Realities of Economic Development in Iraqi Kurdistan, Unpublished, May 2008.

Heshmati A. (2008b), Review of the Recent Trends in Development Economics Research: With Experience from the Federal Region of Kurdistan, in T.G. Rocha (Ed.), *Development Economics Research Trends*, Nova Science Publishers.

Heshmati A. and T.A.H. Chawsheen (2008), The Education Sector at the Federal Region of Kurdistan, Unpublished, May 2008.

Heshmati A. and R. Davis (2007), The Determinants of Foreign Direct Investment Flows to the Federal Region of Kurdistan, IZA Discussion Paper 2007:3218.

Housen-Couriel, D. (1992), Aspects of the Law of International Water Resources, Law Faculty, Hebrew University, Jerusalem, Israel, Mimeo.

Huang, Q., Rozelle, S., Howitt, R., and Wang, J., Huang, J., (2008), Irrigation water pricing policy in rural china, Paper presented at the American Agricultural Economics Association Annual Meeting, July 23-26,2006, Long Beach, CA.

Hughes, N., Hafi, A., Goesch, T., and N. Brownlowe (2008), Urban Water Management: Optimal Price Investment Policy under University, Australian Agricultural and Resource Economics Society 52nd Annual Conference, Canberra.

Izady R. M. (1996), The drowning of the Kurdish historical and artistic heritage, The Kurdish Life, Number 19, Summer 1996 http://www.kurdistanica.com/?q=node/75, available on October 31, 2008,

Jakson, R.B., Carpenter, S.R., Dahm, C.N., and McKinght, D.M. (2001), Water in Changing World, *Ecological Application* 11(4), 1027-1045.

Johnson, J. and K. Schwartz (2004), Water Economic Publication (1961-2003), College of Agricultural Sciences and Natural Resources, Report T-1-585.

Jowett, A.J. (1986), China's Water Crisis: The Case of Tianjin (Tientsin), *The Geographical Journal* 152(1), 9-18.

Lee, C. (2005), Water Tariff and Development: the case of Malaysia, Center of regulation and competition working paper series, faculty of economic and administration university of Malaya.

Levin, R.B., Epstein, P.R., Ford, T.E., Harington, W., and Olson, E. (2002), U.S. Drinking Water Challenges in the Twenty-First Century, *Environmental Health Perspective* 110, 43-52.

Lipchin, C. (2006), A Future for the Dead Sea Basin: Water Culture among Israeli, Palestinians and Jordanians, NRM-Natural Resources Management, Fondazione Eni Enrico Mattei, NOTA DI LAVORO 115.2006.

Lundqvist, J., Appasamy, P., Nelliyat, P. (2003), Dimensions and approaches for third world city water security, *Philosophical Transaction: Biological Sciences* 358(1440), 1985-1996.

Mahzouni, A. (2008), Participatory Local Governance for Sustainable Community-Driven Development: The Case of the Rural Periphery in the Kurdish Region of Iraq, PHD thesis.

Maneta, M.P., Torres, M., Howitt, R., Vosti, S.A., Wallender, W.W., Bassoi, L.H., Rodrigues, L.N., and Young, J.A. (2007), A Detailed Hydro-Economic Model for Assessing the Effects of Surface Water and Groundwater Policies: A Demonstration Model from Brazil, American Agricultural Economists Association annual meeting, Portland, Oregon.

Marcouiller, David W., and Gary Paul Green (2000), Outdoor Recreation and Rural Development, In Gary E. Machlis and Donald R. Field, eds., National Parks and Rural Development: Practice and Policy in the United States, pp. 33-49. Washington, DC: Island Press.

McCauley, A.P., West, S. and Lynch, M. (1992), Household decisions among the Gogo people of Tanzania: determining the roles of men, women and the community in implementing a trachoma prevention program. *Social Science and Medicine*, 34(7), 817-824.

Meinzen-Dick, R.S., Rosegrant, M.W. (2001), Overcoming Water Scarcity and Quality Constraints, International Food Policy Research Institute.

Minoia G. (2007), Gender Issue and Water Management in the Mediterranean, Middle East and North Africa, Fondazione Eni Enrico Mattei, NOTA DI LAVORO 2007:49.

Minoia, P., and Brusarosco, A. (2006), Water Infrastructures Facing Sustainable Development Challenges: Integrated Evaluation of Impacts of Dams on Regional

Development in Morocco, NRM-Natural Resources Management, Fondazione Eni Enrico Mattei, NOTA DI LAVORO 2006:105.

Mitlin, D. (2002), Competition, Regulation and the Urban Poor: a case study of water, Center on regulation and Competition working paper series, pp.37, University of Manchester.

Ohte, N., Koba, K., Yooshikawa, K., Sugimoto, A., Matsuo, N. (2003), Water Utilization of Natural and Planted Trees in the Semiarid Desert of Inner Mongolia, China, *Ecological Application* 13(2), 337-351.

Rathgeber, E.M. (2000), Women, Men, and Water-Resources Management in Africa, Regional Office for Eastern and Southern Africa, IDRC, Nairobi, Kenya.

Ringler, C. (2001), Optimal Water Allocation in the Mekong River Basin, ZEF- Discussion papers on Development Policy, Bonn.

Rockstrom, J. (2003), Water for Food and Nature in Drought-Prone Tropics: Vapour Shift in Rain-Fed Agriculture, *Philosophical Transaction: Biological Sciences* 358(1440), 1997-2009.

Roe,T., Dinar, A. Tsur, Y., and Diao, X. (2006), Understanding the Direct and Indirect Effects of Water Policy for Better Policy Decision Making: An Application to Irrigation Water Management in Morocco, Paper presented at the international association of agricultural economists conference, gold coast, Australia.

Rogers, P. (1991), International River Basins: Pervasive Unidirectional Externalities. Paper Presented at a Conference on the Economics of Transnational Commons, April 25-27, Universita di Siena, Siena, Italy.

Ron, Z.Y.D. (1986), Ancient and modern development of water resources in the Holy Land and the Israeli-Arab conflict-a reply, *Transaction of the Institute of British Geographers, New Series* 11(3), 360-369.

Rubenowitz, E., Axelsson, G., Rylander, R., (1999), Magnesium and Calcium in Drinking Water and Death from Acute Myocardial Infarction in Women, *Epidemiology* 10(1), 31-36.

Ruijs A. (2007), Welfare and Distribution Effects of Water Pricing Policies, NOTA DI LAVORO 2007: 92, Fondazione Uni Enrico Mattei.

Schmitz, T.G. (2002), Measuring Inefficiency in the Presence of an Export Tax, an Import Tariff, and a State Trading Enterprise, *Journal of Agricultural and Applied Economics* 34(1), 81-93.

Seung, CH. K., Waters, E.C. (2006), A Review of Regional Economics Models for Fisheries Management in the U.S., National Marine Fisheries Service, *Marine Resource Economic* 21, 101-124.

Sperow, M. (2004), An Analysis of the Economic Impact of Water Transfers from Agriculture to Urban Uses, Paper Presented at the American Agriculture Economics Association, Denver, Colorado.

Starr, J. (1991), Water Wars. *Foreign Policy* 82, 17-36.

Starr, J. and D. Stoll (1988), eds., The Politics of Scarcity: Water in the Middle East, Boulder, Colo, U.S.A.: Westview Press.

Stijn, S. Jeroen, B. Aymen, F. Marike, D.H., and Luc, D.H. (2008), Estimating the Effect Water Charge Introduction at Small-Scale Irrigation in North West Province, South Africa, Modelling of Agricultural and Rural developmental policies, Sevilla, Spain.

Taylor, R.H., Almas, L.K., and W.A. Colette (2007), Economic Analysis of Water
    Conservation Policies in the Texas Panhandle, Paper Presented at the Southern
    Agriculture Economics Association Annual Meetings Mobile, Alabama.
TEPCO (2004), Pilot Study for Project Formulation for Hydropower Plant Development in
    Kurdistan Iraq, TEPSCO Japanese Consultant Company.
van Rheenen, T., M.A.H.J. van Bavel, C. Graveland and T.A. Selnes (2005), Putting Nature
    on the EU Political Agenda: A Review of Four Policy Dossiers, The Hague, Agricultural
    Economics Research Institute (LEI), Report 6.05.05.
Ury, W., J. Brett and S. Goldberg (1988), Getting Disputes Resolved: Designing Systems to
    Cut the Costs of Conflict, San Francisco, Jossey-Bass.
Wallace, J.S., Acreman, M.C., and Sullivan, C.A. (2003), The Sharing of Water between
    Society and Ecosystem: From Conflict to Catchment-Based Co-Management,
    Philosophical Transaction: Biological Sciences 358(1440), 2011-2026.
Wolf, A. T. (1996), Middle East Water Conflicts and Direction for Conflict Resolution, Food,
    Agriculture, and Environment Discussion Paper 12, International Food Policy Research
    Institute, Washington, D.C. 20036-3006 U.S.A.
Wu, C., Maurer, C., Wang, Y., Xue, S., Davis, D.L. (1999), Water Pollution and Human
    Health in China, *Environmental Health Perspective* 107(4), 251-256.
Xayavong, V., Burton, M. P., and White, B. (2008), Estimating urban residential water-
    demand with increasing block prices: the case of Perth, Western Australia, School of
    Agricultural and Resource Economics Working Paper 0704, School of Agricultural and
    Resource Economics, University of Western Australia, Crawley, Australia.

INTERNET RESOURCES

Dublin Principle 3, (1992), Women and Water Management: an Integrated Approach,
    http://www.unep.org/PDF/Women/ChapterFive.pdf, available on October 28, 2008.
European Commission (2000), Water Framework Directive, http://www.euwfd.com/,
    available on October 28, 2008.
European Union (2002), EU Water Initiative, Water for Life, http://www.euwi.net/ available
    on October 28, 2008.
FAO, Women and Water Resources, FAO Focus, http://www.fao.org/FOCUS/E/Women/
    Water-e.htm, available on October 28, 2008.
Moran T. (2004), The Environmental and Socio-Economic Impacts of Hydroelectric Dams in
    Turkish Kurdistan, http://diggy.ruc.dk:8080/handle/1800/403, available on October 28.
National Commission for Women (2007), Water and Women, Research Foundation for
    Science, Technology, Ecology, http://wcd.nic.in/ar0708/English/Chapter-10.pdf,
    available on October 28, 2008.
Rural Women Securing Household in Jordan, (2006), Gender and Water Alliance, Submitted
    by: Rakin Village-Jordan, http://www.genderandwater.org/page/752, available on
    October 28, 2008.
UN (2008), UN Water, Gender, Water and Sanitation, A Policy Brief, Water for Life (2005 -
    2015), http://www.un.org/temp/waterforlifedecade/pdf/un_water_policy_brief_2_
    gender.pdf, available on October 28, 2008.

STATISTIC MATERIALS

FAO, FAO Projects-Iraq, Food and Agriculture Organization-Iraq.

FAO–IRAQ (2008), From Emergency to Development, Medium-Term Strategy for FAO Assistance to Iraq, Food and Agriculture Organization of the United Nations.

General Directorate of Irrigation and Surface Water (2008a), Directorate of Irrigationand Surface Water-Erbil, Ministry of Water Resources, Kurdistan Regional Government, No. 88.

General Directorate of Irrigation and Surface Water (2008b), Directorate of Irrigationand Surface Water-Erbil, Ministry of Water Resources, Kurdistan Regional Government, No. 373.

General Directorate of Irrigation and Surface Water (2008c), Directorate of Irrigationand Surface Water-Erbil, Ministry of Water Resources, Kurdistan Regional Government, No. 951.

General Directorate of Planning and Follow Up (2007), Ministry of Agriculture Profile, Directorate of Statistics, Kurdistan Region-Iraq.

Iraq Ministry of Industry and Minerals Commercial Investment Summit (2008), investing in Iraq's Industrial Sectors "Public and Mixed", Summit Report.

Ministry of Water Resources (2008), General Directorate of Investigation and Design, Council of Ministers, Kurdistan Regional Government.

UNDP (2005a), Iraqi Living Conditions Survey 2004, Volume 1: Tabulation Report, Ministry of Planning and Development Cooperation, Baghdad Iraq.

UNDP, (2005b), Iraqi Living Conditions Survey 2004, Volume 2: Analytical Report, Ministry of Planning and Development Cooperation, Baghdad Iraq.

UNDP (2005c), Iraqi Living Conditions Survey 2004, Volume 3: Socio-economic Atlas of Iraq, Ministry of Planning and Development Cooperation, Baghdad Iraq.

UNICEF (2000), WATERfront, A UNICEF Publication on Water, Environment, Sanitation and Hygiene, New York USA, Issue 14.

UNICEF (2001a), Assessment of the Water Resources of Dohuk Governorate – Northern Iraq, UNICEF, United Nations Children's Fund, Montgomery Watson Arabtech Jardaneh.

UNICEF (2001b), Assessment of the Water Resources of Erbil Governorate – Northern Iraq, UNICEF, United Nations Children's Fund, Montgomery Watson Arabtech Jardaneh.

UNICEF (2001c), Assessment of the Water Resources of Sulaimanyah Governorate – Northern Iraq, UNICEF, United Nations Children's Fund, Montgomery Watson Arabtech Jardaneh.

INDEX

D

F

G

H

I

S

T

U

V

W

Y